SO GOD MADE A
grandma

caring, faithful, creative, devoted, wise,
generous, resilient—just like you

LESLIE MEANS
HER VIEW FROM HOME

TYNDALE
MOMENTUM®

A Tyndale nonfiction imprint

Visit Tyndale online at tyndale.com.

Visit Tyndale Momentum online at tyndalemomentum.com.

Visit the author at herviewfromhome.com.

Tyndale, Tyndale's quill logo, *Tyndale Momentum*, and the Tyndale Momentum logo are registered trademarks of Tyndale House Ministries. Tyndale Momentum is a nonfiction imprint of Tyndale House Publishers, Carol Stream, Illinois.

So God Made a Grandma: Caring, Faithful, Creative, Devoted, Wise, Generous, Resilient—Just like You

Copyright © 2025 by Leslie Means. All rights reserved.

Cover and interior illustration of floral pattern copyright © cristatus/Shutterstock. All rights reserved.

Author photo copyright © 2024 by Bronwyn Gillespie Photography & Design (Bronwyn Gillespie). All rights reserved.

Designed by Dean H. Renninger

Published in association with Folio Literary Management, LLC, 630 9th Avenue, Suite 1101, New York, NY 10036.

All Scripture quotations, unless otherwise indicated, are taken from the Holy Bible, *New International Version,*® *NIV.*® Copyright © 1973, 1978, 1984, 2011 by Biblica, Inc.® Used by permission. All rights reserved worldwide.

Scripture quotations marked KJV are taken from the *Holy Bible*, King James Version.

Scripture quotations marked NLT are taken from the *Holy Bible*, New Living Translation, copyright © 1996, 2004, 2015 by Tyndale House Foundation. Used by permission of Tyndale House Publishers, Carol Stream, Illinois 60188. All rights reserved.

For information about special discounts for bulk purchases, please contact Tyndale House Publishers at csresponse@tyndale.com, or call 1-855-277-9400.

Library of Congress Cataloging-in-Publication Data

A catalog record for this book is available from the Library of Congress.

ISBN 979-8-4005-0535-5

Printed in China

31	30	29	28	27	26	25
7	6	5	4	3	2	1

To Mom and Dad.

♥

We love you.

Contents

Introduction 1

PART 1
So God Made a Grandma Gentle 5

PART 2
So God Made a Grandma Wise 31

PART 3
So God Made a Grandma Redeemed 67

PART 4
So God Made a Grandma Creative 97

PART 5
So God Made a Grandma Faithful 127

PART 6
So God Made a Grandma Graceful 159

PART 7
So God Made a Grandma Generous 189

PART 8
So God Made a Grandma Resilient 223

PART 9
So God Made a Grandma Devoted 255

PART 10
So God Made a Grandma to Leave a Legacy 281

Conclusion 309
Acknowledgments 311
About the Author 313

Introduction

LESLIE MEANS

I hadn't opened this Bible in years. A gift on my confirmation day, it was packed away when I left for college, along with trinkets and embarrassing photographs from high school. There it sat—in a dark, tattered grocery store box, next to a dollar-store homecoming crown and a yearbook that read "Shoot for the Stars: Class of 2000."

I unboxed it again during my family's recent move to our forever home. My name is inscribed on the front; the cover was pristine.

Not the look you're going for in a used Bible.

I took it from the tattered box and placed it on a shelf next to my first book, *So God Made a Mother*.

And there it sat, yet again.

The next part of this story is what I like to call a "whisper story."

You might call them God winks, intuition, or just coincidence, but I call these moments God's whispers—nudges from the Holy Spirit.

Nearly a year after the Bible's unboxing (and twenty-eight years since it was first gifted to me), I thumbed through its pages and discovered this photograph.

It's a picture of my maternal grandmother and me in 1997. I am wearing her wedding dress—the one she wore to marry my grandaddy in 1947. They were celebrating fifty years of marriage and wanted me to walk down memory lane in Grandma's dress.

I couldn't button the back, so the lane was shortened to the living room, but I shimmied my way into it and snapped a photo with my beloved grandma anyway.

I hadn't seen this photograph since high school, when I'd tucked it into a place I knew would be safe.

But on this day, when it fell from the pages of my Bible and floated gently to the floor, I remembered Grandma and her unending love for me.

INTRODUCTION

And it was this day we finalized our plans to write the very book you're holding.

"Okay, God, I hear you," I told Him. "Thanks (again) for the whisper."

I pray this book takes you down your own memory lane—when you first tasted your grandma's cookies or delighted in her beautiful home. Or perhaps you are a grandmother, and you find joy and comfort in reading the stories of other women in this season of life. Or maybe you are grieving, praying for a wound to heal, or searching for comfort and community. Or you're a forty-something woman like me, grateful for your mother, who is now a grandmother to your babies, and you pray, someday, you can be half the woman she is.

One of my favorite things about putting this book together was talking with my mom about my grandma—someone I didn't get the privilege of doing life with as an adult. I called Mom nearly every morning while I was writing, and talking with her helped me learn more of my family's story.

And that's the beautiful gift of this book.

So God Made a Grandma connects women—no matter who we are, no matter what stage of life we're in, no matter what memories and dreams we tuck away in our hearts.

This book is for the love-givers. The tradition-keepers. The heart-holders. The memory-makers.

This book is for you. We hope you find your own whisper story tucked inside its pages.

xo,
Leslie

PART 1

SO GOD MADE A GRANDMA

gentle

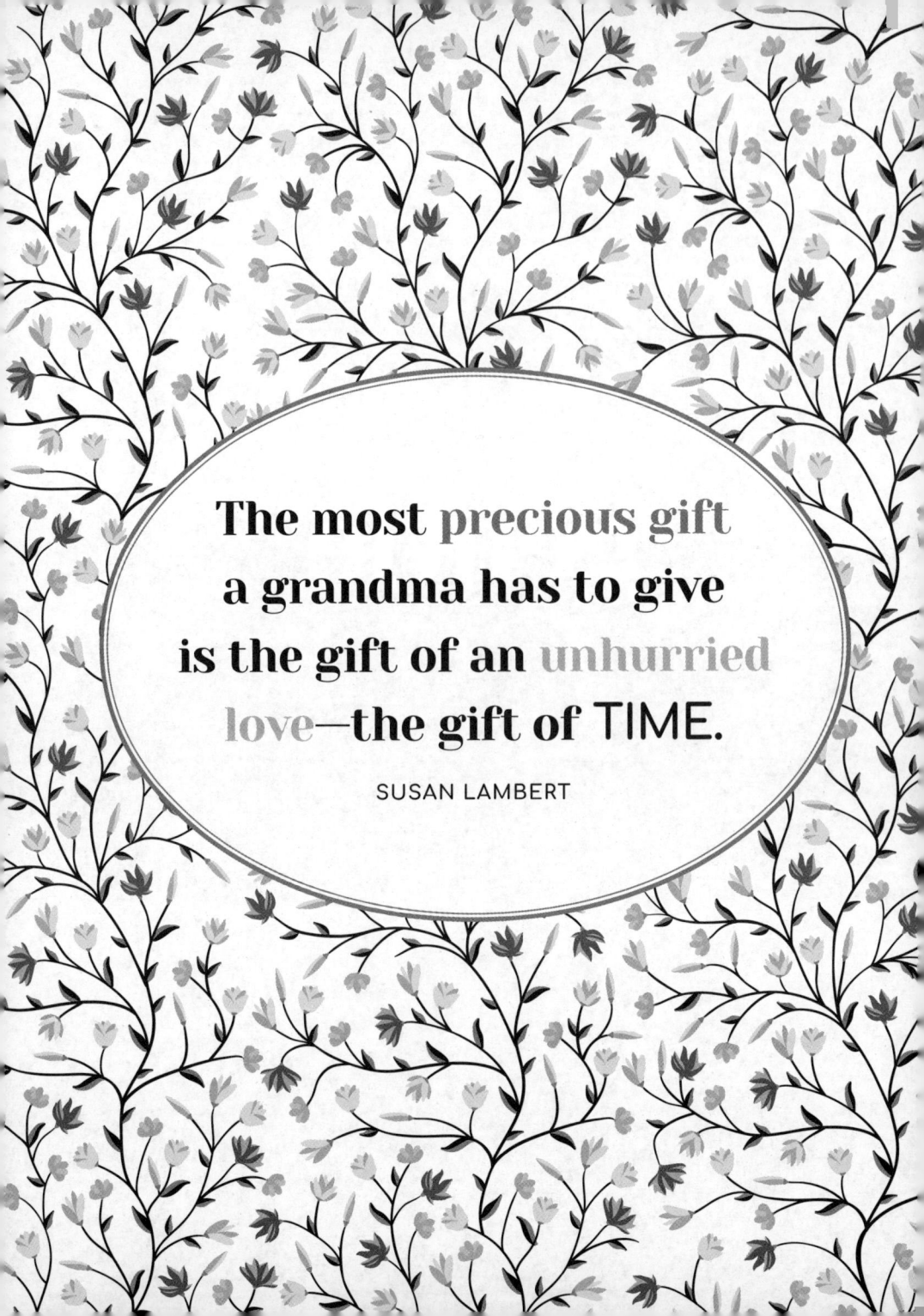

The Tea Set

LESLIE MEANS

My paternal grandmother, Vera, died in her early seventies. Grandma didn't have much. She was raised by a single mother, who I'm told was loved by many.

And I sure loved my grandma.

When Mom and Dad moved to the farm, Grandpa and Grandma moved into town. They owned a small home near the grade school, which was convenient for me.

I walked home many days after school, probably when Mom was working and Dad was in the field. On those long afternoons between school and supper, I'd sit with Grandma and watch *Wheel of Fortune* or play a mean game of Uno. Sometimes when she was resting, I would wander around her home and casually glance (aka snoop) in boxes, drawers, and anything I could get my hands on.

One thing that always caught my eye—a treasure I couldn't wait to discover—was her glass cat tea set.

It was in perfect condition and came with little spoons, plates, saucers, and even a small container for milk and sugar. She kept it in a hutch near the kitchen. I don't recall ever removing the dishes from their glass home. Still, I spent hours staring at their dainty details, and I even used to reach in and use the spoon to stir imaginary milk and sugar into imaginary coffee.

After Grandpa died, she was never the same. A tiny woman, she struggled with diabetes for most of her adult life.

Maybe she knew she wouldn't be around long or was simply preparing for the inevitable, but at some point, she started leaving names on items around her home so we'd know how to divide all her things properly.

One day, I opened the lid on that small glass teapot and found a note written in her shaky cursive that read simply, *Leslie*.

Grandma was planning to give the cat tea set to me.

I was honored.

I was thirteen when Grandma died. She was seventy-three. The tea set relocated to my childhood room.

I kept it on a shelf for everyone to see for a while. But after a few years, I was too cool to have something childish on display, so I decided to pack it away. CDs and pictures took its place.

It stayed hidden in a shoebox for twenty-five years.

When we moved into our forever home, I unpacked boxes and discovered the cat tea set.

My then-five-year-old son, Keithan, named after my dad, Keith (Vera's only son), was with me.

"What is that?" Keithan asked.

I told him about his great-grandma and her tea set.

He wondered, for a moment, if he could play with it.

"Do you want to get Ella and Grace to play with you?" he asked me. (His older sisters were fourteen and twelve at the time.)

"I would love to have tea with *you*, Keithan," I told him.

He stirred the imaginary milk and sugar. I poured him a second glass of tea. Finally, we clinked our glasses together for a well-deserved imagination celebration.

Then he helped me carefully place the tea set in its rightful place—the glass hutch near my kitchen.

"It looks so nice, Mom," he told me.

I agreed. Grandma would be so proud.

That tea set takes me right back to Grandma's house—and the feeling I had whenever I was with her. It's what grandmothers do, isn't it? They love us in quiet ways and teach us to find the beauty in simple things, in a life well lived.

I hope these next few stories remind your heart of that feeling—I know they did for me.

Grandmothers Live for the Details

KIT TOSELLO

After my widowed mom retired from decades of secretarial work, her kitchen table always held a grouping of three items: a beautiful English floral cream pitcher filled with erasable pens; a small sunny-yellow legal pad; and a bottle of petal-pink nail polish.

The floral pitcher Mom used as a pencil cup had been a thank-you gift from my husband, something he'd purchased on a business trip while I remained home, sick during my first pregnancy and needing my mother's care. The erasable pens? A necessity, given Mom's daily crossword habit. Ever the secretary, she also employed them to record an endless series of lists on her little yellow legal pad. Lists I couldn't make heads or tails of. See, Mom often used a combination of letters, curlicues, lines, and circles—the secretarial shorthand she'd relied on for rapid notetaking throughout her professional life.

As for the nail polish, I suppose after all those years as a typist and stenographer, speedy fingers and pretty hands had become Mom's trademark.

My petite mother rejoiced in choosing a grandmother title, finally landing on "Gram." It wasn't long before it became apparent Gram Doris had a superpower: If her grandkids took an interest in something, so did she. Dinosaurs? Olympic figure skaters? *Hannah Montana*? She did the research.

As the grandkids aged, so did Gram Doris—and those lists on her yellow legal pad grew beyond to-do lists into to-remember lists. Reminders of the ever-changing interests and happenings in my three children's lives. This became even more important once we moved a state away.

Between visits, she and I stayed connected across the miles through lengthy phone calls. Was my mother's memory declining at all? If so, I hardly noticed. Thanks to her efficient notetaking, she always remembered what the kids were up to. With her trusty yellow notepad at her side, Mom might say, "How's Marissa enjoying her new ballet class?" or "Did Chelsea and her little friend get things worked out?" or "How is Sean's wrist healing?"

Then came the day Mom called to cheerfully wish me a happy birthday—a day early. My heart squeezed with sadness. Still, after shaking off her embarrassment, she followed it up with a timely inquiry about each of the kids.

More time passed, and after a dangerous fall, Mom decided to move to assisted living. Still, although her balance was unreliable, her notetaking about the grandkids was not.

"Was Marissa able to change college roommates?"

"Did Sean decide to go on the mission trip?"

"Has Chelsea written any new songs?"

Nothing in life prepares you for the first time you walk into your mother's world when she is no longer in it. After my mom passed, I scanned her room with its buttery walls and her butterfly bedspread, sniffing her pajamas, longing for signs of her presence—this one small woman who faithfully loved me and my children in such large ways.

And there they were. Her pencil cup full of erasable pens. Her soft-pink nail polish. Her small yellow legal pad. As usual, Gram Doris's final notes on the pad were hard to translate unless you happened to know shorthand. Weird lines. Curlicues. But also my kids' names. Tears pressed. These were the updates I had given her during our final phone call before she entered the hospital, never to return.

Some years have passed since that tender day when I gathered Mom's last yellow legal pad as if it was a treasure of infinite worth. Today, Mom's English floral "pencil cup" adorns my desk. And—joy upon joy!—I have two grandchildren of my own. Which means I now understand something about Gram Doris I couldn't have grasped back then: those shorthand squiggles had been much more than memory-nudges.

Every inky curve embodied her grandchildren's presence in her heart despite their physical distance. Every line testified to her bottomless love. I know this because between visits and phone calls, I find myself longing for the same kinds of updates about my grandkids.

"Is four-year-old Leon still into *Bluey*?"

"What is eight-year-old Olivia's favorite book today?"

Turns out, these little bits are the golden nuggets of grandparenthood. There is nothing trivial about the details that make each grandchild unique—hearts and minds growing, interests taking root, personalities blossoming. We grandmas cherish it all.

When, someday, my memory and handwriting go wobbly like Gram Doris's, I'll still be storing up every detail about my grandchildren in my heart. And if necessary, on a sunny-yellow legal pad.

Kit Tosello, author of *The Color of Home*, writes bighearted small-town novels and loves making bubble tea for her grandkids. Find info and inspiration at *KitTosello.com*.

Unhurried Love

SUSAN LAMBERT

I never thought I would feel the soft closeness of a tired toddler leaning against my body at the end of a long day ever again.

I thought the days of roaring dinosaurs and fast red toy race cars had well and truly passed me by.

And as hard as this empty-nest mama tried, I simply could not remember.

I could not remember all the lasts.

I could not remember the last time I carried your heavy, tired body on my hip as we walked home from the park.

I could not remember the last time your soft little toddler hand tucked inside mine to keep you safe when we crossed busy roads together.

I could not remember the way your bright eyes sparkled when you learned something new.

I could not remember the sound of your voice when "I love you, Mama" rolled off your lisping toddler tongue for the very first time.

I thought all those precious moments were over forever.

But then I became a grandma.

And suddenly, I found myself in the season of second chances.

A second chance to take in all the beautiful parts of childhood.

A second chance to feel it all again, without the heavy weight of responsibility that stole some of my joy the first time around.

A second chance to fill the love tank of my children's children.

And as this season of second chances unfolded, I began to understand the most precious gift a grandma has to give is the gift of an unhurried love—the gift of time.

Time to be fully present this time around.

Time to stroll slowly and be fully immersed in endless grandchild chatter.

Time to feed the fish and find birds nesting in trees.

Time to stop and look at planes and clouds and nighttime stars.

Time to embrace them with an unhurried extra layer of unconditional grandma love.

Time to sow seeds of love and faith into a new generation.

What a privilege it is to be a grandma.

Empty-nest mama, wife, and grandma Susan Lambert believes the power of faith and sharing stories changes lives. Find her on Instagram @mamastories_.

Of Course She Can

KELLI BACHARA

The other day, my son's stuffed animal got a tear in it. Upset, he asked me, "Do you think Memaw can fix it?"

"Of course she can," I answered,

It's the same answer I have whenever my daughter asks, "Can Memaw watch us when you leave?"

"Of course she can."

There's a question that often swirls around my head when I think about my mom: *What would we ever do without her?*

She's the one who brightens our days with her treats, her creativity, her energy, her ideas.

She's the one we call when we need the recipe, when we're looking for advice on how to handle a tough situation, or when we just want to talk to the person who truly loves us more than anyone else on the planet.

She's my mom, the one who has loved me since I was known to exist. And she's their grandma, loving them like a mom does—but somehow better.

I never had a grandma like my kids have. I didn't know the absolute treasure it is to be raised by a mom and *her* mama. What a blessing to be loved so deeply by two hearts that hold a child so dear, who would do anything for them.

GENTLE

I truly dread (and sometimes sit too long in) anticipatory grief when I think about the day she is no longer with us.

I know I shouldn't, but it's a reality of life. And I fear the hole in my kids' hearts will feel almost as big as my own.

Because what would we ever do without her?

But the thing is, a grandma's love extends beyond her life here on earth.

It lives in us. It's wired into our DNA.

God made her love special and fierce like that.

When she's not physically here, there will be a huge void in our lives, to be sure.

But even from heaven, can she remind us we are covered by her love and bring us that unique mom and grandma comfort like she always did?

Of course she can.

Kelli Bachara is a wife and mom of four from Minnesota. She loves writing, pickleball, Jesus, and her smoking-hot husband.

Lessons in Loss

KAREN PETERSON

Tucked away in a dark corner of my closet is a mug I hold dear. Looking at it makes me sad, but I can't bring myself to throw it away. It's my only connection to a grandchild I won't meet until I get to heaven.

The day my daughter, Beth, announced she was pregnant, my husband, son, and I were sitting in a restaurant with her and her husband, Michael. She offered me a gift bag. When I opened it, I saw the mug. It said, "Not Your Average Grandma." My husband and I looked at each other. I let out a whoop. "We're going to be grandparents!" My son was going to be an uncle. We jumped for joy and hugged each other and cried. We had waited so long for this day.

We took a group photo.

It's hard to look at that photo now.

The call came a few days later. Beth was crying. "I think I'm losing my baby." We were out of town, and I felt helpless. We prayed with her, but we couldn't be there physically. When we finally got there, she had miscarried. I held her in my arms while she sobbed. She described for me the agony she experienced, all the while knowing where it would lead. It seemed like a dirty trick had been played on her and on our family.

My husband likes to say, "When they're young, they sit on your lap. When they're older, they sit on your heart." My heart felt that weight as I watched my daughter and son-in-law walk through the whys and what-ifs of losing their baby. They tried to act like everything was okay so we wouldn't worry. They carried on normal conversations and laughed and joked with us, but I could see they were heartbroken. I prayed that as they struggled, they would be able to integrate what had happened with their faith and come out stronger for it. But I worried. After all, I'm a mom. And I longed to be a grandmother.

One of the hardest parts of being a parent is watching your children suffer. I wanted to comfort my daughter, but I didn't know what to say. I felt awkward talking about her miscarriage. I finally told her, "Something must have been wrong with the baby. That's why the body rejected it," as though that would comfort her. I cringe now, thinking of the pain those words must have inflicted on her heart.

A similar scenario repeated itself a few years later when my son, David, and his wife, Holly, invited us out to dinner. We were still in the parking lot on our way into the restaurant when they could no longer contain their excitement. "We're going to have a baby!" they told us. We hugged them and cried and jumped for joy. It had been a long road for this couple, full of waiting and fertility treatments. We sat down to eat and, between bites, talked about their hopes and dreams for this little one and what we as grandparents could do to help them.

When the call came that Holly had endured a miscarriage, we were heartbroken. But this time, I knew to be more sensitive. Platitudes were not appropriate. I knew just to be there, to listen, and to pray. Always to pray.

My daughter-in-law loves plants. During one of our visits, I gave her a prayer plant. My voice broke as I told her, "We're giving you this plant so every time you see it, you're reminded we're praying for you. And if something happens to this plant, we'll give you another one because we're not giving up praying for you."

God has been gracious since those days of sorrow. He has made us grandparents three times over, with another one on the way. I'm comforted by the thought that those little grandchildren I haven't met yet are being spoiled by their other grandparents and great-grandparents in heaven. Here on earth, I've learned a lesson about supporting my children and their children during difficult times. Now I stay away from platitudes and instead listen or just sit with them and say nothing. I'm learning to give my children and my grandchildren to God.

And to pray. Always to pray.

Karen Peterson speaks and writes about her passion: building healthy Christian marriages and families. She blogs at *To Grow a Family*.

Grandmothers and Friends

ALI FLYNN

As my wedding approached, my soon-to-be mother-in-law called my mom from the dressing room of a bridal store and asked her to come down.

She was trying on dresses, and as a mom to two sons and an only child, she wanted another opinion. She was nervous; was it the right style? The right fit? Was the color too close to my mom's dress?

An hour later, she ran out of the store to greet my mom, giggling like a schoolgirl. Immediately, I knew it—these two different yet remarkable women would be lifelong friends, two moms leaning into the opportunity for friendship.

Months later, they were hand in hand, lighting a candle at our wedding, and their friendship was sealed. They were not just friends; now they were family. They chose to put their adult children and future grandchildren front and center. With many phone calls over cups of hot tea, they laughed and prayed, building a lifelong friendship. A friendship that would model, mold, and shape traditions to span generations.

Once they became Nana and Grandma, they supported each other through stressful times at work, health scares, heartache, and loss. My children—their grandchildren—saw a bond that will impact them for the rest of their lives. They saw Nana and Grandma spending time together laughing in the kitchen on holidays, telling stories of the past, and cradling young babies while singing lullabies. They saw Nana and Grandma sharing family recipes and faith—and most importantly, praying with and for one another. They saw two women who loved each other and their grandchildren unconditionally.

Many years have passed since their laughter echoed in the kitchen, but Nana continues to keep Grandma's spirit alive now that she's gone. Each year as the peepers come out and birds begin to chirp letting us know spring is approaching, a warm Irish soda bread appears on our kitchen counter. It's Nana's little reminder that Grandma is forever with us.

She makes the bread using Grandma's family recipe, and I can only imagine as she stands at the counter, hands covered in flour while measuring raisins, how many conversations she recalls with her old friend, Grandma.

Now my girls stand next to Nana, aprons covered in dusty flour, as she teaches them how to make Grandma's bread. It's a balm to their souls and a beautiful reminder of Grandma. It's a recipe Nana also holds close to her heart and wants to pass on so her grandchildren never let go of their Grandma, her sweet friend.

When I listen to my mom share stories of Grandma with my kids, my heart is full.

I'm blessed these two women decided to come together rather than be at odds with each other, as many in-laws are.

I'm blessed they formed a friendship based on respect and understanding, communication and compassion.

I'm blessed these two women, who didn't always see eye to eye, put their differences aside, saw the big picture of a healthy family dynamic, and acted on it.

I'm blessed by two women who modeled what being a kind, compassionate woman and friend truly means.

But most importantly, I'm blessed my children had Nana and Grandma love them "a bushel and a peck and a hug around the neck," while sharing a warm slice of Irish soda bread.

Creator of *Hang in There, Mama*, Ali Flynn offers encouragement to moms while reminding them they are not alone on their motherhood journey.

In the End

MIKALA ALBERTSON

It doesn't matter, in the end, the size of your house or the quality of your clothes. That petty disagreement you can't get over or the title behind your name. The wrinkles around your eyes or those fancy vacations (or lack thereof). The number on the scale or in your bank account. Your awards or accolades. The resentment you've kept buried deep in your heart.

None of it matters, really. We can let it go.

Because what matters are the people.

What matters are the relationships. The connections built over decades, some hard fought and largely flawed.

What matters is the making of us—the people mixed together with all that love and all those memories into one loud, imperfect family. The family left behind when my grandmother died.

We celebrated her life in a way she would've loved. With chicken salad and homemade ice cream spread on plastic tables in eastern Nebraska. With children in wet swimsuits running in from the rec hall pool to cram a few cookies into their mouths before sprinting back to the water. With uncles playing rounds of cornhole and aunts giving earsplitting screams through shrieks of laughter when someone finally got an answer right in family trivia. With stories, all of us laughing and crying in turn. With hugs, long and close. And with tears mingling on our cheeks.

What matters now is how we remember her.

Remember her hands kneading dough for cinnamon rolls or German kolaches?

Remember how she loved polka music?

Remember her teddy bear obsession and that ridiculous sound one of the teddies made that sounded more like cows mooing?

Remember her funny accent? Her laugh? Remember the story of how she cut her boys' hair? Or that time she tucked a one-hundred-dollar bill up my sleeve on Christmas?

Remember how she loved babies (especially squishing their chubby little feet) and violets (south-facing window, talk to them every day, water from the bottom)?

Remember . . . *her*?

She did the best she could to love her family. This family. Us.

In the end, it's all that matters.

Dr. Mikala Albertson is the author of *Everything I Wish I Could Tell You about Midlife: A Woman's Guide to Health in the Body You Actually Have.*

A Grandma Shows Up for Her Grandchildren Before They're Born

JENNY ALBERS

"Are you scared?" my mom asked.

"Yeah," I croaked into the phone, my cracking voice giving away the tears in my eyes.

Her question might seem an unlikely response to a pregnancy announcement, but my mom offered the exact one I needed. I *was* scared, and her question told me she didn't expect me to pretend otherwise.

Not many people understood this pregnancy announcement wasn't a standard one. This was a pregnancy announcement steeped in grief. One bound by uncertainty, on the heels of a stillbirth. The announcement from my previous pregnancy still lingered in the air, unfulfilled in ways too sorrowful to sufficiently describe.

So, yes, I was scared. Afraid of enduring the heartache of another loss. Fearful another pregnancy would end in unspeakable grief. Terrified of delivering a baby but coming home empty-handed. Again.

My mom understood this.

Though she didn't explicitly say it, I knew the thought of watching me endure another loss scared her, as did the idea of losing another grandbaby. A mother is deeply invested in the well-being of her children, and a grandmother in the well-being of her grandchildren, no matter their age or life stage.

Days later, after an unexpected OB appointment, I hesitantly made another phone call to my mom with an update. I was just days into my second trimester, and there were already concerns. I had been told to stay off my feet, to get as much help as possible for daily tasks and responsibilities, to take it easy in every way—all to help prevent complications and keep my baby growing inside my womb for as long as possible.

"Do you need me to come?" my mom asked. I didn't need to respond; she already knew the answer was yes.

So she came. Again and again, she showed up. But she wasn't just showing up for me—she was showing up for the baby I was carrying. Her grandchild. The baby we both wanted to hold in our arms.

My mom understood what was at stake. My heart, for one, but more importantly, my baby's life . . . her grandbaby's life. She was determined to do what she could to help bring this child safely into the world. Despite a calendar full of other commitments, she was committed to showing up for her grandchild—even before the baby was born.

Because that's what a grandma does.

During those long months of my anxiety-filled pregnancy, my mom's love for the grandchild housed in my womb showed up in the form of service. Love looked like cooking meals for my family and preparing freezer meals for when she wasn't there. It looked like standing in for me when I couldn't pick up my young daughter or participate in play as actively as I had before these restrictions. It looked like sacrificing the time, energy, and freedom semiretirement is supposed to provide, all in the name of caring for me and my unborn baby.

As time tiptoed by, her love showed up in the form of grocery shopping, washing dishes, doing laundry, and cleaning up after my family even though she was supposed to be done with that stage of life. She picked up where I had abruptly left off when an ultrasound suggested my pregnancy was high risk.

More than seven months after that phone call announcing my pregnancy, my mom showed up again. This time, anticipating the arrival of the baby she'd helped care for. But the baby didn't come. Not yet. And I know she felt it too—the disappointment, the fear, the anxiety.

Two weeks later, she showed up again and at last held in her arms the baby she'd done everything in her power to protect—her grandson. All eight pounds, fifteen ounces of him.

My mom started showing up for my son before he was born, and now she has the privilege of showing up to watch her grandson grow from a baby into a boy. I can't think of a better gift for any grandchild—or mother.

Jenny Albers is a Midwestern wife and mother, and the author of *Courageously Expecting: 30 Days of Encouragement for Pregnancy after Loss.*

Grandma Put the "Home" in Homemade

NATASHA SMITH

I traced her steps across the kitchen as I sat at the end of the table, legs swinging back and forth, watching her prepare a Sunday feast. Her favorite light-blue apron outlined in white eyelet ruffles was tied at her waist, and it shifted and swayed as she methodically stirred fresh-cut collards from her garden in the huge pot on the stove.

She walked from the chess (what she called a standing cabinet) to the counter, from the kitchen sink to the stove, and back and forth again. Her hands covered in flour, she was making homemade biscuits, of course, which paired delectably with her homemade pear preserves. All the vegetables she cooked were homegrown and fresh from her garden. She made just about everything you could think of from scratch, including her famous chocolate fall-apart cakes.

Grandma Emma's house was the go-to house after church. Many would stop by to see the family and, of course, see if they could get a plate of food and dessert. But they didn't have to think twice because there was always food there. And with open hands, she gave graciously and generously.

Grandma Emma was a homemaker if I've ever seen one. Everything she made was homemade, from food to handsewn quilts. Her quilts were so heavy I could hardly move under them in bed, but during the winter, they kept us warm and cozy under her love.

At her house, homemade food was and still is the language of love. To go to Grandma's house and not get something to eat when it was offered was like cussing. You'd better grab a plate, eat, and get a glass of freshly squeezed lemonade to wash it all down.

Every time I went to visit Grandma Emma when I was younger, whether it was on a Sunday afternoon or for an overnight stay, I could find her either at the stove or in her rocking chair by the window. In the summer, the window would be cracked to let in fresh air. She'd sit there while she made conversation with guests. I loved being in that small sitting room adjacent to the kitchen, people-watching with her, seeing who was coming in and out of the house, and watching how Grandma loved on them all. It seemed like the entire town would file through to "say hey to Miss Emma just for a little while."

At five feet and a few inches tall, Grandma Emma was what you'd call small yet mighty. She raised eleven children, mostly on her own. She had a village, but she was the one who held it together. She was always sowing her love, time, faith, and talents into the lives of those around her—her family, friends, and the community. You can tell by the way people still come by the house today, especially on Sundays. They stop by to see if Miss Emma is up to seeing visitors (and, of course, to grab a plate of food on their way out).

She made such an impression on me with her beautiful spirit and how she loved me and those around her that I named my first baby girl Emma in her honor. God has truly blessed the work of her hands, and she has been able to see generation after generation.

Now when I visit, I find her either in bed or in her chair by the table. She needs extra assistance these days, but at one hundred years old and counting, her mind is as sharp as a tack. She speaks softly but with strength. Though she's changed physically, her heart is still as big as the sun, her smile as radiant as the moon. Her laugh is as jovial as ever and fills a room with warmth and joy. The heartfelt "You know I love you" she offers every time I see her floods my soul.

Though she hasn't been able to make anything homemade in years, Grandma Emma's presence means everything to me—and makes everything and everyone around her feel at home.

Natasha Smith is a certified grief educator, wife, mom, author, and North Carolina native. Find her books on Amazon and connect on social media @imnatashasmith.

Three Tiny Bibs

KRISTEN HOUGHTON

My grandmother lost three children, all under the age of three, over a period of seven years. Between the ages of twenty to twenty-seven, my grandmother had more than her fair share of grief—and I didn't know about any of it.

She never spoke about it; no one in the family did. I was twelve years old when I asked my mother why Nana never really smiled. My mother hinted that Nana had endured "family hardships" but gave no specifics, no context for my grandmother's sadness.

I didn't understand her emotional pain until the summer I had a miscarriage.

I had a loving relationship with my grandmother. She was always there; she rarely left her house—a sweet Italian lady who was happy to see me whenever I stopped by. I loved that she called me Bella, the Italian word for *beautiful*. There was always food cooking at her house; it smelled of lemon, basil, and fresh herbs. She made the best chicken soup I have ever tasted. Her Thanksgiving stuffing was out-of-this-world delicious. Her lemonade, made with fresh lemons, is a big part of my happy summer memories.

But as much as I loved visiting her, I sensed a certain reserve that kept affection at arm's length. As a teen, I attributed it to her generation, one that didn't openly show displays of affection. I would kiss her hello and goodbye, but as far as saying "I love you," she only said it in response to me. I was the one who always initiated it.

"I love you, Nana."

"I love you, too, Bella."

Still, I knew that my grandmother loved me. Her seeming lack of affection was just part of who she was, the same as the neatly coiled bun and old-fashioned bib aprons she wore. It was just Nana.

These days, we want to know everything about our ancestors—who they really were, what happened in their lives, every little detail—to somehow help us know ourselves better through their stories. But in my grandmother's day, painful things that happened were rarely, if ever, discussed, even within the family. Whether it was from the desire to shield family members from things too personal and painful to talk about or a misplaced feeling of guilt over not having been able to prevent tragedy, her generation kept a great deal of pain inside.

I'd been married for two years when I became pregnant. Three months into the pregnancy, I miscarried. My emotions ran the gamut from sad to angry to hopeful for another pregnancy and back to sad again. The sadness always won. It was now a part of my life, and I didn't know how to help myself. Sadness followed me, my constant companion.

One day, I was sitting in my garden when I heard someone knocking on the gate. I was surprised to see Nana on the other side, holding a small package in one hand and a tall bottle of lemonade in the other.

"I want to sit in your garden, Bella, and drink lemonade with you. I want to talk to you," she said.

We settled into deck chairs in the shade to drink lemonade. My grandmother handed me the small package and told me to open it. Inside were three tiny baby bibs embroidered with the names *Jimmy*, *Rudy*, and *Eda*.

I looked at Nana in confusion.

She touched my hand. "Those are the names of my children, the ones who died," she said.

I shook my head. *Died?* Nana had children other than my mother?

"I kept the bibs in a closet for more than fifty years just to keep their memories in my heart. But today, I bring them to you so you can know I understand your hurt."

As we sipped lemonade, she told me about her first three children. Generoso "Jimmy" was born in Italy when Nana was twenty. He died during a flu epidemic that swept Europe, and she felt as if her heart would never heal. Her second son, Rudy, died a "crib death" in New York City a few years after she immigrated to the United States with my grandfather. Her first daughter, Eda, a sweet little girl who had an unknown heart ailment, died a few months before her third birthday.

I was stunned. "I didn't know, Nana. I'm so sorry. Why didn't I know?"

Nana told me her tragedies weren't something you talked about, especially to children. She kept the pain inside.

She also told me when she found out she was pregnant with my mother, she was upset. She didn't want another baby because she couldn't go through another loss. But my mother thrived and was a healthy baby. She was a good child who became a wonderful woman. Nana thanked God for my mother.

We talked and cried together, and I came to know more about my grandmother in the late hours of a warm afternoon than I had ever known before. That she had kept her sadness to herself so as not to burden anyone else was heart-touching; so was the fact that she came to be with me, to help me with my own sorrow, which, though painful and sad, was nowhere near what she had endured.

That afternoon, our hearts connected in a way only two women's hearts ever can. I saw Nana as a beautiful light, one of bravery shining through grief in the form of three tiny bibs.

Kristen Houghton is a WNYC bestselling author who writes the popular series A Cate Harlow Private Investigation.

PART 2

SO GOD MADE A GRANDMA

wise

The greatest gift I can give the world is **strong, kind, cherished** children and grandchildren who've never doubted for a moment how **very** LOVED they are.

KRISTA WARD

The Knowing

LESLIE MEANS

I cheer for my kids.

I yell encouraging words during soccer games, basketball games, and dance competitions. I'm the mom who sits in front of music recitals and plays, standing and clapping to make sure my kids know I'm proud of them. I snap photos, give high fives, and send as much encouragement to my kids as possible.

I yell so my kids hear me. I also yell encouragement for their teammates. Sometimes, if the other team does something well, I'll yell for them.

I do this because my mom did this for me.

I still hear her voice yelling, "Go, Leslie, GO!"

Even though I wouldn't admit it then, her cheers helped me run faster during those track meets. She made me feel important, seen, and loved.

I still remember that feeling, and I'll do everything I can to ensure my kids do too.

Now, my parents and my in-laws do the same for my kids.

They show up when they're able, cheer when they can, and watch when their grandkids sit on the bench, score the winning basket, or desperately try to get that volleyball over the net.

Of course, it doesn't matter if our team wins—they aren't there for the game. They're there for their grandkids.

I didn't understand it then, but now I know showing up is more valuable than any gift or trinket. It doesn't need to be perfect, planned, or even on time—it's one of the best gifts we can give our loved ones.

Just show up. For the big stuff, yes, and the little things too.

I realize this isn't easy for everyone. Sometimes, parents and grandparents live hours away.

But you can send an encouraging text message, make a quick phone call, write a letter, or say a prayer before they hit the court or go onstage.

Just show up. It's the greatest gift we can give.

Grandmothers seem to know this instinctively. They just have a clearer vision of what's important, don't they? It shows in the way they love everyone around them—their kids, their grandkids, their friends, their neighbors. Maybe that wisdom has been hard-fought, or maybe it evolved naturally as years passed. Either way, it's priceless.

In the next several stories, you'll catch a glimpse of that gift, and it's a wonder to behold.

The Secret Life of Grandmas

DEBBIE PRATHER

Can I tell you a secret?

I sleep with a grandpa.

And, by that, I mean, I share a bed with a grandpa, and we don't *always* sleep.

Can I tell you something else?

Sometimes we get silly in the kitchen, and I dance with him in a way that I'm sure many wouldn't consider to be, ahem, grandmotherly.

This probably makes you crinkle your nose, and I get it. I really do. My grandparents never thought about that forbidden three-letter-word, much less had it. I'm not even certain how our family line continued.

But, after thirty-four years of matrimony, I still view my beloved as the twenty-four-year-old I married, not as "Pop," as he's known these days. He reminds me daily that he sees me not just as "Nonny" but as his bride.

Despite having grown kids and grandchildren, we haven't been willing to embrace the notion that we're in the older category. Mirrors constantly argue this point, but we stick out our tongues at them and move on. A retirement association has sent us more than a few unrequested flyers urging us to join, but we quietly slide them into the recycling bin.

It's not just mirrors and mailers that remind us of our age (and the stigma attached).

Recently, at a dermatology appointment, the young doctor's assistant lectured me about using sunscreen daily. She said, "And make sure to rub it into your hands." Then she added with a sassy tilt of her head, "You don't want grandma hands."

"Why not?" I replied, biting my tongue to answer politely. "I am a grandma."

Later, I wished I'd said, "There's no greater blessing than having grandma hands!"

Grandma hands can rub backs and foreheads, bake cookies and make pancakes, help, hug, and hold. I plan to continue with the aforementioned and so very much more. I'll savor this season for as long as my heart beats and my lungs inflate with air.

The serious side of me can't deny it's hard getting older though. My worst fear when our three were growing up was that I would be taken too soon and our children would have to grow up without a mother. I'd experienced the loss of my father when I was a teen, and I never wanted them to know that life-altering heartache.

By the generous grace of God, I've lived beyond my dad's age, and I have the blessing of two beautiful granddaughters. I know, in the natural order of things, they will, at some point in their lives, have to say goodbye to me. I've learned not to dwell on these morbid thoughts, but at times I agonize about making the absolute most of these years we have together.

That's another secret: Grandmas are no different than you. They have fears, worries, and insecurities. They love their family and friends and don't ever want them to be hurt or sad. Like you, they want world peace and safety for all children and people around the globe.

Just as I didn't know what it was going to feel like to be a mom until I became a mom, I didn't know what it was going to feel like to be a grandmother until I became a grandmother. What I've found is that I'm me. (Well, me along with the reemergence of the "I'd run into a burning building, stand in front of a speeding freight train, and lay down my life for you" kind of crazy love for two little ones that has captured me with the same savage intensity as when ours were small.) I don't have everything figured out. Sure, I've matured, evolved, and acquired patience and a yielding ability that only dozens of trips around the sun can provide, but the essence of who I am hasn't changed.

Being a grandmother is the greatest season of life, as most would tell you, but paradoxically, it's mixed with the bittersweet wistfulness and sand-through-the hourglass awareness that's present when you're beyond the halfway mark.

Just when you have more confidence and clarity of purpose internally, outward qualities you used to appreciate about yourself can crumble and fade. Losing vibrancy in appearance can hold us back if we let it. But why should we? What and who do we hide from? The judgment of humans who are growing older by the second also?

Grandmas are the same as you. They have wants, needs, and desires. They want to have passion and romance, even when the world tells them that at some point it's all just supposed to stop. They sometimes act younger than their age and behave in unexpected, un-grandmotherly ways because their inner selves are still who they were decades ago. They don't want to become insignificant; they want their lives to continue to matter.

And therein lies the most important secret: If you ever have a day when you walk past a reflection of a grandma and wonder how to relate, what you could possibly have in common with her, or what she has to give, dig down deep and remember. You could very well be looking at yourself—only older.

---

742 I Love You holds special meaning to Debbie Prather, her husband, and their family—the reason her blog is so named.

I Don't Have a Grandma, but I Do Have Marlys

AMY ALLENDER

"Hey, are you home? Wondering if I could come by." Tears blurred my vision as I read and reread the text. I closed my eyes and attempted to take a steadying breath but could only manage to force a jagged bit of air down my throat and release it as another sob.

The worst of the panic attack had passed and given way to the ugliest of ugly cries. Several months earlier, I had experienced a mental health crisis, complete with all the trimmings: suicidal depression, self-loathing, self-harm, panic, and crippling anxiety. I'd begun to recover but still found myself in that precarious place between learning a new, healthier way of thinking and being thrown backward into the abyss.

Unpleasant news had just led back to the abyss.

Amid all the irrational thoughts cycling through my head like a washing machine with something to prove, one piece of logic broke through: *It's not safe to be alone.* That's practically Depression 101. That's why I'd taken out my phone. That's why I'd drafted the text.

I didn't want company; in fact, I craved solitude. My desire was to handle things alone, aiming to preserve the facade of being a good wife, friend, and ministry leader. Although I hadn't yet heard the term "high-functioning depression and anxiety," it perfectly described my situation. Despite my adept concealment, my world had crumbled, and each day was a battle to regain my sanity.

I forced my trembling finger to hit "Send."

The reply came almost instantly, "Come over anytime. I'd love to see you."

Fifteen minutes later, I knocked on a familiar door.

There was Marlys. The woman I'd met at church. The woman who invited me over for movie nights. The woman I admired for her wisdom, ability to learn, and independence. As a military spouse, I was states away from my family, but Marlys had become like family.

"I'm sorry to come over like this. But I really think I need to be with someone," I said, uncomfortably aware of my puffy eyes and stress-induced odor.

Her face was kind, only gently concerned. There was no alarm or over-the-top reaction. Just a solemn "Come on in, sweetie."

I curled up on the sofa. She brought the tissues.

She listened while I shared the unfiltered truth of my struggles. I confided in her about the depression I tried to mask, the shame I felt, my debilitating anxiety, and the therapy that had slowly begun to work. She nodded while I explained I'd been living in a nearly empty house since my husband left for his Air Force assignment and I stayed behind to wrap up the move. "I just don't know what to do. It seems like things are never going to be okay again," I said.

I needed a grandmother. But both of mine were gone.

Grandmothers enable a special brand of vulnerability. You can be transparent with a grandmother in ways you can't with a peer—or even a mother. Her vantage point is one only afforded by age. Her wisdom is deep and hard-won, but she is approachable and safe. She is not easily shocked, having weathered life's trials. Her very presence is proof love can be recovered from devastating heartaches. After all, she is both loving and easy to love.

I needed a grandmother. And there she was.

Marlys had a husband in assisted living, stepchildren, grandchildren, and great-grandchildren of her own, yet she made room for one more. We shared no DNA, but when I needed a grandma, genetics didn't matter. It was love that counted, and there was plenty to be had.

She leaned in and shared the profound sadness she had endured in her own life. She didn't offer false reassurances or downplay the severity of the situation. Instead, she showed me through her own experiences that, with faith, tragedy can be transformed into something meaningful. She taught me the sorrow we hold today can be written into the joyful narrative our lives will ultimately tell.

When it seemed like there were no more words to say, she said, "Where are you sleeping until it's time for you to move?"

"On an air mattress in my bedroom. The movers came a couple days ago, but I have some pots and folding chairs," I replied.

"Go home. Pack a bag. Get your toothbrush. You're not staying in an empty house by yourself. You're staying here tonight."

I stayed with Marlys for the next month.

It's been almost a decade since the day I knocked on Marlys's door. Now, when I look in the mirror, I notice faint lines and gray hairs beginning to emerge. Signs of age. When I'm tempted to lament the passage of time, I remember that pivotal day and grab on to hope. Aging gives us the opportunity to be the grandmother—biological or otherwise—someone will lean on. We can embrace the wisdom gained from life's trials and allow time to cultivate a compassionate spirit within us.

We can find hope in growing older. We can eagerly anticipate the moment we'll become the wise woman who opens the door to someone in need of a grandmother.

Amy Allender is a speaker and writer whose superpower is transforming overstimulation, burnout, and negativity into fun, order, and peace. More at her eponymous website.

I Wonder

KRISTA WARD

I wonder if I'll slow down.

If I won't be so tied up in the hustle and bustle and beautiful chaos that consumes my days right now. If I'll be able to simply relax into my role, like a cozy, well-worn sweater on a chilly autumn day. If I'll be able to take my sweet time loving and listening and holding and helping, in much the same way I do now, yet somehow completely different.

I wonder if I'll savor the moments.

If I'll look at them through an entirely new lens, knowing how fleeting this time is, cherishing each millisecond for what it is. If I'll sit with them and watch the birds flit from tree to tree, ice cream dripping down our sticky fingers on a sunshiny day, in much the same way I do now, yet somehow completely different.

I wonder if I'll settle into my role.

If I'll no longer get so caught up in the little stuff, the stuff the years have taught me doesn't truly matter, and allow myself to just be. If I won't spend my days questioning whether my loving them is enough, instead knowing and trusting that the greatest gift I can give the world is strong, kind, cherished children who've never doubted for a moment how very loved they are, in much the same way I do now, yet somehow completely different.

I wonder if I'll find unflinching confidence.

If I'll trust myself in a brand-new way, employing the wisdom I've gleaned over years of highs and lows of raising my own children to feel like they just might be getting the best version of me. If I'll carefully choose my battles and listen more than I talk and give them my all, without hesitation, in much the same way I do now, yet somehow completely different.

I wonder if I'll laugh over spilled milk.

If little messes and mishaps will feel like less of an inconvenience and more of an opportunity for grace and learning. If we'll giggle and talk about how sometimes those silly cups seem to slip right through our hands as we grab rags to soak up the puddle, in much the same way I do now, yet somehow completely different.

I wonder if I'll serve dessert before dinner.

If I'll feel a sense of freedom in knowing not everything has to be so by the book, remembering from the days with my own little ones it's the unexpected that often brings incomparable joy, memories that won't soon be forgotten. If I'll set cookies fresh from the oven atop the counter, eager hands and stomachs waiting impatiently for a predinner treat, in much the same way I do now, yet somehow completely different.

I wonder if I'll read all the bedtime stories.

If I'll no longer feel the nagging of the dishes in the kitchen sink or the school lunches that need making as we snuggle on sheets covered with cars and trucks and buses and planes. If we'll sing songs and make up silly stories and read as many books as our hearts desire, worried far less about what else needs doing and far more about those sacred, sleepy moments together, in much the same way I do now, yet somehow completely different.

I wonder if I'll be like them.

If I'll be the comfort and wisdom of Granny, the strength and steadfastness of Nanny. If I'll be the best parts of my own mom and mother-in-law, the women I've been fortunate enough to watch blossom into grandmas right before my eyes. If all the remarkable ways they love and encourage and support will become pieces of my own heart, in much the same way they are now, yet somehow completely different.

WISE

But I don't have to wonder if I'll fall hopelessly in love.
If I'll thank God each and every day for such incredibly precious lives to love.
If I'll bask in the immense beauty of this new season of life.
And if I'll trust there's no grander title I've ever held than Grandma.
I know I will.

Krista Ward, creator of *Kisses from Boys*, **is a wife and mom with a heart for encouraging others through every messy, beautiful moment of motherhood.**

Oma

SAVANNAH LYON

When you have an Oma whose first language is German and second is English, you might find yourself amused by her words.

She mixed *tomatoes* and *tornadoes*, which was slightly confusing to five-year-old me when both existed in the same season. She called cucumbers *cacoomers*, which she grew in the homestead garden—all that was left of the land her husband's grandparents pioneered in the 1800s.

Every Sunday, family dinner was pot roast, and she would say, "What we don't have, we won't eat" in her thick German accent. Later, she'd scold, "Clean your plate so it will be a nice day tomorrow."

She's been gone for a few years now, but I often replay a video of her at a restaurant trying my favorite green drink made of tart vegetables. She puckered her wrinkled, thin lips and said, "Oh, Savannah, that could kill a horse." And I laugh, at her reaction and at my own laughter recorded in the video.

Oma told stories so outside my reality they sometimes seemed like fairy tales. Growing up, she lived near a castle. One story goes that she snuck in and was locked inside, like her own real-life version of Rapunzel.

Once she was asked to help a farmer; her task was holding the reins of a horse hitched to a wagon. When the horse yawned, she thought it was going to bite her head right off, so she dropped the reins and ran away. She never recovered.

Other stories were nightmares. She was deathly afraid of the dark—a phobia that never left her, even at ninety years of age.

Sometimes, when she was brave, she talked about the war. How she and the other children her age had to go to youth camp.

She told us about her neighbor who said the blood of the youth was on Hitler's hands. He was never seen again.

On her way to school, she passed the bodies of anti-Nazis hanging from trees.

"You keep your mouth shut," her father warned sternly. A slip of the tongue, and that would be her or her parents or her older siblings. Life was not unlike a game of poker, pretending and keeping secrets. It's no wonder she lived afraid of the night.

It was barely spoken about, but sometimes she told us about the Mormons and Jews her family hid in the basement. When it was safe, she would sneak them food, coffee, and the newspaper. After the war, they hid German soldiers from the American army. The soldiers had been drafted—forced, unwilling. Sometimes I wondered if she feared being caught, even here in the United States, even sixty years later.

Her family lived near a concentration camp where people with disabilities were taken. Many years after the war, she returned to visit with my mom and aunt. "Oh, the smell," Oma said, remembering the stench of burned bodies that filtered their air and the horror of it all.

Oma lost siblings during the war. Her older brother, called into mandatory army service to guard Hitler's palace, was killed in an air raid, not allowed to take shelter. Her sister left the foxhole to retrieve a watch gifted by their father. She didn't make it back, hit in the head by a brick during the air raid. Later, the family discovered her father had been buried in a factory for three days. I can only imagine the terror she must have felt.

When my daughter was in seventh grade, her class studied the Holocaust. What a coincidence, maybe, that they teach this in middle school, the students the same age as Oma and Anne Frank were at the time. Middle school really is its own kind of dark night of the soul.

Oma's memory was already fading, but these early years of her life remained strong in her mind, as is common with dementia. She was invited to share with the class about her life. She spoke of growing up in Nazi Germany. Of the youth camp. Of the war.

And then she repeated with great emphasis: "They were just like you and me. They were no different. There was no reason . . ."

Of all the things Oma had to say, those words were her most important. Her legacy for future generations.

Savannah Lyon loves her kids, dogs, and Jesus too. She writes encouragement for embracing faith in the messiness of life on her website and socials.

And Just like That, I'm a Grandmother

CINDY FARR

I wasn't the mom who was yearning to have grandbabies. I figured it would happen when it happened. We had our boys later in life, and they seemed to be in no rush to marry and start families. We had gotten used to retirement and grown children. Then the sweetest and most adorable little baby boy joined our family.

I am thrilled with this little guy. I want to be helpful and involved but not overbearing and pushy. I have been thinking about a guide (okay, specifically ten gentle suggestions) for all of us Mee-maws, Honeys, Mimis, Nanas—grandmothers.

1. **Things have changed.** Yep, little things and big things. Babies now sleep on their backs, and they don't have bumpers in the crib. They have a SNOO instead of a bassinet and sleep with white-noise machines, eliminating the need to put your baby on top of your dryer to get the same effect (don't judge me, it worked). Formula is different and bottles are better. Face it—anything you used for your kids has now been replaced with safer, shinier, and improved products. This is not a bad thing. It just means you keep quiet and observe; we no longer know the latest and greatest.
2. **Everything is a big thing.** No one has the right to measure your problem. When it is *your* problem, *your* baby, and *your* life, it's big.

So don't minimize anything. Your baby not wanting the bottle after nursing all his life was a huge problem (okay, that was me). It's all real and happening for the first time, and no one wants to hear "little children, little problems." Nope. *My* problem. Big. Huge.

3. **This is not your baby.** You do not get to have the big moments. If that baby takes his first steps when he's at your house, it never happened. Do not take the little guy for his first haircut (yep, that one happened), and don't pierce those little ears. Mom and Dad get those firsts. Let them have them. All of them. You had your turn.

4. **Never drop in unannounced.** Really? We need to be told this? It's not hard to call and check to see if it's a good time. And if it's not a good time, don't breeze in anyway. If anything, the baby means they need *more* privacy.

5. **Don't judge. Be supportive.** Okay, two things, but they go together. Few people know what to really expect when they have a baby, and many have never actually cared for one (me again). They will figure it out. I was determined to sing a lullaby to my newborn. I didn't know any lullabies. I rocked him in my arms, singing while reading the words to "Hush, Little Baby." Such a tender moment that could have been ruined by judgment or ridicule. I eventually learned the words and always remembered the support, which in this case translated to not laughing at me. (And now I can giggle at the thought of it.)

6. **Be a giver.** Are the new parents exhausted? Bring dinner. Offer to hold the baby while they eat (bonus!). Offer to babysit to give them a break. Check in on them. Ask if they need anything at the store. You don't need to do this every day; just help when you can.

7. **Follow directions.** If you have been told a specific way to care for the baby, do it. Follow the bedtime routine, observe playtimes and naptimes, and do what the little one is used to doing. 'Nuff said.

8. **Know your limitations.** My friend took care of her grands their entire first year. My children do not expect this, which is great because I know I couldn't do it. Maybe your limitation is physical, maybe it's time, or

maybe it's just a matter of preference. Time spent together should be enjoyable for everyone. Don't set yourself up for failure.

9. **Set a precedent.** Like a first baby, the first grandchild is kind of a guinea pig. We figured out what worked and then we did the same thing for all three boys. It worked for a lot of things. When it comes to grands, be consistent. Siblings notice when they aren't treated the same. Be realistic and have fun—start some traditions!

10. **Love, love, love.** These grandkids are blessings. I look back at our child-rearing years and wonder how we did it all. So busy with kids, work, church, community, school, sports—such busy lives. We fit *so* much into each day. Now we should enjoy these precious grands. Just love them! It seems like such a simple task.

I'm pretty sure I'm going to mess up some of these things. I probably already have. I wasn't a perfect mom, and it's looking like I'm not going to be the perfect grandmother either (perfection is overrated, right?). But I do want to continue to be in my children's and grandchildren's lives, and I know one thing for sure: I am all in on number ten.

Cindy Farr blogs at *Tropical Life, Food and Fun* and currently lives in Pass-a-Grille, Florida.

The Best Gift I Ever Gave My Teenager Was Her Grandmother

SANDRA SAMOSKA

"I'm going to Grandma's house."

I looked up as my teenage daughter came downstairs and grabbed her keys. "Is everything okay?"

She slipped on her shoes and slid her phone into her back pocket, smiling and shrugging her shoulders at the same time. "Yes," she said, "I just wanted to hang out, and she said I could come over."

I watched out the window as she climbed into her car, smiling faintly at her disappearing taillights.

There are many things I've given my children through the years, both tangible and intangible, but one of the best things is the chance to form a close relationship with their grandmothers.

It can be so easy, especially when children are small, to be consumed by the day-to-day decisions and worries of parenting. Without conscious thought, I could have easily relegated my children's grandmothers to the role of familial obligation or emergency babysitter. A grandmother is so much more than that though. She is an opportunity, a gift we can give our children of a person who will be there for them and love them forever.

Partly because we live close by, but mostly because of who they are, my mother and mother-in-law have been fixtures in my children's lives since they were born.

They took turns watching the kids when they were small so my husband and I could go on dates. They cheered at school plays, choir concerts, and ball games. They kissed skinned knees, sang at birthday parties, and played board games.

All those moments, big and small, laid the foundation for these special teenage years. My teenagers don't need babysitting or Band-Aids anymore, but now more than ever they need to go to Grandma's house.

Grandma's house is welcoming. It's a second home you don't have to clean, a place you can take your shoes off and sprawl on the sofa. My children know where the snacks are and that there are always special ones on hand just for them.

Grandma's house is quiet. Not so much for lack of noise but for lack of demands. My girls' grandmothers give them the time, space, and sometimes the silence my teenagers need. The girls know they can talk if they want or be quiet if they don't. They can discuss school, boyfriends, sports, music, faith, fears, or the way they want to get their nails done. There is no pressure to spill their secrets, but their secrets are safe if they're offered.

Grandma's house is safe. There is never any question of acceptance. The door is always unlocked, time is always made, and the joy felt in their presence is constant, honest, and visible. My teenagers can leave their masks at the door, knowing their true selves are exactly what Grandma wants to see.

Grandma's house is peaceful. When my daughters go to Grandma's, they know they're guaranteed time away from friend drama, sibling aggravation, and parental demands. They know their grandmother has rules and values that must be followed, but there is no pressure to perform or pacify anyone else.

When my daughter came home from her grandma's house that day, I could tell something inside her had shifted and settled.

"How was it?"

She glanced at me as she hung up her keys. "It was good."

"Did you do anything special?"

My daughter, this almost-adult with my hair and her father's eyes, shook her head and smiled a little. "Nope, we just sat outside for a while. I helped her pull some weeds."

That was it. Nothing special or elaborate. No big adventures or expensive outings—just quiet time pulling weeds with her grandmother.

I never know exactly what they talk about on these visits, but time spent at Grandma's house is never wasted. Sometimes, I believe, my teenagers receive wise counsel from a trusted source. Sometimes they simply get time and space to process their own feelings. Most times I think ice cream is involved, although I never ask about that part.

Some gifts in life are fleeting.

Some are expensive.

Some are fun for a while but quickly lose their shine.

The gift of a grandmother is a treasure that grows in value the longer you have her. And for a teenager, the gift of a grandmother is priceless.

Sandra Samoska teaches for her local BSF and writes about faith and family on *Outnumbered*. **She lives with her husband and four kids in Texas.**

My Kids Don't Have Their Grandma's Eyes, They Have Her Heart

MARALEE BRADLEY

Sometimes I wonder if my mom knew, if she sensed it or had a premonition.

We were standing in the toy aisle, and I can still see the scene play out in my mind, some thirty-five years later. There were so many dolls of all different colors and shapes and sizes. She asked which one I wanted. I picked one with a skin tone very different from my own. She paused. She asked me if I wanted this one instead—the one with blue eyes and blonde curls, like my own. But I didn't. So she happily bought the doll that looked nothing like my other dolls. Nothing like me.

I've often wondered if it was then she envisioned a different life for me than the one she might have originally pictured. If she imagined me with kids who looked nothing like me and nothing like her or the family we came from—the ancestry she's always been so proud of. I've wondered if that was the moment she started preparing to become a grandma who doesn't need a biological connection or a physical resemblance in order to be fully invested in the lives of her grandchildren. The grandma my kids have been so blessed by.

In my early twenties, I became the house mom in a group home for teens. Immediately after graduating from college, I took on the responsibility of loving and caring for a house full of boys who had been through some of the hardest realities you can imagine. And I loved them so deeply. I saw that love reflected in my mom's eyes when she came to visit. She needed to see for herself that I was okay, that this was going to be okay. When I watched her interact with these young men, I knew just as I was built for this, she was built for it too. I wasn't going to take the conventional path to motherhood, but she would be with me every step of the way.

During the international adoption process, my mom was nothing but supportive. After I became a foster parent, she earned a new level of respect from me as she learned to live side by side with me in the uncertainty of the foster care world. We both learned how to love deeply and hold loosely. I could count on her to understand both my joy and my grief when a foster placement turned into a forever one. My family was so happy for our gain in the addition of this child into our family, but we deeply felt the loss the biological family was experiencing. My mom was there for it all.

Her home had dolls in every color. The books on her shelves took on the look of the family we were creating. She learned about hair and skin care, and we had the hard conversations about what it meant to be a multiracial family. She was in it with me because she loved these kids, without ever needing to see her face reflected in their features. That wasn't what mattered.

And because of her ability to set those things aside, what has been transmitted instead of physical resemblance has been her timeless values. These kids all take piano lessons from Grandma as she imparts to them a love of music. They go to her for wisdom when they face hard times because she is a constant source of love and support. They prefer her sugar cookie recipe and her pancakes and her spaghetti to anybody else's. When they sing a favorite hymn, they think of her because they know how much she loves those songs. They sleep with the special quilts she made for them. They look forward to eating the traditional Swedish foods she makes because they are part of her family, even if they don't share her ancestry. She has grafted them in, and they are grateful.

I never had a baby girl with blue eyes and curls like mine. My family is a lot more diverse than my mom may have anticipated as we stood in that toy aisle. But I think she somehow just knew. She knew God built me to love any child as my own. She knew I could take children who needed a family and offer them mine, filled with love, stability, warmth, and nurturing.

She didn't choose this journey or this family for me, but she's a grandma who's with me every step of the way. And we are all the better for it.

Maralee Bradley is a mother of eight kids, and each one is her favorite.

The Hurry

MEHR LEE

"What's the hurry?" My mother's words were more gentle than reproachful.

I only half listened to her, as I was elbow-deep in a backpack taking rapid inventory, my fingers brushing over the essentials.

Snacks? Check.

Diapers? Check.

Wipes? Check.

Sippy cups? Check.

Spare pair of pants? Check.

Sandwiches . . . where were the sandwiches?

Frustrated, I shoved my hand down a bit deeper and found them. The top of the Ziploc bag had burst open, and peanut butter and jelly now smeared my fingertips.

"Ugh." I looked at my hand as I pulled it from the bag. "Let's go, kids!" I hollered. "I'm just going to wash my hands, then we're out the door. Nina will help get your shoes on."

My mother shook her head but gave me a knowing smile as I brushed past her toward the bathroom. We'd made plans to head to the park together that day. I was grateful to spend time with her, but having her help was an added bonus.

The windows of my living room were open, inviting the smells of early summer and sunshine. The outdoors were calling, and I was in a rush to answer.

If only I could get my children to cooperate and get a move on.

As I washed the oily residue off my hands, I looked around at the mess. I'd need to leave some time after the park to pick up the discarded towels and pajamas littering the bathroom floor.

There was so much to do. We had to get this day started. The clock was ticking.

I walked out to the living room, thinking my mom and kids would be waiting by the door, but instead I found them nestled together on the couch as she read them a book.

I paused and listened to the gruff, villainous voice she'd always invoked when reading this same story to me as a child. "That Sam-I-am! That Sam-I-am! I do not like that Sam-I-am!" My little ones giggled as their Nina transformed into the grumpy Dr. Seuss character.

"Guys, let's get our shoes on and get going." They looked up at me, the unwelcome disruptor of story time. "It's already getting late, and we'll only have a few hours at the park before we have to get back for naptime," I pleaded.

My mother sighed and stood up, so the kids followed suit.

When we arrived, the park was already swarming with children. Big kids dangling from the monkey bars. Little ones racing down the slides. Toddlers tripping through the sandbox. Babies cooing in the swings.

We got there at a great time. The trees encircling the park offered their leaves as a bit of shade. The area was dappled in sunshine, warming the play space just enough. I knew in a couple of hours, midday sun would creep overhead and the heat would become too much. We'd head home then. I'd planned our exit before we even stepped foot in the park.

As we walked toward the gated entrance, my daughter stopped to look at newly blooming flowers. They glowed with lovely shades of blushing pink and watercolor purple. But we didn't have time to dillydally. "C'mon," I said, taking her hand. "Let's hurry up so we can get a swing."

My mother looked over. "What's the hurry?"

"I want to get *in* the park." I gestured toward the playground as families continued to file through the gate.

I huffed in resignation as my mother knelt down and talked to my girl about the different types of flowers.

They dillied *and* dallied, burying their noses in the petals.

I could feel the minutes ticking down in my head. It was like my mother was on another planet where time didn't exist.

My son tugged at my sleeve, eager to scale the beckoning jungle gym a short distance away. "I'm going to bring him in," I said to my mom.

She smiled and waved me off. "We'll be in when we're done here."

Over the next hour, we made our way around the park, my eye always on the clock, making sure time was distributed wisely. Fifteen minutes on the swings. Twenty minutes in the play structures. Ten minutes on the slides. Saving some precious time and energy for the monkey bars and seesaws.

Soon the kids needed their snack before a hangry meltdown ensued.

Realizing I'd forgotten the backpack in the car, I asked my mother to keep an eye on both kids while I ran out to grab it. When I got back to the park, I noticed so many other parents with a mindset like mine.

A mother corralling her two little girls to a nearby table. "Hurry up and finish your snack so we have enough time to play!" she said to them.

"Get moving—we have to get you to practice soon," a father said, dragging his son off the slide.

Another mother frantically gathered up her belongings, calling her kids to her side. "Come on, Auntie is meeting us for lunch, and we have to get home to clean up."

They all looked so hurried. So rushed.

Then I saw my mother with my children. She was sitting on the ground beside them as they played. One of the kids would say something, and she'd tip her chin up to the sun and let out easy laughter. Her hands would be busy with a toy one moment, then she'd pause to rest her palm on their cheek or back or shoulder. She'd wait for them to look up at her, and they'd delight each other with mirrored smiles.

We had so many days like this when the kids were little. Life was so full, but through the hustle and bustle, my mother's words always nudged the corners of my mind: "What's the hurry?"

I was spending so much time hurrying from one experience to the next, rushing toward a place of joy, I left myself little time to breathe in the beauty of it all. Truth is, sometimes I just couldn't help it. We didn't have a lot of time, and I really wanted to get to *all* the things with them. Enjoy all the places.

But there's wisdom that only comes with experience, and my mother had gained it.

Time isn't what's precious.

Time isn't the dictator of joy.

It's not about how many places you can get while time allows.

It's not how many minutes you spend in those places.

No, time isn't precious.

The time we have together—that's what is sacred.

The moments when the clock melts away and all that matters is breathing in the joy of togetherness.

That's what is precious.

Today, my children are grown.

My mom has gotten older.

Life is still busy, but busy in the way that the hustle belongs to them.

We work around their schedules, carving out time to visit with their grandmother. They don't run and play and curl up beside her like they used to, but I still adore watching the slow and easy way she sits with them. How her eyes roam over their faces and soak up their words.

Whenever we're together, she leans into the magical love only a grandmother can know with her growing grandbabies.

Sometimes I catch her eye, catch her thought.

I know she's wondering when they'll say they have to go.

I see her brow knit together, wondering when the spell will break.

And I just look at her and smile, as if to say, "What's the hurry?"

Mehr Lee is the writer behind the blog *Raise Her Wild*. Her heart is happiest in nature, alongside her amazing children and awesome husband.

The Sparkle in Her Eyes

BETH HOFF

"This has been the best Christmas of my entire life," my mother-in-law said with a smile as she watched her lively bunch of grandkids enjoying new gifts all over her living room.

I nodded and smiled in agreement, thinking how glad I was we'd chosen to celebrate my youngest daughter's first Christmas here in West Virginia with my in-laws. I could tell how much it meant to my mother-in-law.

"It makes me wonder if this is my last," she almost whispered, her gaze fixed on the chaos of empty wrapping-paper tubes being used as makeshift swords.

I searched her eyes, but she shrugged and smiled and moved on to another topic. So I shook off the odd statement.

The following summer, we made the three-hour drive again from northeast Ohio to the farm in West Virginia where my husband grew up. As our car climbed the winding gravel driveway to the familiar log house at the top of the hill, the girls could barely contain their excitement.

Mamaw Joe, as they called her, met them on the porch with big hugs and the promise of a weekend to remember.

As always, she delivered. She had a pile of gifts, art projects, cookie dough, and sparklers waiting for her granddaughters' arrival. I could tell their squeals of delight instantly made all her planning worth it.

Seeing her blossom into a grandma was inspiring. A retired teacher, she always had a bag of tricks. A creative idea. A fun project. But what I loved most was the sparkle in her eyes. The way she'd put her hand on her hip when she disagreed with you. How her eyelids fluttered slightly when she was being feisty. She had a zest for life that was contagious. She didn't see problems—she saw opportunities. Life was a grand adventure to Mamaw Joe, and nothing could hold her back from enjoying it to the fullest.

It was a year of firsts. First Christmas, first birthday, first words, first steps.

And then, a first we never expected.

The phone rang on September 1.

"Okay, Mom, we love you. We'll be praying," I heard my husband say. His mom was being admitted to the hospital for testing.

Three short weeks later, she was gone.

Her words from Christmas echoed in my head: "I wonder if this is my last." Somehow, she knew.

In the aftermath of funeral planning, outfit choosing, and meal coordinating, I sat holding my fifteen-month-old daughter in my arms. As I stared into her tiny face, the suffocating weight of grief hit me.

Not the grief of what I lost, or even what my husband lost, but the grief of what my sweet little girl lost. She faced a lifetime without her grandma. No more birthdays together. No more Christmases. No more books or snuggles. No more *I love you*s. No more porch hugs or sparklers in the backyard. No more magical moments. But worst of all, no memories. At barely a year old, I knew my baby would never even remember Mamaw Joe herself.

I felt horribly cheated, like something so beautiful and precious—a lifetime of love, support, adventures, and prayers from a grandma—had been stolen from my little girl, and I was powerless to do anything about it. So I sat in my sadness, mourning on behalf of my green-eyed girl and a future forever changed, a grandmother she'd never know.

But something happened: The little green-eyed beauty began to grow. And she is feisty. I remember the first time she thrust her hip out to the side, rested her hand on it with flair, and told me, "No." That's when I saw the sparkle in her eyes—a tiny glimmer of the grandma she barely knew.

It was just the beginning.

As weeks and months passed, she developed mannerisms that make her the spitting image of Mamaw Joe. The way she walks, the cadence of her voice, how she flutters her eyelids when she's feisty. Mannerisms she never witnessed in real life but somehow embodies perfectly.

But even more is the way she approaches life as a glorious adventure. My daughter laughs in the face of challenges and loves with the ferocity of a mama bear. Her heart boasts courage and a depth of wisdom far beyond her years.

And every time I see that sparkle in her eyes, I see Mamaw Joe. Her sparkle lives on.

Beth Hoff is a fun-loving wife, mother of three, and lover of Jesus. She blogs about marriage, motherhood, and intentional family culture at *Favorite Families*.

Don't You Just Love Her?

AMY BETTERS-MIDTVEDT

Kate was walking slowly through the grocery aisle talking about the tight spots she'd been navigating in her world. High school is not an easy time, and my girl was deep in all the things that are so hard to talk about. But it was not a comment on how helpful I was that came next; instead, it was this: "Mom, when I am in a bind, I just think what Momere would do. It has never steered me wrong."

I smiled at the comment, happy in my soul that her grandmother, my mother (nicknamed Momere by her grandchildren early on), was a factor in any sixteen-year-old's decision-making. I mean, how great is that?

As I reached for the yogurt to add it to my overflowing cart, I looked at Kate and thought about how my mom has been there not only for her but for all thirteen of her grandkids since day one. I was brought right back to the moment I became a mother. My mom was at each of my births (I like a party in that room, if I'm honest), so when my beloved obstetrician held up my firstborn and declared, "It's a girl!" Mom was by my side.

Feelings I didn't know a person could experience washed over me. I couldn't even name them, but I knew I was in the middle of a miracle. A whole new human was suddenly here, and she was also somehow mine.

As the doctor handed my baby to me and my husband leaned over to kiss her sweet and somewhat goopy head, my mom peered over the bedside and spoke what I remember to be the first words spoken after my daughter was born, words that helped my heart make sense of it all.

"Don't you just *love* her?" my mom said with joy in her voice, like someone who has been sitting on a really fun surprise finally revealed.

My mother's one sentence crystallized that moment for me. I was the mother of a daughter. I was feeling what she had felt when she first held me. Three generations of women were now in that room, and my mother and I were the same in a way we never had been before.

The *love*. Now I knew the love.

And my mom knew an all-new love, too—the love of a grandparent who is all in.

She just *loves* them. Thirteen grandkids in thirteen years, and they all get all the love. And that love has shown up for us in all the ways.

So much time spent. Taking over for a day or a night so we parents could work or just breathe without worry. Pushing strollers through the mall and sitting on hard bleachers watching sweet grandkids singing their hearts out on stages in elementary schools. Back-to-school shopping dates and dinners out with the college kids to catch up and to spend time forging a more grown-up relationship.

So many excuses for fun. Something to celebrate? Something gone awry? Just need a ride home? Momere will scoop you up and talk it through and get a little something for you from the drive-thru along the way.

So many hard moments of just stepping in, especially in the teenage years of random tattoos and broken curfews and general madness, ready to listen without judgment and with wisdom my kids sometimes prefer over mine. I recalled various moonlit nights, my parents in the screened-in porch, one on either side of one of my tall kids, talking them through some hard spot as I listened from inside the cottage, grateful for the additional help in the heavy lifting of parenting teenagers.

And when the chips were down, as they had been lately for Kate, her Momere was a go-to for wisdom in all the things. And time and again, the wisdom of grandparenthood was there to fill in the gaps of my parenting.

It is impossible when you are the parent to have the same softness and flexibility of a grandparent. The seed of it is planted deep, ready to sprout when the grandchildren arrive. This parenting-once-removed is a thing that can see them through in a way that the right-there parenting from me and their dad just can't. We are still in it, more worried and strict, without the softness of having seen things wash out over a generation.

I came back to reality as we hit the frozen food aisle and Kate said, "That Momere, she is just the best isn't she?"

"Don't you just love her?" was the only thing I could possibly say.

Amy Betters-Midtvedt is a mom, educator, speaker, and author of *You'll Make It (and They Will Too): Everything No One Talks about When You're Parenting Teens.*

PART 3

SO GOD MADE A GRANDMA
redeemed

Jesus is in the business of redeeming imperfect things—and that includes RELATIONSHIPS.

LESLIE MEANS

The Unspoken

LESLIE MEANS

I thought my grandmother was perfect. Surely, God created her better than the rest—full of wisdom and love, and with a knack for making the best chocolate chip cookies.

How could she do anything wrong?

As we grow older, we learn life isn't full of glitter, rainbows, and perfectly baked goods. Instead, it's made up of flawed, sinful humans simply trying to make their way through it all.

What's the saying? Just wait until you're a mother, and you'll understand?

Or maybe that's just what my mother said to me.

When I was growing up, I didn't know the nuances of my mom's relationship with her mother-in-law, my beloved grandmother.

But a few years ago, I learned my grandmother wasn't perfect.

Is anyone? (If you're wondering, the answer is nope, only God is.)

I was forty before Mom opened up to me about her relationship with her mother-in-law. I've been with my husband for twenty years, so as a wife, I understand Mom's frustrations. As a mother, I understand my grandma's perspective too.

In my childhood, I sensed none of the pressure points mothers and daughters and in-laws navigate. Now that I'm one of those adults, with the benefit of time and wisdom and life experience, I understand we all are flawed. We're sinful humans who make mistakes, and family is complicated, even when it's cherished.

But Jesus is in the business of redeeming imperfect things—and that includes relationships.

Sometimes time brings understanding. Sometimes it doesn't. Families are complicated—feelings, even more so. Whatever your own family relationships look like from generation to generation, there is power in honesty and peace in grace—you'll see it in the stories up next.

Precious Things

KIRSTYN WEGNER

My grandmother was not a warm woman. Honestly, as a child, I was a bit afraid of her.

Though she was not even five feet tall, she was an intimidating figure with dark, intense eyes beneath scowling brows and a beautiful, full mouth whose smiles had to be earned. She was a glamorous, fussy woman whose home was an extravaganza of precious things arranged just so.

Each room was a museum of sorts, an exhibition of collections: thimbles and spoons in wooden display cases, Avon perfume bottles and fancy lotion jars on the bathroom counters, porcelain figurines and Faberge eggs in glass curio cabinets, and silver trinkets and ornate lamps on every elegant end table, with dozens upon dozens of miniature elephants, their trunks raised for luck, peppered in between.

Precious things, all of them.

We were not allowed to play with them.

As a child, I both loved and dreaded going to her house.

I had to exercise tremendous restraint there. I was enamored of the beauty around me—her home was a wonderland, and I wanted to touch every tempting, precious thing in it. I wanted to cradle the Faberge eggs in my hands, to spritz her Avon perfume onto my wrists, to take her elephants on a jungle safari through the carpet, to open her cabinets and play with her porcelain figurines like toys.

I succumbed to temptation exactly once. I opened the glass cabinet door and removed the porcelain figurines to play with them. When she saw me, she scolded me, tore them from my hands, and returned them to their exact places on the shelves.

She must have seen the hurt in my eyes. She held out a battered deck of cards. "Here," she said. "Let's play with these instead."

I looked at this peace offering with grim disdain. Their edges were brown and worn, eroded by decades of use. They smelled strangely of a fustiness that was not quite overpowered by her Avon hand lotion. They were, as well-used cards tend to be, slightly sticky from being handled by so many different hands.

They weren't the precious things I'd wanted to play with, but they would have to do.

Her standoffishness vanished when she took a deck of cards into her hands. We started with simple games: Old Maid and Crazy Eights, Go Fish and War. When I'd mastered those, we moved on to more complicated games: Pfeffer and Cribbage, Hand and Foot and Polish Poker, Golf and Garbage, Rook and Seven Up, Kings in the Corner and Rummy—so many I can't remember them all.

Every time I went to Grandma's house, we played cards. It was always a family affair—my parents and siblings joined in, as did my aunts and uncles and cousins, and eventually my own children. We spent hours crowded around her table, swapping jokes and slapping jacks.

Precious things, those moments.

They became more precious after her cancer diagnosis, even more so when she entered hospice care.

The last time I saw my grandmother, she looked so different from that beautiful woman I feared in my youth. Cancer had taken away so much of her—pounds of flesh and tufts of hair—but gone also was that vain pride she'd taken in her earthly treasures.

"Whatever you want," she told me, "take it."

I could hardly believe the offer.

"Take it and use it and enjoy it, like I never did." She offered a feeble smile, sensing my reticence. "Go on—I can't take it with me where I'm going," she said.

Cancer never did steal her wit.

I stood, paralyzed by the generosity of her offer, by the magnitude of its meaning: She was going to leave me, and soon all I would have left in her place would be a handful of precious things.

They seemed worthless now.

"They're just things," she said. "I'm sorry if I ever made them out to be more than that. Where your treasure is, your heart will be also. *You* are my treasure, Kirsey. I love you."

I love you.

Those were not words she used often.

I swallowed, savoring them. "I love you too," I said.

The phrase felt unfamiliar on my tongue. We'd had no practice with these words. They were undoubtedly true, but we didn't use them—they were too precious to be used, dusty from sitting undisturbed in the curio cabinets of our hearts. What a waste it had been to leave them locked away.

She squeezed my hand and shooed me off, granting her permission. I waded through her precious things with eyes blurred by welling tears. I think it brought her a sort of peace watching me choose my own inheritance, knowing her beautiful things would be loved. I made my selections: two gold-framed mirrors, a dozen miniature elephants from her massive herd, some perfume bottles, a dish of Japanese silver, a handful of trinkets, the birchwood logs from her fireplace.

Beautiful things, to be sure, and I was grateful for them. But they no longer felt precious.

I also took two fusty decks of cards and a Cribbage board, items that conjured memories not of scoldings and coldness but of warmth and togetherness and laughter and fun. Truly, of all the things I inherited from my grandmother, those memories were the most precious.

But those playing cards, still scented with Avon lotion even now, are a close second.

Kirstyn Wegner lives in rural Minnesota with her husband, daughter, stray cats, and a revolving cast of foster children. Her blog is *The Frustrated Epileptic*.

I Never Planned to Raise My Grandchild

COURTNEY MOUNT

I'll never forget the day my phone rang, with my daughter on the line, saying, "Mom, I'm going to be homeless. I need you to come and take your granddaughter home with you." I had been a grandma for exactly 365 days. As I drove, I worried and prayed, both for my own child and for the little one I would be parenting for the foreseeable future.

Arriving at the apartment, I packed the things she would need—high chair, diaper bag, random clothing—then began loading her car seat into my van. Hugging my daughter, I left the driveway carrying the emotions of her broken heart and my own, too, along with her little girl. I knew my first task would be to hold the baby's first birthday celebration, even though her own mother couldn't attend. I drove home, stopping to buy a chocolate cake, ice cream, and a few party favors. I wanted her to have photos of her first birthday despite the chaos she was going through.

Gathering around the dining table with my other children, my mother, and my grandmother, five generations were present for this impromptu celebration. We placed a hunk of chocolate cake in front of the baby and a party hat on her head; she hungrily dug in. We took smash-cake pictures with frosting smeared on her face from ear to ear as she enjoyed every bite. Being with my grandchild on her first birthday, despite the sorrow, was a reminder that as mothers and grandmothers, we strive to make the best of what life sends our way. I could not control this situation, but I could do my best to make life as normal as possible for her.

Then she began her new life at Meme's house. This part was easy! I was still raising young children of my own; our home already included a toddler just nine months older than my granddaughter. Overnight, I was raising nonidentical "twins." I would breastfeed my toddler at the same time I rocked and bottle-fed my granddaughter. At dinner, a high chair stood at either side of my place. I fed each toddler a bite, then quickly shoveled in my own food. I spent the next few months dressing my granddaughter and all my young daughters—her aunts—in matching dresses. She fit perfectly into the space as the baby of our home.

We often played in the yard, where she learned to walk and then run behind the bigger children. Bathtime was a noisy event with four little bodies lined up in the tub. She even began to call me "Mama" because everyone else in the house did. Over that summer, life settled into a normal routine. This tiny ball of energy was always on the move, climbing on tables and running around shrieking with joy. As the school year resumed and we gathered around our homeschool table, I had to purchase a baby gate to block off the school area. Every time I turned my head, she would be on the desks, writing in schoolbooks with gleeful toddler abandon.

When October arrived, so did another call from her mother. She felt it was time to reclaim her place as the provider for her baby. She arrived one morning and loaded the high chair, diaper bag, and clothing into a friend's car. As we said goodbye, she strapped the car seat and prepared to drive away with a piece of my heart. The house seemed much quieter without my granddaughter's toddler joy. My own little girls were lost without her to play with each day. My older sons missed her giggles, as did her Poppy and I. She left a huge hole in our household. A few days after she left, I found her tiny pink tennis shoes. We had somehow misplaced them the day she moved; now, they were a reminder of her summer spent with us.

As my granddaughter has grown, she has no memories of her time living with us other than the photographs I added to her baby book. To her, I will always be her Meme, but in my heart, I will cherish those nights spent rocking a baby not quite my own but in need of a loving home.

I never intended to raise my own granddaughter, especially not while I was raising my own family. But sometimes, the hard things that come to us in life remind us exactly what family is all about: coming together, stepping in, lending a hand—and knowing when to let go.

Wife, mother, and author Courtney Mount writes on motherhood, surviving child loss, and Jesus. You can find her on FB/IG at *Millie's Miracle 2020.*

Without Her

ASHLEY ADAIR GARNER

"It's coming for us all," he said. I stared at my grandpa while twirling the new diamond, her diamond, on my right ring finger with my thumb. I pushed it into the other bands every time it made a full rotation, then nervously cracked all the knuckles on both hands.

I wasn't sure what to say or what to do. So I leaned my head against the frame of the closet door, the same closet where, as a child, I'd waited all year for the okay to venture into the room with its four-post cherry canopy bed. Waiting for the go-ahead to start dismantling the top closet shelf.

That's where the ornaments were.

The flocked teddy bears in their golden swings ordered from an Avon catalog. The glass tree with the lights on the bottom flashing red-green-red-green that she let me set on the coffee table beside the heavy clay manger. And the most exciting, most delicate ornaments—the ones I waited and waited for. The collection of hollowed-out eggshells with ribbon trim and tiny people inside. Every year they numbered fewer and fewer. But every year, I waited for them. I marveled at them—and her.

She packed them in layers of old shopping mall bags and tissue paper, each one meticulously labeled inside a larger box of different ornaments, also labeled.

I looked up at one of the large boxes. Two Christmases ago, I had taken it down and put up a tiny tree in the living room. Why hadn't I done it again last year? She wouldn't have remembered anyway. My grandpa had barely even turned it on two years ago. No. There wasn't any room for that now. Now there was only staring into a closet that used to hold wonder and now held my dead grandmother's nice dresses.

My uncle helped. My dad drank. I pretended it wasn't happening.

I'll never forget where I was when I learned she had Alzheimer's: standing in the kitchen of a rental house on a snowy day, while my then-four-year-old stared out the window at the snowflakes.

Little slips became big slips, which became the same questions repeated every twenty minutes, then ten, then every few sentences. Some days it was 1975. Some days she was tired. Some days her hips hurt. Some days she was dizzy. Months turned to years, then turned to more years, and still she was alive. Not her, exactly, but she outlived all the timelines associated with a disease that robs its host of their independence and humanity, little by little.

The magnitude of a life without Eula Mae sitting in the faded khaki recliner asking us if we were cold and why we weren't wearing socks when it was eighty degrees and sunny outside. I couldn't comprehend it—so I didn't.

"You can't go to heaven without your shoes on," my uncle said while I dug through meticulously labeled shoeboxes. I looked up at him. If I was weary, he was . . . what, exactly? For the last decade, his life had been entirely on hold. There were tears in his eyes. "That's all I'm going to say." And it was. He walked away, and I held up taupe and black and navy, my arms feeling like lead weights moving through peanut butter. When he came back into the room, I was riffling through her underwear drawer. "You can't meet the Lord without your panties on."

When we wrestled with the thought of heaven and hell, we all knew where Eula Mae was sitting. We discreetly packed underclothes and collectively acknowledged if she wasn't dead already, the embarrassment of strangers touching her panties would have most certainly have done her in.

How exactly do you reconcile with something so tremendous while also doing the things required after a death of this magnitude? I've never really thought it fair that after someone dies, those most intimate with that person's life have to go into planning and decision-making mode. I just wanted to lie down, not talk to the florist behind a grocery store kiosk about why I don't really like roses but if that's what everyone else thinks, it's fine.

"It comes for us all."

Nearly a year has passed, and I think about my grandpa's words often. Death is the great equalizer, the only inevitable, and all the other cliché terms, but the most uncanny thing about death is how we all keep living. We stay here, tethered to our earthly home, with only memories and an ache that never gets smaller—the box around the hollow, hurt spot growing while the wound never really scabs over.

She was so much more than words, but then, if we're fortunate, isn't everyone's grandma? And maybe, that's the lesson here: If we feel this empty without her, how full she must have made us, with snacks and love and traditions. Mostly, though, she filled us with a legacy I will carry always.

It does come for us all. And when it does, it reminds the ones left behind just how blessed we were.

Ashley Adair Garner is an artist, writer, mom, devoted partner, advocate, and dog lover living in Knoxville, Tennessee. Find her on Instagram @loladietcola_ and @bestnesthome.

A Grandma's Love Is Transformative

KRYSTAL SIEBEN

"That baby should have a jacket on," my mom said in disapproval as a frazzled mom carrying a toddler passed the windshield of our 1990 Ford Probe. I looked up and went back to doodling in my fifth-grade yearbook.

"You know why there are so many problems with kids today? Daycare—the kids are always in daycare," I overheard my mom saying to our neighbor as I helped my little sister off the slide. I nodded in approval, making a mental note I should, one day, be a stay-at-home mom.

"Babies shouldn't always be carried around in those buckets. It's no wonder there are so many issues with attachment and all of that today," my grandma said as she sat with my mom at her fancy glass table eating lunch.

These comments were made in my presence more than twenty-five years ago, but I can still hear them as if it were yesterday.

I've heard it said our mother's voice becomes our internal voice, and I believe it.

I also believe most people attribute their good fortune to their own choices and abilities. Rather than seeing an easy or capable child as a gift, they see them as an achievement, something they created for themselves. That, somehow, they had the formula for a healthy child, a smart child, a "good" child.

My mom was definitely one of those people—until she met and loved a little boy with bright blue eyes, the sweetest sense of humor, a thick head of hair, not a mean bone in his body, and an autism diagnosis.

My firstborn struggled, and so did I. The first few years of his life were some of the hardest of mine. The way he cried if someone laughed too loudly when he was as young as six months old. The way he screamed if I left him with anyone other than my mom. His lack of words. The lies I told myself about what was going on with him.

Through the first years of his life, my mom had a front-row seat to his heartbreaking struggle, and she also had a front-row seat to my pain: my mama heart breaking as I tried to navigate uncharted waters, my anxiety climbing with each missed milestone, my voice breaking as I told her over the phone how people judged us, judged him.

And finally, when he was three, the diagnosis. *Autism.*

It wasn't because I carried him in an infant seat. I wasn't spared because I stayed home. It wasn't because, as his mom, I did something wrong.

It was because this is who he's meant to be.

God uses the most extraordinary measures to help us all grow. I truly believe there is no one who could change my mom as much as this angelic little boy. It would take the bluest eyes, the gentlest little hands, and the enduring goodness of this innocent child to transform a mother who passed a lot of judgment into a grandma with a new perspective.

All those ideals she had in her mind for mothering were replaced with grace, compassion, understanding, and a new love. A grandma's love.

It takes a big person to admit they were wrong. It takes a humble person to confess (out loud) that maybe they don't have all the answers. And it takes the absolute strongest person to change that internal voice and break a generational cycle.

My mom recently told me a story about going grocery shopping with my grandma. They'd seen a school-age child having a meltdown after his mother had told him no about something.

In what I'm sure was a tone just loud enough for them to hear, my grandma said if her kids had behaved that way, there would have been swift consequences.

"And so I just said, 'You know, Mom, there are many reasons for a child's behavior. You never know what's going on with people,'" my mom proudly recounted. She spoke as if she never would have considered agreeing with my grandma's view on the subject.

I smiled. I kept talking. I felt so proud.

And I realized just how transformative a grandmother's love is.

Krystal Sieben is Minnesota proud and loves photography, animals, old friends, family, God, and running her nonprofit, Three Little Burdes. Visit Instagram for nonprofit information.

Ladles of Gravy in Heaven

MEG DUNCAN

I fanned smoke pouring from a hot skillet as the fire alarm announced another dinner at the Duncans'. Tapping the familiar button to silence the beeping, my husband and two boys gathered around the table.

Although I still say the fire alarm is trigger-happy, my family knows it as the dinner bell. Despite books and blogs claiming otherwise, I am proof cooking isn't for everyone.

I have burned, undercooked, and over-seasoned all types of food. My cooking isn't terrible every day—there has been a time or two I nailed dinner, and most nights we sit down to something really quite edible. But cooking doesn't come from my soul. Instead of being made with love, it's usually thrown together with obligation—the planning, preparing, and cleanup are part of my daily drudgery.

I imagine a lot of parents probably feel the same way, but there's one person whose cooking settled deep into my soul.

My Granny Fern poured out her love in ladles of thick gravy over homemade mashed potatoes plated beside her famous fried chicken, buttered biscuits, and pistachio salad (which she called potassium salad).

Her handwritten recipe books, a collection my family now considers one of our most treasured heirlooms, were merely a formality. Cooking was her craft, and she knew it well.

When we gathered for a meal, whether it was just my brother and me at her kitchen table or a big family meal in the dining room, she tended to each diner with great care. She never let a fork scrape the plate until someone cried "uncle," and even then, she shook her finger at their nose and reminded them the pie was coming.

Meanwhile, her seat was empty and her plate usually went unfilled. As she buzzed around our chairs, we urged her to sit down and eat, but she rarely did. Instead, I often found her munching on leftovers as she cleared the table.

Years later, I realized this was Granny's ministry.

I don't recall any deep theological debates with Granny about what it meant to live out God's Word, but I remember the conversations around her table while she quietly poured coffee.

From Grandpa's work buddies to her ladies' group from church, there was rarely a day she wasn't cooking for someone.

Sometimes it was barefoot neighbor kids sharing our grilled cheese and tomato soup lunch during a quick break from exploring the creek or playing baseball in the field out back.

Other times it was out-of-town family passing through who knew they could stop by for a hot meal and good conversation at Fern's house.

Granny did what she loved, and God used it.

Really, God uses everything. Even the things we aren't good at, He brings together for good. In Granny's case, it was her terrible driving, which God used to help others and teach her passengers to fully trust in Him.

Granny was known as the woman who drove into Hannibal National Bank, sideswiped the city clerk's car (which was parked in his driveway), and slammed her brakes in the middle of Highway 61 every single time she realized she'd forgotten to go to the post office.

Since my mom didn't drive and my dad worked a lot, Granny was also a chauffeur for my brother and me. She took us all the millions of places teenagers go.

I saw a lot of things on the way to singing lessons or school functions, or on the many days I pretended to miss the school bus because I knew she would get me french fries from Wendy's on the way home.

I often looked out the passenger window in confusion as fellow motorists greeted us with an extended finger or mouthed words I didn't understand until I was allowed to watch PG-13 movies.

Granny also drove around her church friends, many who were widows and couldn't drive anymore. She sat in doctors' offices holding their hands as they waited for a diagnosis, attended funerals of people she'd never met, and walked around the store checking items off someone else's grocery list.

I have wondered before if I could ever love the way she did, until I finally realized I can't. I was created to love in a different way.

I think God uses my cooking just like He used Granny's driving.

Despite my usually meager mealtime offerings, the time we spend around our table as a family is cherished. We often sit long after our plates are scraped clean, chatting about the simple things and hashing out the hard stuff. It's where we come back together after life sometimes pulls us apart.

And although I wish my kids could experience Granny's cooking, I believe with all my heart she is now standing over Jesus with a ladle. Since He died on the Cross to save us from our sins, I guess the least we could do down here was send her up with the best fried chicken we had to offer.

Meg Duncan is an author and a contributor to the bestseller *So God Made a Mother*. She writes on Facebook at *Meg Duncan—What a Life*.

Someone I Used to Know

ANDREA L. CORSI

My daughters and I drove three hours to see my grandma yesterday, to the house that holds seventy-six years of her memories and so many of mine. Thanksgiving dinners with a dozen dogs underfoot. Hiding out in the back room with cousins. Trying to dislodge the old coin painted into the cinder-block garage. Escaping to the worn playground down the street. So many old feelings, which made that three-hour drive feel longer than usual.

My grandma and I never understood each other because we were opposite ends of a color spectrum. She was red, born in the coal mines of Scranton, Pennsylvania, one of eight children, with a ninth-grade education. She married her childhood love after the war and still lives in the house they built together. I was violet, with my books and writing and college degrees. I was never her favorite grandchild—that place was reserved for my brother, simply because he was the only boy. He was the person who would carry on the family name, and I resented the significance she placed on a name and a gender. I was not even the favorite granddaughter; as one of seven, there were always others who needed her more.

But she wasn't who I wanted her to be either—so different from my friend's grandmas. There were no birthday cards in my mailbox through the years, no presence at regular Sunday dinners, no cheering from the bleachers.

But by ninety-six, she was deep in her dementia, and it was finally time to visit her while there was still time.

My daughters and I made cookies the night before—chocolate chip, her favorite—and in a one-hour photo envelope, I brought a year's worth of our memories: soccer games, school awards, birthday candles, and days at the Jersey shore. We knocked on her aluminum side door, and I half expected to be greeted by the smell of turkey in the oven, a back room of treasures to discover, a cousin asking where I've been all this time.

But there were none of those things in the tidy old house we walked into.

We talked about my daughters. How proud I am of their school sports and club activities. She asked about the repairman for her radiators, then asked the same question a minute later. I mentioned the weather—more snow coming next week. We talked about the house and the new neighbors across the street. She looked at the pictures one by one, without recognition reaching her eyes, and she asked about the repairman for the radiators again. The girls explored the house, looked at the pictures on her bookshelf, and pointed to one from when she was young. My grandma smiled, and I realized she didn't recognize herself.

I started to see it then. Maybe it was because time had passed and colors change, but Grandma wasn't red anymore and I wasn't violet. Or maybe the space between us, on a spectrum or in my memory, wasn't important anymore because our different colors were never strong enough to hold the weight of the big things—life, time, family, health.

As we were leaving, she took my younger daughter's hands in hers and said, "You look like someone I used to know." And somehow, in words she didn't even understand, forty-one years of colored feelings faded.

My daughter has my eyes, my face structure, my childhood pre-braces smile. And after all our history and all dementia has taken from my grandma, she remembered me.

A former psychologist-turned-writer from New Jersey, Andrea Corsi can be found with a book enjoying a sunrise cup of coffee or spending time with family.

Living Vows

SARAH LANGO

I came across the words scrawled on the tattered page of a birthday card that had been in storage for decades—words in the unmistakable, sloppy cursive of my late grandmother. Alongside the cheerful words of a typical birthday greeting and good wishes for another year was this quote: "Broken things can become blessed things if we allow God to do the mending." The words struck me, not because they are unique, but because she wrote them—a woman who knew firsthand the reality of brokenness.

If you were to observe a family gathering where all four of my grandmother's children, nineteen grandchildren, and twenty-five great grandchildren and counting got together, you would find the best kind of chaos: children running around playing tag or basketball, intense games of cards, discussions about life and God and even politics, and of course a bounty of casserole dishes that arrive full and leave empty. You would hear prayer and laughter. You would never know that this legacy was birthed not from laughter but from pain.

In 1953, my grandma Martha immigrated to the United States from her home in Canada. Though many people immigrate for a better life for themselves, she did so for the opposite reason—to help provide a better life for someone else. She became part of a service team that worked in a Mennonite children's home in rural Kansas. Though she never lived in an orphanage herself, she knew well the pain of being without a parent, losing her own mother before she reached adulthood.

It wasn't long before Martha met JT and they married. On that day in 1956, I imagine Grandma had the same dreams we all have: get married, start a family, and live a happy life—but things are never quite that simple. In 1969, after having four children and building a family farm that required tending, Grandma's world started to break. It became apparent Grandpa JT was battling severe mental illness that impacted everything in their day-to-day life. He was plagued with paranoia, lack of motivation, disillusionment, and an overall unkindness that, in many ways, tainted the family unit.

His mental illness required Grandma to not only care for her four children but also care for her husband as if he were a child himself. She courageously walked into the role of both mother and father, picking up all the slack and labor required for a family farm. She carried the physical and financial burden on her own in a time when that was almost unheard of, while continuing to care for her spouse—a spouse who caused public humiliation at times, a spouse who seemed to have given up, a spouse who surely wasn't holding up his end of the bargain any longer. Though Grandma was encouraged by some to cut her losses and leave Grandpa behind—a decision everyone would have understood—she instead chose to selflessly and compassionately stay by his side, loving him in the most real way until his last breath.

For years, my grandmother's life was lived in the shadow of brokenness. And yet that's not how I remember her at all. I wish I knew more about her life. I wish I'd asked her about pain and coping and faith and resilience. But I remember Grandma for puzzles put together at the kitchen table, homemade strawberry jam, and snack picnics on the back deck. I remember her for dozens of storybooks read aloud, *Adventures in Odyssey* around the radio, and quilts put together piece by piece. I remember her for fruit salad in crystal bowls, big bear hugs, and a kind of humble wisdom I could not possibly fully appreciate until I knew the life she had lived. Some might say hardship was the very yarn with which Grandma's life was woven, but today a beautiful tapestry exists—threads of pain, faithfulness, hardship, and goodness—and a legacy lives on. That legacy gives us courage to face our own pain with the same resilient spirit.

When I asked my mother about my grandma, she told me, "I know Momma loved Daddy even though he was sick. She was faithful in loving Jesus and her broken husband all while leading our family with such strength, faith, wisdom, and love. She loved and served others in spite of the brokenness she dealt with for so many years in her own life. She knew one day the mending would get done."

Isn't it interesting that I don't remember a single broken thing about Grandma? What I do remember—the good and fun and wise parts of her—those are surely the mended things.

Wife, mama, writer, disability advocate, and coffee lover Sarah Lango writes about God's goodness in hard places. Find her at *Gracefilled Growth*.

Sober Grandma

CAROL MOORE

My mom is a recovering alcoholic. I am the youngest of four kids, and she took her last drink when I was eleven. Now she is a sober grandma to nine grandchildren.

She wasn't a bad mom—in fact, she was a beautiful mom, weary and vulnerable and trying to raise four kids with a husband who traveled for work. The days were long, and the needs were endless. She took comfort in a glass of wine at the end of the day. Or a few of them, every day. And while she still managed to meet the logistical needs of a lively and active house full of kids, alcohol took her away from us. What was numbing her ache was also numbing her presence.

There were no grandkids yet when she looked this dependence straight in the eye and said, "No more." I think God graciously gave her a few years to heal and grow and find new ways of coping in a world that made her heart almost too heavy to beat before He gave her grandkids. He is so kind and wise that way.

When grandkids did come along, she was ready. As one exquisite little soul after another entered into our healing family, my beautiful mom, now a beautiful grandma, was completely present. She had learned skills through a recovery program and was applying them to her life. She was brave. She stood up to her fears and to her feelings of inadequacy, and she found her worth—something she had never seen before in her life. She no longer had to hide from her weak places but instead could embrace them and nurture them back to strength. And she was present.

Being a grandma wasn't about having the responsibility of holding everyone together. It wasn't about exhaustion and loneliness. It wasn't about feeling inadequate or incapable of measuring up to the impossible standards mothers set for themselves. It was about love. It was about holding babies against her chest through their entire nap. It was about the smell of their skin and the feel of their warm cheeks against her own. It was about counting eyelashes and memorizing the curve of their tiny noses. This sweet grandma pushed strollers through shopping malls and neighborhoods and doctors' offices with a joy that could not be measured. She didn't have to hurry through the sweet moments to catch up on the arduous tasks of managing a home and a family and a husband. She could just be still. She could be present.

As the number and size of grandchildren grew in our family, her sober presence was foundational. She listened as they told her stories of sports and school and friendships, good ones and difficult ones. She attended sporting events and recitals and graduations. She hosted celebrations and opened her home to anyone who wanted or needed to enter. She was a friend and a soft place for everyone to land, no matter how easy or difficult the season was. She was present.

My mom's decision to choose sobriety gave my siblings and me a rock to lean on as we tried to figure out how to raise our own kids. She gave each one of us what she didn't have when she was parenting us: something sturdy to hold on to. She gave us a companion, a ride or die, a call any time of the night because something or someone was too hard. She gave us a reason not to numb our own ache of loneliness and overwhelm. She gave us her time so we could escape for a night with our spouse to recharge our hearts. She was present.

As her grandkids got bigger, so did the issues of life. Relationships and breakups. College applications and rejections. Career decisions and uncertainties about the future. She was the easy place all of them could go. There was no judgment or condemnation. They would never be rushed to get through the story. She was wise, and they knew it. And when the day came when one of her grandchildren would battle their own addiction, she was there. This sober grandma knew what to say when no one else did. She was the one who had the right to confront with love and to advise. She was the lifeline because she once walked in the same shoes and learned how to take them off. She was present.

I know my mom regrets the years blurred by wine's seductive lie of comfort. I know perhaps we didn't get as much of her as we all needed. But her brave decision and commitment to get and remain sober for the rest of her days gave this family, expanded by nine, such a beautiful gift. She showed us you can fall into a deep hole and climb back out. She showed us you don't have to run from vulnerability and imperfection. As a grandma, she showed a whole new generation how much they were loved and noticed and valued. She showed all of us that God gives second chances to do something a different way.

And while none of this came easy, she was present.

Carol Moore, a wife, mom, parenting-teens advocate, and author writes on building lasting relationships with our kids. Find her on FB/IG @heymom.co.

Motherhood, Part 2

SYLVIA SCHROEDER

I am a grandma. I scoop baby bodies as they fly past on fat little legs and swing them high into the air. I sniff diapered bottoms and cut up hot dogs into little un-choke-able bites. I hold toddler hands to cross streets and sing about wheels that go round and round.

And sometimes, as my flying airplane spoonful dives into the open-mouthed hangar, I think, *I've been here before.*

It's like watching a black-and-white film that stutters and skips between then and now. At times, I am young. I see my own child in the high chair. And dimly in the background, I hear sages with smug faces warning, "Don't blink."

Other times, images of my children ghost across the faces of my grandchildren and I feel the grand tiredness of my years. Then I draw in my breath and remember: *I am a grandma.*

Grandmahood looks like mommyhood elongated into part 2. It sounds and smells like another go-round of yesterday. Tantrums, screams, and sirens meld with sweet lullabies. My brain shifts between déjà vu and brand-new, never-done-this-before until it's a cauldron of baby food mush.

I am the mommy of the mommy, a secondhand learner to a new way of doing what I thought I already knew. The baby I birthed holds the controls, and I am her sidekick, which means I must bite my tongue and strive to please.

Am I doing this right? I wonder. *Are the mistakes I made as a mother on display in this second round?* We did it one way; they do it another. Is it her responsibility or mine when he drops the phone into the toilet? When should I scold, and when should I reward? And what about the grand comparisons between us and the other grandparents?

Suddenly, in the throes of grandmahood, I am an insecure mother again. *Should I do more? Did I do too much? Do any of them even like me anymore?*

It's like mom guilt gone sour.

Don't get me wrong—I'm thrilled to be a grandma. But grandmas should be gentle and sweet. I'm not quite there yet. I am impatient and cranky, and sometimes I feel downright mean.

"Gamma, I get in bed?" a little voice asks.

I can feel his face next to mine before I open my eyes. He is there, eye level.

I am supposed to say sweetly, "Let's get back into your bed for just a little longer."

His parents are gone for a few days, and Grandpa and I are in charge. I am so exhausted. I haul him in, and he puts a little hand on my cheek, like a blessing for grace received. He can't read my heart.

Grandmothering oozes all the feels, including some of the bad stuff I thought I'd left behind with motherhood. The bad bits are still alive in me—and apparently doing quite well.

I feel their rise as I fumble with the enigma of the stroller. *Open, shut them, open, shut them, give a little clap-clap-clap.*

All manner of technology has procreated since my children were little. Alexa clearly broadcasts the mutterings of my ineptness to the entire household.

As I straddle the back seat, I try to remember my son's instructions on car seat hook-up and buckle tension. With one leg up on the cushion, I pull with all my might. My grandson searches me with terrified saucer eyes.

Pack 'n Plays? They are evilly designed to bring grandmas to their knees.

I love my grandchildren with the kind of love that melts my heart and waters my eyes. I am so grateful for each one of them. But I never imagined I'd feel so unprepared for what I expected to be second nature.

This lack of confidence humbles me. It gently reminds me that Jesus put me exactly where I am. In the same way He chose me to be the mother of my children, He saw the grandma I would become. He saw me in this wrinkled flesh and declared, "I want her to be the grandma for those children."

Grandmahood calls me into a new journey of trust and dependence on Him, much the same as when I had my own children. Grandparents are like God-designed bridges to Jesus. Like a child, I know I still have much to learn.

"Don't forbid the little ones to come to me," Jesus told His disciples. And He took the little ones into His arms.

I am a grandma strategically placed. I carry generations in love and prayer. With intentionality, I place them in Jesus' loving arms.

In this privileged space where little hands press against my cheeks and velvet arms slide around my neck, distractions grow quiet.

I am in mommyhood part 2, awed by its sacredness, honored by its choosing, and privileged by its sweet joys.

I am Grandma, and this is God's calling.

Sylvia Schroeder is a wife, mother, and grandmother to fourteen grand-marvels. She loves connecting God's Word with real life at *When the House Is Quiet.*

PART 4

SO GOD MADE A GRANDMA

creative

Sometimes a grandmother's COOKING is synonymous with LOVE.

JENNI BRENNAN

The Gift

LESLIE MEANS

As I write this, I'm eating the second-to-last piece of cheesecake in our fridge—a birthday gift from my mother to my husband.

Yes, I saved him the last piece. Although you know I wanted to eat it.

My mother is the most creative person I know. She thinks of things differently than most. The salutatorian of her class in 1967, she became a secretary and wife right out of high school. Not long after, she added mother and soldier's wife to her résumé.

When the farming crisis hit in the 1980s, she had to find a way to help support her family of six. Recently, I learned she had a choice: go to school to become a nurse (an occupation that offered good pay and flexible hours) or start her own bakery in town.

She was known for her cakes. Still is. She made wedding cakes in the basement of our farmhouse and delivered them all over the county.

Her creations were hot commodities, or so I'm told.

But a bakery business is risky, even for the most beloved bakers. So she took a safe path that would most certainly pay the bills.

I was just two when Mom decided to go to nursing school.

Her work provided much-needed income for our family, and since she could switch shifts with other nurses, she never missed my school activities—a gift I didn't truly understand until I became a mother.

Although she hasn't sold her cakes since the early eighties, Mom continues to bake for her family. One Christmas a few years ago, she gave my sisters and me each a frozen pan of lasagna with a letter that read,

> During the year ahead, you will receive a Mama's Recipe (cook's choice) delivered to your door once monthly.

Dad came along during these deliveries too.

Each month, they brought goodies to our doorstep. We got pie and soup, meatloaf and bite-size cakes, salads, and desserts fit for the season. Each delivery also included a kitchen tool we could keep, like a new baking dish or serving tray, and a copy of the recipe.

It was a stunning, delicious gift, and I loved the break from cooking one night each month. But I think my favorite part was the opportunity to spend a little more time with Mom and Dad. I will cherish their beloved gift forever, and I hope to do the same thing for my kids someday.

I shared their gift on social media—it went viral, as we say in this business. Hundreds of women reached out to let me know they planned to give their children the same gift the following holiday season.

"Now that's pretty cool," Mom said.

I'm not surprised she came up with such a creative way to love her grown daughters though. Grandmas have a way of tapping into a special brand of brilliance and giving you a new way of looking at life. Sometimes it's a gift you didn't know you needed. Sometimes it's an art project she plans and executes with the grandkids. Sometimes it's a bouquet of yellow tulips on your doorstep just because she knows they're your favorite.

Grandmas are a creative bunch, and you'll meet several of them in these next few stories.

We're Gaga for Her Fun

ALYSE BRESSNER

"You can use a mason jar for anything!"

It was a Saturday morning when she walked through the door, arms full of mason jars, assorted craft supplies, and those words of creative wisdom. It's not every day a florist and "jack-of-all-crafts" walks through your front door—but for us, it's a weekly occurrence.

That talented woman just so happens to be my mother-in-law and my children's grandma, who they lovingly call Gaga. I can't recall exactly how we landed on that name, whether it was my infant son's babbling or some variation of grandma that just stuck, but since "going gaga" over something means excessive enthusiasm, there isn't a better name in the world for her.

I've always considered myself "craft capable." My talent level falls somewhere between Pinterest-worthy and preschool open house night. I'm not great, I'm not awful—I'm just capable. I can frost a cupcake, draw a decent-looking dog, and even sew a small hole (if someone else threads the needle).

Gaga is different though. She makes bakery-worthy spritz cookies from scratch and decadent chocolates by the dozens. She creates elaborate patchwork quilts with her grandchildren's favorite colors and characters. She sews matching pajama sets with material they pick out during long strolls down fabric aisles.

One Saturday morning, instead of her usual craft supplies, she brought souvenirs from her recent vacation: long-sleeved surf shirts, one for each grandchild. The bright white waterproof fabric featured a black outline of an old-school pickup truck carrying surfboards.

The shirts were well made, their quality reflected by the $30 price tags hanging from the sleeves. As she gifted them to my eight-year-old son and five-year-old daughter, I thanked her for the generous and thoughtful gesture. I was grateful to have such pristine, high-quality swim shirts for the kids this summer. But she had a different idea.

These shirts had caught her eye because they were perfect canvases. The outlined pickup trucks begged to be painted, the surfboards splashed with color. Immediately, my son headed to the craft bin and pulled out the fabric paint I'd bought just days earlier (a decision I soon regretted).

He carefully chose his colors, laying broad brushstrokes of bright orange on the truck's outer panels. He blotted red on the rear, dabbed yellow on the tailgate, and finished with a swooping stroke of brown down the running boards. My perfectionist self breathed a sigh of relief. It was still wearable, endearing even. But he wasn't done.

Looking up at Gaga, he asked if he could continue his painting. The vast amount of white space left on the shirt was unacceptable and needed to be filled immediately—and he had just the idea for how to do it. With an encouraging nod and an enthusiastic "Sure!" she gave her approval.

Taking the largest paintbrush he could find, he laid down thick black lines, painting a square smack-dab in the middle of the shirt. He filled the center with mustard yellow and added two giant blue eyes to finish off the portrait of his favorite video game character. Now he was done.

His paint strokes were messy and uneven, and little splatters randomly covered the once-flawless fabric. Much of his work seemed to have no rhyme or reason, yet Gaga smiled warmly, admiring his creative expression. So did I. Watching his face light up as he worked in complete creative freedom was worth every penny of the shirt's cost.

But of course, Gaga already knew that.

She knows the joy that comes from painting outside the lines, the delight of creating something one of a kind. She sees creative potential in anything and everything, from mason jars to fabric scraps. And she teaches her grandchildren to do the same—like miraculously crafting a toilet paper roll into a beautiful butterfly, as if it had been a cardboard caterpillar the entire time.

Among all the wonderful gifts Gaga gives my children, the gift of creativity surpasses them all. It's a gift they get to unwrap daily. They enjoy creating handmade presents to bless others like she does for them. As they grow, they'll use that gift to mold their own definition of beauty in a one-size-fits-all world. And when life feels hopeless, they'll remember how their grandma could take something destined for the trash and turn it into a wondrous work of art.

That's the thing about creativity—it translates across all facets of life, from painting to problem-solving, molding clay to mindset shifts. And just like those beautiful quilts Gaga made for each of her grandchildren, that kind of gift will be passed down for generations to come.

A Midwest mom of two, Alyse Bressner shares an authentic view of stumbling through life, marriage, and motherhood on her blog, *She Writes Flowers*.

There Weren't Any Words

LISA LESHAW

We gathered at the Thanksgiving table for pre-dinner munchies and our family tradition of asking each person to describe their best blessings and favorite memories of the past year. I had saved a special announcement for this special occasion, one I'd learned about weeks earlier but chose to wait and disclose in the presence of my favorite people. I told everyone in advance I had something quite amazing to share with them.

After fifteen years working at the corporation that had become my second home, the chairman of the board informed me I had been selected to become its next president. *Whew. Whoa. Wow.* I could barely contain my exhilaration but managed to hold out until just this moment.

My sweet daughter—newly pregnant with her first child, our first grandchild—was seated beside me. It was her turn to share her blessings. I listened with abundant love, one person to go. It was breathtaking to hear her describe this growing life, exquisite to be part of this momentous new season. I'd already picked out our grandchild's "my first" everything: onesies, rompers, Christmas and Hanukkah bibs. To say we felt bathed in extraordinary bliss, gratitude, and joy couldn't come close to expressing the truth. There weren't any words.

Then my daughter moved on to part 2 of her blessings. I think I recall the gist of what she was saying. I think. I admit after hearing the first couple of sentences, I might have blacked out for a second. Her words all blended together, sounding garbled. My thoughts were so jumbled I didn't speak right away. Or maybe at all. There weren't any words.

My daughter had just announced she and her lovely husband wanted me to become their nanny for our soon-to-be-born grandchild. As in, provide full-time care Monday through Friday, 7:00 a.m. until 4:00 p.m.—extra when her work required evening commitments. The arrangement would stay in place until kindergarten enrollment.

Having recently accepted her dream job as principal of an elementary school, my beautiful daughter didn't know at the time of her hire that she was expecting. The district was willing to grant a six-week family leave while the assistant principal took over; if she requested additional time, there was no guarantee of her position remaining available.

My daughter mentioned having peace of mind knowing her baby would be in the safest, most loving hands when she left for work each day. I was honored and humbled. And speechless. There weren't any words.

I believe I smiled, and the smile likely froze on my face. I do recall squeezing my husband's hand under the table in an unspoken gesture that said, *What in the world do I do now?*

"It's your turn!" my daughter exclaimed. And I took my turn without ever mentioning the milestone I'd reached, or how I'd been bursting with exhilaration at having reached it. When everyone shouted, "Tell us your exciting news!" I replied, "How could anything top what's already been said?" and grabbed a mozzarella stick to dip in marinara.

That Monday, I notified the board I was resigning the position I'd never had a chance to start. Soon after, Baby Michael and I began our odyssey.

The early days brought lots of spit-up and colic, and every time a colleague called to say hello and how they wished I hadn't left, I wondered if I'd made the right decision.

Then one day, a cherub face looked up at me and smiled for the first time, and I never had to wonder again. Michael learned to walk under my watchful eye, but I pretended he didn't take his first steps by himself until my daughter came home from work so she could experience this epic milestone.

His first word was *cheese*, so I figured he should learn a variety. By three, he could identify American, cheddar, mozzarella, and Swiss. Gouda always posed confusion.

The two of us spent our mornings on stroller walks through the park, watching seagulls skim across the water and ducks skid in like runners sliding into second base. I'd never noticed that during a gentle breeze, the highest leaves on a tree sway differently than the lower dwellers until my grandson yelled, "Look, Nanny!"

Oh, how he opened my eyes to a new and magical world. When we were seated on a blanket together in the park, Michael asked me to close my eyes and listen. There was a wonderful lesson to be learned. He taught me that clouds can whisper. To this day, I believe him.

Early afternoons were reserved for the Pooh song, which we sang to every creature we came across and to each other while huddled in the rocking chair. Weather permitting, we caught raindrops on our tongues, and during the winter, we built grandma snow ladies on the front lawn, complete with granny glasses and purses.

In the late afternoon hours, we frolicked in the treehouse fighting fire-breathing dragons. Once they were defeated, we rewarded ourselves with fruit snacks and fruit punch and stories about how brave we were.

The best illustration of who Michael and I were together didn't occur during my five years as his Nanny, but rather took place when he was in first grade, when family members were invited to his class to participate in "Meet My Hero" day. My daughter and son-in-law were each convinced it would be them on his hero page, but when we saw Michael's paper, it wasn't either of them. It was me.

The paper said, "Meet my hero: my Nanny. She loves me and she's always there for me. She watches me play soccer." Below the words was a picture of a rather young-looking lady with long, yellow hair, a red bow, and the biggest smile.

I never did become the president of a corporation.

I became something so much more.

There aren't any words.

Lisa Leshaw is humbled to be among this breathtaking group of writers whose stunning words leave forever imprints and indelible ripples on needing hearts and souls.

Here's to the Wild Ones

JAYMI TORREZ

While many of the best grandmas are the classic kind—the quiet, loving, soothing kind—there's something about the wild ones.

My grandma wasn't soft and gentle. She didn't bake cookies, she didn't teach me to knit, and she didn't take me to feed the ducks or visit the library. God didn't give me one of those grandmas.

No, God gave me Nana—rip-roaring, fun-loving, good-time Nana.

Visits to her house meant unlimited snacks and late nights giggling. She'd let us join her line dancing classes or take us to Yosemite to go on a zip line. While other grandmas were taking their littles to the movies or maybe shopping, Nana took us on epic adventures into San Francisco or to a weeklong outdoor camp all by herself.

Time with Nana meant dancing in the kitchen with country music blaring. It meant walks to get Slurpees and sleeping all together in her condo in the city. It meant getting in all kinds of predicaments (like a trip to the middle of the lake on a paddleboat that ended in sobs, screams for help, and a frantic rescue by my uncle) but always getting out of trouble together.

Nana loved Betty Boop and looked a lot like Dolly Parton. Her hair was big, her clothes were modern, and she was always chasing the latest trends. She was also impulsive. She'd call to say she'd sold her house and was moving in with us or that she'd eloped with her new boyfriend to Tahoe. She'd give someone a whole new name if she thought theirs didn't suit them (I'm so sorry, Elizabeth-turned-Dolores) and could always be counted on to show up a little (a lot) late.

Nana smoked cigarettes and rode public transit. She thought there was nothing a Pepsi and a couple of Tylenol couldn't fix. She picked cotton in Oklahoma as a kid to help feed her family and started a thriving business when money got tight. She had a little bit of a temper and a whole lot of spirit. She quite literally threw things at people who underestimated her, then turned around and threw big Christmas Eve parties for those very same people.

And yes, maybe that makes her sound like a wild one. Probably because she was. But Nana did everything big, and that includes how she fought, how she lived, and how she loved.

She gave me so many gifts a more traditional grandma could not have. She was tough as nails and never backed down from a fight. She beat cancer and heart disease, showing us life is about beating the odds, not giving in to people or battles seeking to bring you down.

In a world full of pressure to take care of the kids and make a beautiful home and do everything just right, Nana managed to show me life doesn't have to follow some laid-out plan. Life can be about silly detours and messy delays. It's never too late to start again, and you are never too old, too small town, or too feminine to do the things you want to do.

Nana taught me to seize the moment. She showed me how to find joy in the everyday and to always seek fun. She taught me relationships matter, but so does taking care of yourself. She taught me life is short, and if you get the chance to say yes to something (whether it's bull riding or a second chance at love), gosh darn it, you should really say yes.

The world needs the soft grandmas who bake bread and watch classic movies while snuggling on the couch. There is no question about that.

But it also needs the rebel Nanas. The boisterous, full-of-life, nonstop, on-the-go grandmas who teach us to take life for all its worth, leaving not a single moment unlived.

She made a lot of mistakes, like so many of us do. But I always knew Nana loved me. She was there for me, and she cared deeply about me. Instead of conforming to what the world wanted her to be, she brought me along to witness the slice of life that was so uniquely hers.

Nana taught me to chase joy, to find the fun, and to always live for the now. And what an unusual and beautiful gift that has been.

So tonight, I'll dance in the kitchen with my daughter. I'll crack open a Pepsi and put on one of her favorite songs, questionable lyrics and all. Tonight, my baby girl and I won't dance like no one is watching—we'll dance like Nana is.

Jaymi Torrez is a writer and teacher of tiny humans. On weekends, you'll find her with family, baking too many goodies, or talking to houseplants.

Grandma's Meatballs

JENNI BRENNAN

When I was in elementary school, we had to contribute a family recipe celebrating our heritage to the class cookbook. I instantly knew what I would submit: my family's meatball recipe—because surely we were Italian.

While all my friends were having turkey dinners on Thanksgiving, my mother was busy cooking her grandmother's meatballs. After opening our gifts from Santa every Christmas morning, my family would gather for a meal accompanied by those same meatballs. Same with Easter Sunday. The Fourth of July. New Year's Day. Any weekend. Those meatballs were a constant at every holiday feast and family party. Eventually, they became more than just a staple at our table—they became part of the foundation of my family's story. (But not because we had any Italian heritage; it turns out my Irish/English grandmother just really liked her mother's meatball recipe.)

The truth is, even though the recipe made it into the cookbook, the meatballs were never really that good. They gave almost all of us instant heartburn, they stained tablecloths and shirts, and they were some of the blandest meatballs any of us have ever tasted. But they were synonymous with love. They connected four generations of women, who all stood in their kitchens following the same recipe, preparing them the same way, and sharing a similar experience with their families. They provided consistency and ritual, comfort and predictability, tradition and connection.

So it was no surprise that by the time I became a mother myself, those meatballs found their way to our table on every holiday too. For many years, my mother would prepare them at her house, then transport them, piping hot, to mine, where I would host the entire family. The tradition of hosting family meals had transferred from my mother's generation to mine, but the meatballs remained hers to make. Somewhere along the way, my son, the oldest grandchild in the family, fell in love with them and began affectionately referring to them as "Grandma's meatballs."

As my son got older, he asked before every holiday if my mother would be bringing her meatballs. The question wasn't really about the meatballs, though. We all knew if my mother was coming to a holiday, so were her meatballs. My son, in his infinite old-soul wisdom, was starting to understand the fragility of life and anticipate the inevitable changes that make their way into all families. He seemed to know we were heading toward a day when the answer to his question about Grandma's meatballs would be no.

The day our inevitable loss finally happened, I swear I heard my ten-year-old son's heart break. My own heart shattered too. There is no pain quite like seeing your child hurting and knowing there's nothing you can do to shield them from grief. My mother would never spend a holiday with us again. She would never make him another pan of meatballs.

The next holiday, I made Grandma's meatballs myself and put them center stage on our table. For many holidays after her death, I couldn't make them without crying or pounding my angry fists into the raw mixture. I would curse silently as I stirred my mother's meatballs into the sauce, furious at the world for being so unfair. I wanted to ban meatballs from my home. I wanted to forget about them. I wanted to rip the recipe into tiny pieces. But it was etched too deeply in my memory and in my heart. I couldn't let them go.

Before every holiday and family party, my son made sure I would be making Grandma's meatballs. My answer was, and always will be, yes. We will keep making room at the table for Grandma's meatballs.

Years later, although the hurt is still there, I no longer cry when I make Grandma's meatballs. Instead, I try to conjure up memories of the good times.

As I roll the mixture into balls, I picture my grandmother and great-grandmother standing in the kitchen with a young version of my mother, teaching her how to make what would eventually become a recipe named for her. I try to picture what it will feel like to one day transport these meatballs, piping hot, to my son's house, to sit at a table with my own grandchildren as he tells them his memories about Grandma's meatballs.

I wonder if every generation in my family has learned the same lesson from Grandma's recipe. Perhaps as certain as the heartburn that will result from eating them is the insight they provide. They offer connection to our family's story—our past, our future, our hurts, and our hopes. Maybe every time Grandma's meatballs are shaped, each generation learns to mend the pieces of their broken hearts and find hope for the future.

Maybe that's exactly the kind of recipe every cookbook should include.

GRANDMA'S MEATBALLS

Sauce

3 or 4 twenty-eight-ounce cans of crushed tomatoes
8-ounce can of tomato paste
2-3 tablespoons minced garlic
parsley flakes to taste
oregano to taste
dash of sugar
salt and pepper to taste
4-5 slices/pieces of any cheese

Meatballs

3-4 pounds ground hamburger
2 eggs
1 1/2 cup bread crumbs
parsley flakes to taste
salt and pepper to taste

Mix sauce ingredients in large stock pot on stovetop and let simmer on low heat, stirring occasionally. Mix all meatball ingredients by hand and form into balls. Place into 350-degree oven for about thirty minutes. Do not overcook or completely cook in the oven. Add to the sauce and let simmer, the longer the better. Continue to stir so bottom does not burn.

Jenni Brennan is a grief therapist, college professor, and podcaster. She is the founder of *Changing Perspectives Online* and author of *Confessions from the Couch*.

Ladybug Tattoos and Aching Hearts

KELLY CERVANTES

"I have an idea that is going to shock you," Mom said to me one morning.

Except it wasn't just any morning; it was the morning after my nearly four-year-old daughter passed away due to complications from epilepsy and a neurodegenerative disorder. I felt like I was navigating the world underwater. Lights were dimmer, sounds were muffled, and movement was disorienting. Can something still shock you when you're in physical shock?

"On Adelaide's birthday, what if we got matching ladybug tattoos?" She was looking at me with a soft smile on her face and a mischievous glint in her eyes. My mother's typically meticulously crafted appearance was instead puffy from tears, with no effort made to cover the circles of exhaustion beneath her eyes. Out of respect for my dignity, I personally was avoiding all mirrors.

Lots of mothers and grandmothers have tattoos—*my* mother is not one of them. My mother couldn't understand why I didn't want to include crystal glassware on my bridal registry. I can count on two hands the number of times I've seen her leave the house without her hair and makeup done. And when I asked to get a tattoo in high school, I was met with the threat of my parents rescinding their offer to pay for college. Thankfully, my frontal lobe had developed enough by that point to resist the urge to get one anyway.

For months following my daughter's death, I was so consumed with my grief it was hard for me to comprehend that other people were also grieving my daughter. I mean, of course they were, but also, what day was it? When was the last time I'd eaten? And where did these flowers come from?

There are support groups and retreats for all kinds of loss, from spouse to parent to child. But so often the loss of a grandchild is overlooked. It shouldn't be. I am a firm believer that there is no grief hierarchy—loss is loss, and all grief deserves and needs to be experienced and processed. With so much focus on the lost child's parents (the arbitrary winner of the made-up grief Olympics), who is supporting the grandparents? After all, grandparents aren't just grieving their grandchild; they are hurting and worried for their own child as well.

My mother once wrote,

> I have a bright, beautiful, healthy daughter, but she does not, and this just breaks my heart more than I can put into words. I love my sweet little Adelaide with all my being, but the truth is, my priority in this devastating situation is my daughter, my beautiful Kelly. I would do anything to take away Kelly's pain. If it was in my power, I would give my life in exchange for Adelaide's health. But alas, it is not in my power. As a matter of fact, grandparents have very little power when it comes to grandchildren.

I have a deep understanding of what powerlessness feels like. Every time I held Adelaide during a seizure, I was consumed by it. But afterward, I could message the doctor, make a plan to adjust medications, or at a minimum record the details in a seizure diary so we could look for patterns. The only thing my mother could do as Grandma was love her granddaughter unconditionally and support her daughter. So that's what she did.

For the last month of Adelaide's life, Mom moved into our basement, sleeping on a barely comfortable pull-out couch, doing what she could to take care of our family so we could, in turn, take care of Adelaide. She stole moments with her granddaughter when we needed breaks. In doing so, my mother gave me the greatest gift I could ask for—time. Time with my dying daughter without the distraction of laundry, meals, or cleaning.

Today, when I look at the ladybug tattoo on my wrist, I don't just think of my daughter—I think of her grandma, who succeeded in shocking me with her suggestion of getting tattoos. A woman who grieves not just for her granddaughter but for her daughter as well. A grief that can feel helpless and unseen. A complicated grief with little support or understanding from the outside world.

A grandma who, like me, has a little red bug just behind her ear.

Kelly Cervantes is an award-winning writer, speaker, and advocate known for her blog *Inchstones*, bestselling book *Normal Broken*, and nonprofit work with CURE Epilepsy.

A Swift
Force of Nature

STEVIE SWIFT

Grandma Hazel became a Swiftie in the 1930s. Of course, in the twentieth century, "Swiftie" was just a nickname assigned to us Swifts, not a label for Taylor fans.

Hazel grew up in the roaring twenties, a South Dakota farm girl with a wild streak who joined a group of friends to run off to Seattle. She met Grandpa there, a Swift, born December 13, the same day Taylor would be born about a century later.

At first glance, Hazel and Taylor don't have a lot in common beyond the shared last name. Hazel was more likely to be covered in mud than sparkles, and I doubt Taylor would stick her head in the oven to dry her hair, as Grandma was famous for doing.

But I see some similarities.

While she worked as a waitress on the ferry between Vashon Island and Seattle, Hazel paid attention to the men who left the island and who they met on the other side. Women at that time weren't even legally allowed to have their own bank account, but Hazel didn't have a problem owning her own voice to call those men out on bad behavior.

Hazel didn't write songs about her exes—she was married to Grandpa until the day she died. But when she was mad, you might find her candling eggs and dramatically reciting "The Charge of the Light Brigade," which I think is pretty close.

She was herself.

When I ask people about her, this is the comment I hear most. She was who she was. She was *fully* Hazel.

She was a smoking, cussing, pants-wearing, shoe-hating, chicken-raising, baby-loving force of nature who ran away from the farm only to make one of her own and fill it with a crop of Swifties.

I can't quite imagine Taylor processing chickens or refusing to even *look* at a newly constructed house when there were perfectly good old farmhouses on the market, but there's more than one way to be a force of nature.

I was nine years old when Grandma and Grandpa's farmhouse burned to the ground. I have a snippet of memory of standing in the remains of their home, sifting through ash for salvageable items.

Grandma died shortly after the fire. On the heels of her death, a huge windstorm rolled through Western Washington. Seventy-nine homes were destroyed, and thousands were damaged. Widespread power outages and road closures disrupted the region. I told everyone at school my grandma caused the storm.

If you hang around us Swifts long enough, you might hear someone say, "She's got some Hazel in her" about one of Grandma's many descendants. They might mean she has a wild streak or she marches to her own beat or she's stubborn or blunt or mouthy.

They might mean it as a compliment. They might not.

I hope we all have a little bit of her fire, a little bit of her generosity, a little bit of her ability to be herself. I hope we each take those things and affect the world in our own way.

There are, after all, many ways to be a swift force of nature.

Stevie Swift writes fiction, essays, and poems about cheese.

More Than Just a Stool

STACY BRONEC

There's a small hand-painted stool under my desk. I see it every time I sit down, and I use it to rest my feet while I'm working on my laptop. When it's not under my desk, I find it in the pantry, where my youngest child used it to reach a snack on the shelf. My grandpa cut the wood for the stool, and my grandma painted a little girl on it with a blue ribbon in her dark brown hair, holding an ice cream cone. On each corner, there are delicate blue and white flowers. My grandma's signature is on the bottom in her familiar cursive. Along with her signature is the date she gave it to me: March 1987, my third birthday.

My grandma worked as my grandpa's bookkeeper for sixty-five years. Together, they ran a gas station in rural Wyoming. She kept her desk at home, and to this day, I can still hear her fingers clicking over the ten-key calculator, her eyes never looking down at the keys. She was a whiz with numbers.

But creativity was her true passion. She made countless afghans, crocheted doll dresses, and created beautiful paintings. She taught all her granddaughters how to crochet too—though none of us had her talent. My grandparents made stools for each of their four granddaughters, and my grandma personalized each one.

When I married at twenty-nine, I brought my stool to my new home. The paint was worn, one of the scoops of ice cream was missing, and the little girl's face was scraped off, but I still loved it. There were nicks in the wood from being dropped over the years, but my grandma's signature was still legible.

Two years later, a stool showed up in the mail for my son's first birthday. A few years after that, my daughter got her own too. My grandma made stools for my sister's boys and my cousins' kids. I'm sure she made others I didn't know about.

Then my grandma's heart started to give out. She became weaker and refused a second open-heart surgery. No one blamed her. A few weeks after I had my third baby, we drove to my hometown to introduce her to my grandparents. My grandma lovingly held her newest and last great-grandbaby. Over the next year, her health continued to decline, and with each visit we made home, I knew it could be the last time I would see her.

My baby's first birthday came and went. I knew it was too much for my grandma to hold a paintbrush, but part of me was sad my youngest child wouldn't have this special keepsake like her siblings and cousins.

That October, my family and I went to my hometown for a long weekend to visit my parents, and we spent one of the days with my grandma. We watched daytime TV, just like when I was a kid, except *Guiding Light* was no longer on the air and she was resting in her recliner instead of at her desk doing bookwork. Her ten-key calculator was still there but silent—the steady pumping of her oxygen tank filled the room instead of calculator clicks.

In early December, my grandma took her last breath, my faithful grandpa by her side after sixty-eight years of marriage. I felt helpless and sad getting the news over the phone in another state but grateful for the day we'd spent together weeks earlier.

On Christmas Eve, we gathered at my grandparents' house, like we had my whole life. When I opened the front door, I swear I could hear her voice, her familiar laugh. I thought of the countless times she met me at the top of the stairs in a white blouse, a tissue tucked up her sleeve, kissing me on the cheek with her pink lipstick. She always greeted me with, "Hi, Peanut."

But of course, this time she wasn't there.

After dinner, the chaos of opening presents with twenty-three people began. My heart felt heavy—her empty recliner left a gaping hole. We passed gifts around, but there wasn't much holiday cheer. The kids tore off wrapping paper, not worried about the tags. I watched, tracking who received what gift from who. Then someone handed me a package addressed to my youngest child from Great Grandma Joan.

"Nora, this present is for you!" I said excitedly as she tore the paper. Tears began streaming down my face before it was even unwrapped.

A stool.

I wiped the tears from my cheeks as I ran my fingers along the smooth, dark wood. I traced the delicate pink flowers around the corners. I looked up. My grandpa's eyes met mine. "Grandma wanted to make Nora a stool, but she didn't have the energy," he said. "I hope this one she made a while back will be okay."

The room was silent. Everyone stopped opening their gifts, noticing the gift in my hands.

I nodded, unable to speak.

It was just a stool, and of course, so much more.

Stacy Bronec, a writer, wife, and mom in rural Montana, navigates the beauty and challenges of farm and ranch life through storytelling.

Painting Her Memory

ELIZABETH ALLISON

Thomas's lithe fingers unfurled a thin paper strip to reveal the night's question: *If you could paint one thing that would come to life, what would you paint?*

I had crafted the Question Jar, a plastic bin brimming with conversation starters, to spare my husband and me endless Roblox ramblings during dinner, but I was delighted by how enlightening and entertaining the exercise proved. Nightly questions revealed Thomas, our twelve-year-old, was feeling overwhelmed with extracurricular activities, and DJ, our ten-year-old, thought adult parties consisted only of "strange cheeses" and conversations about taxes.

Thomas dropped the paper slip and proceeded to manhandle his French bread while I repeated the question aloud.

"If you could paint one thing that would come to life, what would you paint?"

I was conjuring images of a maid cleaning after my always-sticky children and a chauffeur shuttling them from activity to activity when DJ blurted his response.

"Grandma."

The table froze.

"I would paint Grandma," DJ declared confidently.

My heart split into two, rejoicing in my son's adoration for my mother while lamenting what was lost when she died unexpectedly. Through moments big and small, my mom had been a constant in our lives, a dynamic presence fueled by furious devotion to her children and grandchildren.

She stooped over a plastic tub to lovingly wash three-day-old Thomas after I called her in tears, terrified I would injure my newborn's tiny frame. She lulled Thomas to sleep in her arms two weeks later so I could leave the house simply to walk the mall. She sat by my side in the ER at 2:00 a.m. to reassure me when DJ contracted RSV. Then she tended to us all in the days after.

As my sons grew, they witnessed for themselves a grandma's love. When they performed at the school talent show, Grandma blew kisses and clapped loudest and longest. When the temperature hit one hundred, Grandma called them. "Come use the pool, boys. Then we'll make an apple pie together." When they subsequently detonated flour, butter, and sugar shrapnel onto the counters and floor, Grandma always waved it off. Nothing flustered her when she was with the boys.

What's more, my mom had an extraordinary ability to see, instantly and instinctively, what her grandchildren needed. When Thomas's beloved baby blanket tore, she read the anguish of a boy too embarrassed to admit his distress and returned the next day with sewing supplies. When DJ became despondent during the pandemic lockdown, an apple pie magically materialized on the front porch and happy gasps followed. Days later, a pot of minestrone appeared. Then a cheesy lasagna. And so on until restrictions were lifted.

So consistent was Mom's attention that her sudden absence left a crater I feared we would never climb out of. The family landscape felt incomplete, as if an artist had hastily blotted out her image and left a blank space on the canvas. Who could fill the void? Who could paint her back?

Then an otter appeared in my bedroom.

In the days following Grandma's death, I was shuffling mindlessly in a haze of grief and disbelief exacerbated by an inability to sleep. When I trudged to bed one evening, Otto, Thomas's trusty bedtime companion, was resting on my pillow. I fell asleep clutching the stuffed animal.

The next morning, I asked my son about the gesture. "Did Dad tell you to lend me Otto?"

"No," Thomas answered. "But I knew you could use him." He sounded so much like my mother.

After that night, I noticed how my boys were emulating their grandma. They invited Grandpa to sleepovers because "he shouldn't be alone." They researched TV shows that would make him laugh. They lent me books they thought would make me smile. They revamped a neglected bench at the far end of our yard, painted it Dodger blue to honor Grandma's favorite team, and christened it a place to rest and remember Grandma.

My boys echo their grandma, painting her spirit back onto our family canvas. DJ paints his grandma's compassion each time he sweetly befriends new students at school. Thomas paints his grandma's insight when he sees me dragging and asks if I need a hug. My sons paint their grandma's loyalty when they cheer each other on at sporting events and award assemblies. And every single day, they paint her enormous heart with tight squeezes before bed and in daily, unprompted professions of love.

After the Question Jar was returned to the pantry and the greasy dishes and always-sticky children were washed, it was bedtime. I tucked DJ and his animal menagerie under the covers, swiped the shiny hair from his youthful face, and asked, "If you painted Grandma and she came back to life, what would you say to her?"

"I'd say, 'Thank you.'"

Giant doe eyes gazed upward before he continued. "And 'Can we make one more pie together?'"

Elizabeth Allison is a former educator, fiction and nonfiction writer, and proud mother of two boys. Her work can be found at *The Write Profile*.

Nana's Lasagna

ALANA SMITH

I just can't keep this much grease in here. I mean, how has she lived eighty-three years leaving grease in her lasagna?

I'm holding a colander half-full of ground beef, thinking I should pour the rest in to drain, but I hear my grandmother in my head saying, "You gotta leave some grease in there."

I do as she would, because I cannot cook at all, so who am I to change her recipe? I can make spaghetti and scrambled eggs, and after today, Nana's lasagna—her one and only dish.

Nana is my mother's mother. She is the epitome of a grandmother—so much so that if you looked up the word in the dictionary, her picture might just be there (with the footnote "does not enjoy cooking"). Her stature is short and soft and just right for pulling you into a solid hug. She is gray and slow and lovely. She has an air about her that has always reminded me of Winnie-the-Pooh looking for one of his honey pots.

I've always pictured my grandmother as, well, my grandmother. When I was young, I never thought of her as ever being my age—wrinkle-free and carefree, wearing heels and big hooped earrings. I always thought of her as just Nana.

It wasn't until I was visiting her house with my first baby, pulling the tab across his Pampers diaper, that I stopped to think about her younger days and the five children she had to raise and cloth-diaper. I imagined her pushing safety pins through the fabric, hoping not to poke herself or the baby, and praying the diaper did its job this time.

Five babies in cloth diapers? There would be no time for anything but changing diapers. No wonder she doesn't cook.

I pour tomato sauce into the meat and begin to stir. I keep looking at her handwritten recipe after each step, and I read it aloud slowly, again, as if I am reciting a foreign language.

"Add one fifteen-ounce cottage cheese."

Is that right? Doesn't ricotta cheese go in lasagna?

I pour in the cottage cheese, followed by sour cream, and while the entire mixture looks like one big heart attack, it is starting to smell lovely and rich, like a warm hug in a pot. I scoop out some sauce for the bottom of the dish and begin to layer the noodles, sauce, and mozzarella. I picture my grandmother in her late twenties, assembling a lasagna on her Formica countertop. I imagine this would feed her large family for one day, maybe two, if my grandfather didn't get seconds. She probably dreaded scrubbing this pan.

I decide I like this recipe because it doesn't involve any chopping or measuring. I top the whole thing with cheddar cheese, like the recipe says, and slide it into the oven. She didn't specify if it should be covered or not, so I'm hoping the omission was on purpose.

Good luck, Nana's lasagna!

My boys come into the house armed with Nerf guns and grass stuck to their shoes, and ask, "What's for dinner?"

"Nana's lasagna!"

They are rightfully skeptical; they've never seen me pull a lasagna out of the oven, much less while wearing an apron (I was channeling Nana in the 1960s), but out it comes.

I watch them try a bite with slight apprehension, and then, to my surprise, they keep eating. I mentally file away this recipe as a winner and finish my own plate, swiping the remaining sauce with my last bite of bread, pleased with myself.

As I clean up the kitchen, I wonder if this was my Nana's own recipe, created by trial and error, or if it was passed down to her from her mother or grandmother. I realize there aren't many things that survive the test of time, like a good recipe. It can't be broken like a piece of china or lost like a gold earring. It just holds true.

That is, of course, if you remember to "leave a little grease in it."

NANA'S LASAGNA

Ingredients

1 pack lasagna noodles (cook and drain)
3 pounds ground chuck, browned (leave a little grease in it)

Add to meat:

29-ounce can tomato sauce
15 ounces cottage cheese
15 ounces sour cream

Layer sauce, noodles, and a pack of mozzarella cheese. Top with sharp cheddar cheese. Bake at 350 degrees until bubbly.

Alana Smith is a nurse anesthetist, children's author (*Magic Air: Ten Kid-Sized Steps to Surgery*), and the voice behind the blog *Holy Moly Motherhood*.

PART 5

SO GOD MADE A GRANDMA
faithful

A grandma is the one to ask before Siri, every time.

KRISTA BRATVOLD

The Prayer

LESLIE MEANS

When I'm tired or simply can't find the words to talk to God, I repeat my childhood prayer, which is basically just a list of names. *God bless Mommy and Daddy* and so on.

Many of the people on my list are in heaven now. Is it okay to pray for people already hanging out with Jesus? I suppose He doesn't care.

Hey, Les, it's cool you're praying for your grandma and all, but she's chillin' with me now. We're currently playing a mean game of Uno. But you keep on being you. We love you for it. Love, God.

God and I have unique chats.

But back to the point.

I have added more than a few names to my prayer list in my forty-three years of life—and a few more requests (*Please, God, protect my girl as she starts driving!*) but sometimes, when I can't find the words, I simply list the names as I did so many years ago.

I don't remember my grandparents ever talking to me about Jesus. "That generation didn't say much," Mom told me recently.

But what they lacked in words, they showed in action.

In the early 1900s, my great-grandparents helped start the church where I grew up.

Mom tells me her grandmother—who lived to be 106—was a God-fearing woman.

I hear she made the best pressed chicken sandwiches on homemade rolls and served them at church dinners. I would love to have one with her now.

I know my grandparents' faith was strong because they taught their kids about Jesus, then Mom and Dad passed it on to me.

There have been seasons when God and I have been on rocky terms (tell me this has happened to you too?). I've had questions, and I'm still trying to figure things out, as one does when one becomes an adult, but I've never doubted His love for me—a gift, I believe, given to me years ago with those bedtime prayers.

I pray I'm doing the same for my kids.

"Thank You, Jesus, for all my blessings," my seven-year-old whispered as I tucked him in one night.

"You know, buddy, you can talk to Jesus anytime, anywhere!" I reminded him.

He nodded.

"I know, Mom, but we usually talk at night."

Me too, buddy. Me too.

Whether it's quiet or loud, big or little, old or new, faith provides fertile soil for a family tree. Generations before us often inspire our own walk with Jesus, just as the way we live our own faith lives can impact generations to come.

It's a thread that weaves through families in the most beautiful way—you'll see how in these next several essays.

Mile Marker 302

KRIS ANN VALDEZ

At mile marker 302 on Route 260, the back tire of an eighteen-year-old driver's car blew out, sending his 1976 Mercury Capri careening and landing on its roof. From the passenger seat, his best friend walked away with a few minor scratches. But the driver suffered severe head trauma. They needed to air vac him from the facility in remote Holbrook to a bigger hospital in Phoenix, about 150 miles away.

On the phone, the doctor said hopefully to the boy's father, "I think he's going to make it."

The date was June 14, 1980.

Two decades earlier, my grandma, a spitfire from Long Island, New York, prayed that if God would fill her womb, she would name her firstborn daughter after Mary. She'd been trying to get pregnant for over a year, but it felt longer.

Eventually, she did get pregnant and gave birth to a boy named Richard, after his father—Rick, for short. As if the floodgates of fertility opened to her, she soon became pregnant with numbers two, three, and four, all girls. Remembering her promise, Grandma realized she didn't particularly *like* the name Mary enough to use it as a first name, so she bestowed it upon each of her girls as a middle.

Christine Mary. Cheryl Mary. Carolyn Mary.

After a three-year respite, she had two boys back-to-back, for a total of six kids. Life was filled with the usual big-family things: sharing meals, sharing everything.

When the youngest finally hit nine, my grandparents decided to spend two weeks alone in Europe to celebrate their twentieth wedding anniversary. It would be their first time overseas and the longest stretch away from their children. The day before their trip, they pulled Rick aside. Having just graduated from high school, he was driving up north to the woods with his best friend to go backpacking and fishing.

"Lord, keep us safe on our adventures," they prayed in unison, and hugged.

Rick hopped in his car, waving goodbye. The family waved back, knowing he had a good set of matching tires on his car and an even better head on his shoulders.

Midmorning, Grandma took her girls to the mall for some last-minute shopping. She and the girls ran into a family friend there.

Or rather, the family friend ran to find them, out of breath and pale.

"It's Rick," he huffed. "He was in a car accident."

The family prayed. Oh, how they prayed. Their community did too. A prayer chain, link after link, wound its way through their church and its members.

But Rick didn't make it. At eighteen years old, in a small hospital in the woods, the boy they'd longed for, hoped for, named for his father, died.

Instead of gallivanting through Europe, Grandma spent months hardly leaving Rick's room, fluctuating between numbness and tears.

Grief spread through the family like an illness that couldn't be shaken. At the large trestle table where they took their meals, Rick's assigned seat was empty. And when it came time for nightly chores, "Sir Broomalot" wasn't there to harass his younger siblings with his cleaning antics. Sweeping became a painful reminder of who they'd lost.

He'd been Christine's best friend. Cheryl and Carolyn's protector. The younger boys' hero. Now he was only a six-foot-two shadow in their memory.

The second daughter, Cheryl, had jaw surgery a month after his death. "I sat in that hospital for five long hours," Grandma recounts, "wondering what it would have been like to sit with Rick in his last moments."

She knew how fortunate she'd been to have hugged him goodbye—but still, it haunted her that she hadn't held his hand as he passed into eternity.

On Thanksgiving, the family went to see a movie. It felt like they were consuming time, waiting for the holiday to be over. Waiting to wake up from the nightmare.

"My mind played tricks on me in that season," Grandma says. "I decided the rapture was going to happen soon, because Jesus wouldn't make me suffer this intensely for long. Until then, I could just pretend Rick was away in the military and would be home any moment."

One day, she heard a still, small voice. "Barbara, you have five other children God has given you to care for. You must be there for them."

So she picked herself up and willed herself forward. The grief still hung around, but she didn't wrap herself in its shadow any longer.

As the others grew, Grandma held her breath when each obtained a driver's license, crashed cars, took road trips. She learned to pray—not the bargaining prayers she'd once made—but the sort that ripped her heart out while bringing her inner peace. *Lord, these are Your children. I entrust them to You.*

It took thirty years before my grandparents willed themselves to drive past mile marker 302 on Route 260. A few years after that, they finally let Rick's ashes go, buried in the woods he loved so much.

My grandma is in her eighties now. Every time she talks about Rick, her eyes light up. "I can't wait to be with him again," she says.

A grieving mother never stops missing her child—she only knows how to tuck it away so she can keep existing for others' sake.

When my own infant daughter fell deathly ill with bacterial sepsis, my grandma promised, "We are praying ceaselessly." I knew she would pound the gates of heaven, because while her New Yorker accent softened over the years, her spirit remains in spitfire shape.

Monitors beeping, I clutched the hand of my newborn daughter—PICC line near her tiny wrist, feeding tube down her throat, wires recording her brain activity—and felt some of the same emotions Grandma must have felt the day she longed to hold her son's hand in the ICU. Fear. Hope. Numbness.

What would the future for this little girl look like? Would she even have one?

I wanted to bargain with God, but I knew better. Instead, I prayed what I'd seen Grandma model: *Lord, this is Your child. I entrust her to You.*

And even as my heart ripped, I felt peace stitching me back together.

My daughter made a miraculous recovery. A few years later, my third child, a son, made one too. I'm not done raising these children of mine. I don't know what shadows the future holds. But I do know this: God gave my grandmother the resilience to face her tomorrows and the joy of a reunion to look forward to.

Whatever happens in my motherhood journey, she paved the way to face each day. To be strong for the sake of others. To entrust her children to the Lord.

Kris Ann Valdez is a proud Arizona native, wife, and mother to three spunky children. She's a freelance writer and novelist. Follow her @krisannvaldezwrites.

Fully Loved

TERA ELNESS

I'm not exactly sure how Nana got her name, but I never once called her anything else.

Nana was tiny in stature and gigantic in faith.

She showed me what worship looked like by bringing me with her each time she went to Mass.

I'd watch carefully as people tapped water on their heads while they walked in, how they dropped to one knee before entering the pew, and later how they kneeled.

I remember feeling so small in such a big, holy place—a space so beautiful I wondered if perhaps it was what an art museum in heaven might look like.

Nana would place her hand on my knee almost as a guide to be still. She'd reach into her purse and carefully split a single piece of Doublemint gum—half for me, half for her. She was wise to give my young, talkative mouth a chore to do.

Nana was a lover of all and a hater of none, regardless of what the person looked like.

I will never forget the time I visited shortly after her parish received a new priest.

We sat in the balcony that day, much to my delight. It's funny, I can still clearly remember the view. And when the man they called Father took his place by the altar, I couldn't help but notice he looked *nothing* like the Fathers I had seen at Nana's church before. This Father had long hair and an earring and multiple rings on his fingers, and the expression on my face must have spoken a thousand words, because the next thing I heard was Nana's whisper: "Some don't care for him because of the way he looks, Tera Jeannie, but they seem to forget Who we're praying to." Nana was progressive like that.

I'd spend weeks with her each summer as well as during holidays, and I hated when it was time to leave. I'd cry and she'd cry, and she'd hug me for what seemed like an hour. We had our own traditions, and she gave me space to be me. She listened to my ideas before ruling them out, and she *usually* agreed—even when it meant going Christmas shopping at 3:00 a.m. just to see if people really *do* shop twenty-four hours a day during the holidays.

She made my favorite foods and we'd stay up late and talk about big things like dreams. When I drew her a picture, I was Van Gogh. When I practiced my clarinet, I was Beethoven. When I dressed up in her high-heeled shoes, I was a fancy model. She believed in the girl God had created me to be, and she wasn't afraid to tell me.

She worked hard because she wanted us to have what made our hearts smile, but what made my heart smile the absolute most was being with her, right by her side.

When Nana died, I cried until the well of my tears went dry. But she left me with something that can never be lost: the truth that God is real and good, and that I am unconditionally, unfailingly, everlastingly fully loved.

P. S. I have my own grandchild now. Can you guess what he calls me?

Tera Elness is an author, a speaker, and a die-hard eighties girl. Tera writes daily on Instagram @terajean and Facebook at *Tera's Online Christian Journey*.

May You Always Love Jesus Most of All

KRISTA BRATVOLD

I blinked back tears as I replaced the devotional book on the shelf. I tucked my twin boys and younger daughter into bed, kissed them goodnight, and turned on their lullabies. A few drops slid down my cheeks as I stood in the hallway alone after closing their doors, and my mind returned to those few moments before bed.

That particular devotional was a beautiful book with imaginative illustrations and text that lays out the gospel in a way that calls to your heart. It's one of our favorites, one the kids and I had been reading each night as part of our bedtime routine. But that night, it wasn't the captivating colors or inspiring messages that caught at my heart—it was the inscription on the inside cover.

My parents gave this book to my children as a gift, and inside is a simple note written in my mother's lovely rounded script (which I've always wished I'd inherited).

> To Jayce and Bryce and Brenna
>   From Papa and Nana
>   May you always love Jesus most of all.

That was it—only a few short lines. But oh, the message it holds.

My kids had asked me to read that inscription to them plenty of times, loving to hear it again and again. But that night as I began, they chimed in and quoted it with me, word for word. And that was what made my heart squeeze tight, my breath snag in my chest, and tears press hard behind my eyes. In one short sentence, my mother had encapsulated the one thing, the most important thing, that we could ever wish them to know.

May you always love Jesus most of all.

As we raise our children, as we wade through what sometimes feels like a quagmire of all they need to learn, the weight of responsibility can be so very heavy. We fear that we will miss something vital, that we will neglect an area they need guidance in, that we will basically go about this business of parenting all wrong and leave our children to pay the price—and it can be paralyzing at times. But in the end, if we could hold on to only one thing while all the rest blew away like chaff in the wind, this would be it.

May you always love Jesus most of all.

My mother knows. She passed it on to her grandchildren with all the love she possesses. And now they know too.

Thankfully, God does not call us to do this alone. My mother is always the one I call first, whether my question is about cooking or gardening or getting rid of ants or how to mother these beautiful souls God has entrusted to my husband and me. I call her before I ask Siri, every time. It's because, as a grandmother, she knows. She has been here before, making these decisions, praying over her children, guiding them the best she knew how. And now it's as though all that experience has given her clarity, a way of cutting through the noise and seeing what truly matters.

May you always love Jesus most of all.

This is her prayer for her grandchildren, for these children who belong to God first and to us only second. And oh, how thankful I am they have her. There was a time when my kids were young and I joked they loved Nana more than me—only I was mostly serious. It never bothered me once, because they need her. The way she points them to Jesus, and always has, is one of the greatest blessings they will ever know.

FAITHFUL

Years have passed since that quiet night at bedtime. My boys are taller than Nana, and my daughter isn't far behind. But that devotional book still sits on their shelf, and I know my mother's prayer for them is still faithfully laid before our Father, day after day. She knows what they need—what they have always needed, and always will need, no matter how tall they grow.

May you always love Jesus most of all.

Krista Bratvold is a preschool teacher in North Dakota who loves Jesus, her three delightful kids, her incredible husband, and reading far too many books.

Legacies
Instead of Laps

CHELSEA OHLEMILLER

Some grandmothers have legacies instead of cozy laps to fill. They have grandchildren who either met them briefly or never got the chance to meet them at all. These special grandmothers fill the spaces of heaven instead of the bleachers of sporting events or the auditorium seats of plays and productions.

These special grandmothers aren't like others. They're not like the ones you see on grandparents' day or the ones cheering on the sidelines with wrinkles and gray hair. They're the ones who left too soon, too early—but never left completely. They remain in the hearts of each person who knew them and in the stories retold so those who never got the chance feel as though they did. Their beauty is in the power of love and influence, for they sprinkle their grandmotherly guidance and impact from the promised eternity, from heaven.

They don't get moments and memories. They don't get pictures on mantels featuring smiles and hugs next to their precious grandchildren. They don't get sloppy, cherished handmade artwork or delicately drawn cards. Instead, they monitor from above, witnessing it all with God's companionship. They watch their grandchildren from a different location than anyone wanted, but one that reigns above it all.

I believe God sends whispers in the wind to remind the little ones of their grandmother's love, to remind everyone of her love. I believe He sends butterflies or cardinals at just the right time, a reminder that even though she's not there in person, her love still is. Heavenly grandmothers are in songs on the radio with words that speak directly to our hearts and souls, words that remind us of them. They're in the spaces that seem empty and the faces of those who loved them. They're in the moments it seems they're missing but never truly are. They're in the times some may call coincidence but are actually opportunities for connection.

They're the grandmothers with legacies instead of lives, the ones loving us powerfully from heaven.

These grandmothers sit with a friend called Jesus instead of friends at book clubs or coffee dates. They're missed fiercely and remembered in a way just as powerful as the promise we'll see them again one day. The promise of a reunion or a meeting that never happened this side of eternity.

Those who have this type of grandmother know the effortless impact of their legacy and the constant ache of their absence. They know a grandmother's selfless and unwavering love but also the holes caused by hands they don't get to hold and laps they don't get to sit in. They know the complicated reality of having a grandmother both here and in heaven.

Unlike a grandmother's legacy and undeniable influence, life is fragile and comes with limits. Some grandmothers get to make memories and be part of adventures; some get memorials and remembrance instead. Time isn't promised, and life is unpredictable and often unfair.

But those grandmothers with legacies instead of laps are special ones. With God by their side, they prove they can love and show up for you from anywhere—even from heaven.

Chelsea Ohlemiller, wife and mother of three, writes to inspire and comfort. Her first book, *Now That She's Gone*, is available now.

A Generational Faith

HADASSAH TREU

In the 1980s, I was a young girl growing up behind the Iron Curtain. I didn't know any life other than communist Bulgaria. I just felt the heavy burden of the life I lived—dark, isolated, and filled with pain and despair.

God was not in the picture. No one openly spoke His name. His Word seemed forgotten. Only the visible was real, the things we could see and touch. Everything else was nonexistent.

My home was not a safe place. I lived with the monster of alcoholism and violence that took hold of my father. But there were rays of light that penetrated the thick darkness. God, in His sovereignty and providence, had given me a grandma who knew Him and planted the first seeds of faith in me.

Her name was Anka, but we all called her Baba Ana.

Every day after school, I visited her for lunch. I loved her fried whitefish with a lot of garlic and her thick pancakes with jam and fresh fruits. God prepared a table for me in the desert, feeding my body and tending to my wounded heart too.

My grandma didn't talk about God often because my grandpa was a renowned Communist, and such talks were dangerous in his presence. But by what she shared, I felt her discontentment with her life and a hunger and thirst for Somebody I didn't yet know.

FAITHFUL

There was a small old book at her bedside, hidden below a pile of newspapers. After lunch, I would hop into her bed and read this mysterious book. It consisted of many smaller books, but I soon nailed my favorite—the last one, called Revelation. The words there sent bolts of lightning into my heart, moving me to tears every time, igniting a powerful longing I couldn't name.

These words do the same for me today:

> I heard a loud voice from the throne saying, "Look! God's dwelling place is now among the people, and he will dwell with them. They will be his people, and God himself will be with them and be their God. 'He will wipe every tear from their eyes. There will be no more death' or mourning or crying or pain, for the old order of things has passed away." He who was seated on the throne said, "I am making everything new!"
> REVELATION 21:3-5

It sounded like a dream, a fairy tale stirring a powerful longing. This was the deep cry of my soul: no more crying, no more pain.

I asked Baba Ana a lot of questions about Revelation and the other books in her shabby New Testament. I couldn't understand many of the things she told me. But I understood her family was special. This book belonged to her mother, who I didn't know, and she got it from her mother. They lived in Plovdiv, the second-largest city in Bulgaria, and they secretly met with other special people in their house. I learned they called this a "house church."

Through my grandma's stories, God was drawing my heart to Him, showing me I was part of a godly legacy. These women before me had prayed for my family and me to find and know the true, living God through Jesus Christ.

God is a generational God. The seeds in one generation become mature plants in the next, bearing fruits in even more generations ahead. Everything we do and say matters and causes a ripple effect on the lives of the ones who come after us.

Baba Ana died when I was eighteen, but she lived long enough to experience the falling of the Iron Curtain and the end of the communist regime in Bulgaria.

She also lived long enough to experience the tearing down of the iron curtain erected in my heart, a year before she left this world. God granted her the mercy and joy to see both my sister and me accept Jesus as our Lord and Savior, joining the body of believers and claiming our legacy of faith.

After I heard the gospel and understood it for the first time at seventeen, my heart responded. I shared the Good News with my sister, and she also gave her life to the Lord. Then God brought Baba Ana full circle as my sister sat beside her deathbed in her last hours and minutes, holding her hand, praying with and for her, and gently releasing her into God's eternal embrace.

Yes, God is a generational God, who entrusted me with a legacy of faith. Will I be faithful to steward this treasure and pass it on to the next generations, honoring the memory of my grandma and the women before her?

What will be my legacy of faith? I consider this question when I order my days, make decisions, and interact with my loved ones, that I may reap a golden harvest of all the seeds I plant today.

Hadassah Treu is an award-winning international Christian writer, blogger, poet, speaker, and author of *Draw Near: How Painful Experiences Become the Birthplace of Blessings*.

Grandma, Who Is God?

KIERRA TATE HENDERSON

I remember being a little girl tinkering in my grandma's kitchen, my long puffy ponytails sweeping my shoulders. My grandma began thanking God, suddenly jumping up and down shouting, "Glory! Glory! Thank You, God! Thank You, Jesus!"

I watched and asked, "Grandma, who is God?"

She looked at me with concern and said, "You don't know who God is?" And then she began to testify. I don't recall her exact words, but somehow my little spirit understood what she was saying. It went like this: He is Alpha and Omega, the beginning and the end. He is the Creator of heaven and earth. He's my Father, the One who loves me, and the One who gave His life for me. He's the One I love, and the One I live my life for!

She was introducing me to Someone who had always known me. And it was like I never hadn't known Him.

Throughout my childhood, my grandmother showed me who God is. She tirelessly gave to the poor, attended Bible study, and nurtured so many children, including me. She'd wake me up on Sunday mornings with the sound of gospel quartet music playing, the comfort of grits on the stove, the statuesque presence of an ironing board in the kitchen, and the faint smell of starch in the air. We'd get dressed for church. She'd put on her signature pantsuit and hat, and I'd choose a dress she'd bought for me from her hallway closet. Many times we'd pick someone else up for church too.

During the week, she woke up early in the mornings to pray. Her Bible pages were ruffled, and the spine was well-worn and tattered. She always found the time for the simple and beautiful things. We'd tie a jump rope to the fence and take turns turning and jumping to rhymes from her girlhood. We would eat fruit, drink hot tea, and ride bikes. She created the beauty of my childhood.

When I was about eight years old, I found my grandma praying. She looked at me and said, "Kierra, you are going to break the generational curse of broken marriages in our family, and I am praying for your husband even now."

My grandma mandated to heaven that the seeds she planted in me bring forth a harvest. I felt the charge, but I can't say I welcomed it.

I know I worried my grandmother—my teenage behavior was so elusive that she thought I was on drugs. We laughed about it. But I knew she'd felt that pain before. I was disappointed I caused her that much anguish and anxiety. When my grandmother went through cancer, I gave her my all. I gave everything a nineteen-year-old had to offer. My all was very flawed, but I didn't want to disappoint her again for all she had poured into me.

In my grandma's final season of her cancer journey, she moved away to return to her childhood home. I struggled because for the first time, she was out of my reach.

In our last conversation, she mustered up the strength to fuss at me about responsibility and how I needed to do what I'd been taught to do.

Her last words to me were "Grandmommy is crazy about you. You know that, right?"

I responded dejectedly, "I know."

And unbeknownst to me, our final *I love you*s were exchanged. She knew that would be the last of us. I didn't.

My grandmother's passing broke me.

I abandoned everything she taught me. I didn't know how to live without the most precious person in my life. My grief overtook me, and I lived in the shadow of her death.

But she taught me, "Yea, though I walk through the valley of the shadow of death, I will fear no evil: for thou art with me; thy rod and thy staff they comfort me" (Psalm 23:4, KJV).

The prayers my grandmother prayed during her life transcended her time, and eventually the power of God began to overtake my grief.

It didn't take long before I ran back to the Jesus she'd introduced me to in that kitchen long ago. This time, there was no Grandma. I learned Grandma isn't my way to God—Jesus is. I had to ask my own self, "Kierra, who is God?"

I wish my grandmommy could see I'm becoming the woman she prayed I'd be.

From both our lives, I know just because you don't see something happen in your lifetime, it doesn't mean the prayers go unanswered. Keep planting the seeds; God will bring the rain for the harvest.

Now I have a blessed marriage. I married the one she'd been praying for all those years ago. And together, my husband and I fight the giants that stand in the way of God's destiny for us. We have four beautiful boys who know my grandmother's name, Barbara Tate. Because of her legacy, I find myself praising God in my kitchen, shouting, "Glory! Glory! Thank You, God! Thank You, Jesus!"

All because I ask my children, "Son, who is God?"

And they testify to me: He is Alpha and Omega, the beginning and the end. He is the Creator of heaven and earth. He's my Father, the One who loves me, and the One who gave His life for me. He's the One I love and the One I live my life for.

Kierra Tate Henderson created *Beloved Mama*, a mom blog for generational curse breakers. Kierra lives beautifully in Detroit with her husband and four boys.

A Dance in the Bathroom

REBECCA NEVIUS

My grandma picked cotton as a child. Not your standard extracurricular, but it helped pay for school in the small mountain town of her birth. When she was still very young, her father, who had an alcohol addiction, left their family to start a new one in Florida, and Nana was shipped across the country to live with a sister in Arizona.

I don't know what went through her mind as she sat looking out the window of the bus, weighted southern branches shrinking into the tall prairie grass of the Midwest, Colorado mountains scooping into the Valley of the Sun, where saguaros spread their arms toward the open sky of the Southwest.

Under different circumstances, it would've been a great adventure to travel across the country, but she was a lone girl, thirteen, and leaving behind the only family she'd ever known.

My mom was her firstborn. She used to tell me how living during the Depression had built a kind of grit and character in Nana that nothing else could. So maybe after all she'd already been through, a trip across the country didn't seem like a big deal, but it was. I don't think Nana liked being alone. Proof of the fact, she had six kids after she married Papa. This is why that story struck me as significant when I first heard it—it's strange to think of her sitting alone anywhere. In my memory, she was always surrounded by my aunts and uncles, cousins and babies, friends and loved ones.

She wasn't a prim kind of woman either. Having twelve siblings and six children didn't make her a prim kind of anything. She used to dance in the bathroom of Cracker Barrel and wear silly costumes to Papa's birthday parties. One year, she made my sister and me dress up in tights and raisin costumes with them—we even had to dance through the door to "I Heard It through the Grapevine." The best costume she ever wore had a farm girl dress on the front, but the back side of her and Papa's outfits were cut out to show off nineteenth-century underwear. It was perfectly indecent, and I loved her for it.

She often had to shout to be heard, whether around her large dining table or while we sat talking on her plastic-covered floral sofas. Not because she talked quietly, but because there were so many of us. When she sat in the back row of the church, everyone in a five-pew radius could hear her singing, high-pitched and a little off-key. I loved the way she sang. It was so completely for Him and nobody else.

Sin had left a crimson stain,
He washed it white as snow.

Nana still had some of that thirteen-year-old girl in her, a broken child. But what had started as a lonely life alone on a bus blossomed into a fruit basket of activity and love. It was a love that had so fully imprinted itself on my heart that to lose it would be like losing my own name.

I was in college when it happened. It was Easter. Her shirts hung neatly in the closet, still ripe with the familiar scent of coconut sunscreen, and her gold walking sneakers were by the door, just where she'd left them. A crimson pool of blood—her blood—stained the carpet where he shot her, soaked in so deeply no amount of scrubbing could erase it.

She was the one who once told me, "The world is at your feet." But my world had shattered along with any semblance of safety I'd ever felt. Suddenly, newsreels about tragedy weren't just another five-second spot. They were talking about someone's child, mother, grandmother. They were talking about *my* grandmother.

My mom told the news anchor, "Evil stole my mother, but we will choose to forgive."

At the funeral, news trucks were there broadcasting her celebration of life across Phoenix. Her funeral had a flyover and a folded flag ceremony. She was honored by thousands, but none of that mattered to me. I just wanted her back.

I wanted my family back, the one that talked too much and got stuck on the plastic sofas in the summer. I wanted her to barge in on me getting ready in the bathroom in her holiday-themed apron and talk to me from the toilet. I wanted to hear her voice ring out from the back of the church, to sit beside her just to feel her next to me and breathe in the fumes of her Vaseline intensive care lotion. I wanted to be broken with her, not over her.

After she was killed, I'd frequently go to the university chapel and study the cross at the center of the altar and wonder if she would've lived any differently if she'd known what was coming.

There's something that happens inside when someone you love is murdered. It's as if all the safety you thought existed disappears. You start to check for exits in crowded spaces. You wonder if someone else will come and do the same to you—or worse, that someone else will be taken away.

It became very clear to me I had a choice, just like Nana did all those years before when she got off that bus. Something broken can be the beginning of something wonderful. You can get off the bus and walk toward your whole life. You can leave a chapel with renewed hope for the future. That young girl couldn't have known the whole world was at her feet as she watched it pass by the bus window, yet she lived as though it was.

I could choose to be afraid, or I could live my life like she did, full of love and the fruit of faithfulness to God and others. I could get married and have babies. Grow old and cover my sofas with plastic. I could shout, "Dinner's ready!" and gather around a table. I could wear a funny, slightly indecent costume that makes at least one grandchild laugh out loud. I could sing loudly at church and tell my children and grandchildren, "The world is at your feet," because it really is, and "Don't be afraid," because we serve a big God who has a wonderful plan, even if it means dying the hard way. I could live like she did and not worry about death.

FAITHFUL

As I sat in my university chapel, I imagined her sitting across the aisle, that thirteen-year-old girl wearing a worn-out dress, but also my grandma who rooted for me all my life. I wound my hands tightly, grieving for both, but knowing deep down the next time I visited a Cracker Barrel I would dance to the music in the bathroom—and I did.

Rebecca Nevius is a wife and mother who enjoys writing about the beauty of exceptionally ordinary things and regular squeezy hugs from her three children.

Christmas Countdown

CYNTHIA MURRAY

By October, it was clear my mother would not be getting better. The yellow hue had spread to her eyes, their whites now clouded by illness. The doctors said her medications were no longer effective. Her blood was building up with toxins, and she needed a liver. Would she qualify at seventy-one? A month of testing would determine that.

"But it helps you are nice," they joked, which is a good attempt at bedside humor when you tell someone she's dying.

My mother had dedicated her life to "nice." She was notorious for giving away her family's coats to cold children at her door. She headed food drives, weeded her neighbor's yards, served as a Cub Scout leader, led PTA parties, decorated Barbie birthday cakes, and hand-sewed her children's Halloween costumes and grandbabies' quilts. For decades, she'd been investing in everyone but herself.

True to character, her decline had been quiet. She'd been helping my father through a pulmonary embolism, heart surgery, cancer, muscle atrophy, back surgery, a broken kneecap, pain management, and limited mobility. "I think I'm getting worse because your dad isn't getting better," she said, though she'd never regret her role in his care.

November was full of bouncing between home and the hospital for rigorous testing and observation of her heart and kidneys during her spikes of potassium and bilirubin. She didn't talk much about the odds of finding a rare match or enduring what her doctors described as one of the hardest recoveries in the surgical world. My mother chose to live in joy, watching baking shows, talking about family, and smiling at smudgy grandkid drawings bringing sunshine to the sterile walls.

In her days at home, we continued to talk on the phone about the kids' adorable sayings, sweet birthday wishes, parent-teacher conferences, new levels of growth percentiles, and loose teeth. We'd stop by and read stories in Grandma's lap, and I'd take a photo, both treasuring and fearing.

My sleepless nights brought silent grieving to the surface, but the morning arrived with or without rest. Holidays passed, the turkey was carved, but no word had come on the miracle we needed.

I suppose we all expect our parents to grow old and pass away someday, but I didn't expect to feel such desperation. I found myself wiping stray tears with crumpled napkins in the car at school drop-off, just thinking about how much I still relied on my mom's love, advice, and belief in me as a mother. Imagining her absence was shredding the future joys I planned to share with her. How could I let go when she didn't want to let go either?

As Christmas marked a season of celebration and love, I regretted moving the Advent gingerbread man through what seemed like my mother's final days. She had just been placed in the top position on the nationwide transplant list, waiting for a call, but time was not on her side.

Ornaments and glowing lights crowded my home as I tried to maintain normalcy, but I felt reminders of my mother in my hands: a passed-down recipe, sewn holiday towels, my children's sweaters from Grandma.

Cherishing every opportunity, I drove my mother to deliver Christmas gifts to her neighbors, a final priority on her list. I felt her quietly pulling away, leaving bits of love, just in case.

Her peace was not mine. I prayed, but I could not understand my own prayer. Could I hope for someone else to lose their life to extend hers? Could I ask for someone to mourn a loss I could not yet bear myself? Time, love, and miracles . . . we never have enough.

Then the phone rang. I heard it, felt it, and knew it before she said hello.

We drove through a fog of fear and faith. My kids ran to pack her reading glasses in a bag. We said goodbyes with hope abounding.

The surgery was expected to take ten hours but took only five. My mother's bilirubin levels immediately dropped from 16 to 4.4. Though sleepy and thirsty, she was laughing just hours after her transplant (I made sure of it!). She attributed her resilience and longevity to a love for God, and I could see her countenance already turning a healthy pink.

I'm so grateful to love others so deeply that to consider losing them is sorrow. Though I do not know the donor, I will never forget the woman who gave my mom life. Her gift in her passing is cherished, a selfless hope for life during a tragic end.

I, too, see God in His miracles, especially in His love surrounding a mourning family at Christmastime. I continue to pray for the donor's family, asking for peace and healing beyond my own understanding and memories to cherish.

One day, that's what I will cling to as well, but right now my mother is still here for the hugs. She and my father still cheer at my kids' soccer games and plan Easter egg hunts, and they will soon celebrate their fiftieth wedding anniversary.

My mom was given a healthy liver—and I have a grateful heart.

Cynthia Murray is a grateful mother to four miracles. She loves dabbling in writing, and her heart belongs to her favorite people at home.

So God Made a (Fairy) Grandmother

STEPHANIE HANRAHAN

I had a baby, a two-year-old, and a husband at home with a failing heart.

Without announcing its arrival, heart disease entered my life, and very shortly thereafter, so did a diagnosis of autism for both my children.

That year was a complete demolition and rebuild of my faith and family. A mourning of my expectations, which lasted longer than I care to mention.

Drowning in new diagnoses, I searched for a place to breathe. Like every mom, I needed a break. Unlike every mom, I was breaking.

I found respite in a community group for mothers of preschoolers that met twice a month at a local church. At the time, I didn't have a relationship with organized religion or God, but they offered free coffee and free childcare, so I signed up without asking questions.

At our first meeting, we were split into groups of ten. Ten novice moms and one leader of the pack, our mentor.

The "mentor mom" was more experienced in motherhood, someone a few steps ahead who could offer comfort and guidance to those of us struggling with sleep schedules and intimacy with our spouse.

The mentor moms lined up at the front of the room and one by one were assigned to tables. They all looked the same: kind, well-rested eyes, perfectly coiffed hair (they clearly didn't have toddlers), and reassuring smiles that silently communicated, *I've been there, too, honey.*

As each mentor took a seat at her assigned table, I noticed the one walking toward mine looked different from the others. Her hair was gray, her skin loose and sagging. She had the same kind eyes, which were hidden behind wire-framed glasses, but the message they conveyed was different. She was different.

She was Marylou, my mentor (grand)mom.

Unlike the other mentor moms who had teenagers at home, Marylou was an aging and experienced grandmother. She was forty-four years older than I was, and that fact alone told me we'd never relate. There were too many gaps between our generations. I'd had too many family members, even closer in age, misunderstand me. How could she possibly mentor me, a young mom drowning in diagnoses and disbelief?

Somehow, she did.

As the year progressed, I would come to our meetings with my tears and fears and lay them at the feet of Marylou. I told her how my husband couldn't walk, my son couldn't talk. I shared the doubts I had about my body and the Bible. She always listened with tender grace and answered with tough truths. She never placated me, never put a pacifier in my pain. She just received my woes, then said she'd turn them over to God on my behalf.

When she spoke, I listened. When she prayed, I prayed too.

While the other mentor moms threw parties and wore matching T-shirts with their mentees, I found Jesus because a woman in her eighties grandmothered me with grace.

Sometimes we find belonging beyond our bloodline. Sometimes people are sent to this earth to shepherd us, and they come in the most unexpected forms—like a baby in a manger or a grandmother with graying hair. It's only when we open our eyes to this possibility—that love often looks different, that it mends and molds into the shape we most need, when we most need it—that we can finally begin to believe.

As our year together came to a close, Marylou and I went out for breakfast. Over egg-white omelets and coffee that had turned cold, she handed me a sealed envelope—one I recognized yet had completely forgotten about.

At our first meeting, Marylou asked us to write down our greatest hope for the year, something we wanted and needed. Something we wished God would heal or make whole.

There are a lot of things I could've written on that card, a lot of things I still could. Even though my perspective has changed, my circumstances remain the same.

But at that time, the struggling, unbelieving girl I once was wrote this: "I'm hoping for connection this year. For even just one forever friend."

Seven years later, I don't talk to a single woman my age who was at that table.

But I still have my forever friend. My mentor, my fairy godmother/grandmother, Marylou.

Stephanie Hanrahan is a writer, TEDx speaker, autism activist, and creator of the viral online community *Tinkles Her Pants*.

PART 6

SO GOD MADE A GRANDMA

graceful

My grandma taught me life is wonderful and rich and full, even when it's hard and sorrowful and long.

CAROLYN MOORE

The Coat

LESLIE MEANS

My maternal grandmother was a quintessential woman of the 1950s. My mother said she was proper, and if there was a cliché for a fifties housewife, she was it.

She was beautiful, poised, and always put together.

A stark contrast to today's predominant wardrobe of black stretchy pants and oversize sweatshirts.

Of course, I didn't know Grandma then. I only remember her as a sixty-something-year-old woman with curly hair and shoulder pads, but even then, I recall her gorgeous complexion.

In the late 1940s, she married my grandfather, who had been a soldier in World War II. They lived on a farm in Nebraska, as most of my relatives did.

Money was tight, but in the 1970s when (as my mother tells me) "money was better," my grandfather purchased a gift for his wife: a custom-made coat of mink and leather. The inside tag bears her name: *Noreen*.

I asked Mom what her mother thought of such a coat, especially when extravagant items weren't readily available.

"I believe she was overwhelmed," she said.

To my knowledge, we don't have any photos of Grandma in the coat—no memories to call upon either.

When she passed away and her belongings were divided, somehow I was the lucky recipient of that beautiful coat. My arms are a bit too long and the shoulders are snug, but I wear the coat at least once a year on Christmas Eve in her memory.

When I do, I can't help but feel a little more sophisticated—and a little closer to Grandma. She may have lived in another time, but our very beings are intertwined in a way that's hard to explain.

That's the magic of grandmas.

Even though our lives are separate and unique, we are connected. I feel her in my heart. And I see it in my kids, in the way they laugh with Mom. Beauty and grace glisten in the moments and memories that bind us together—something I hope you'll feel too as you read these next stories.

You're Marvelous

CAROLYN MOORE

It's the first thing I notice when I push open the spatula-shaped handle of the hospital door—the lack of light. The plastic blinds covering the room's large windows are drawn tightly closed.

In the bed, her eyes are closed too. The starched white blanket is pulled up, as always, against her right ear. I have the identical idiosyncrasy when I sleep; genetics are such a funny thing.

I go back into the hall, looking for a nurse. I'm confused, because physical therapy should be underway at this very moment, not an early morning nap.

My ninety-one-year-old grandmother is recovering—beautifully, if I'm bragging—from a total hip replacement, and I'm here to cheer her on.

A nurse spots me. "We're just waiting for palliative care to get things set up," she says with an odd brightness that doesn't match the words.

I blink at her. Palliative care? There's clearly been some kind of mistake. I say as much now.

A look I can't quite decipher passes over her features. "She . . . doesn't want to do physical therapy anymore. I talked to her about it this morning, so we're going to go ahead and get her set up."

I close my eyes and mumble something back, letting the nurse return to her morning rounds. I pick up the phone to call my mother, who's back at the hotel with my three young children. I'd just come over to have breakfast with my grandma, not to be the recipient of surprise news.

The omelet would have to wait.

I relay what I've found and my mom echoes my confusion. Grandma had been doing so well, was almost ready to be discharged home by way of a three-week stay in a rehab facility. "I'll talk to her." I sigh into the phone.

I go back into the hospital room and slit the blinds slightly. She stirs and opens her eyes.

My grandma, this elegant, silver-haired woman with earlobes she loathes ("Too big!") and a twinkle in her eye, has never been just a grandma to me. She's the cloth from which I'm cut, like looking in a mirror (minus the earlobes; mine are perfectly average).

We'd always been close. Visiting her house five hundred miles from my own was a regular and much-loved routine well into my adulthood. She taught me to knit, patiently sitting by my side as a child—cast on, knit, pearl. She took an interest in what interested me and wanted to know about my friends and school and my work and kids. Most of all, she made time for me.

When I was a senior in college, I turned down a White House internship to live with her in South Dakota for the semester instead—a decision some questioned, but I never did. One of my daughters is named Beatrice after her. We're so much the same, and it's something I've always cherished.

"Hi, Grandma," I say now. "What's going on?"

She tells me she'd like to go home, that she's had enough with the therapy. Of course, she can't go home until she's rehabbed—the assisted-living facility she lives in isn't designed for skilled nursing. I watch the understanding settle across her lined, beautiful face when I remind her of this. The way home is through the pain, the hard work, the frustration.

Isn't it always.

"I've had a beautiful life," she says, almost childlike, a slight question. I know, then, what she needs to hear, because it's the same words I'd crave.

"You have," I agree. "And if you want to stop everything . . . it's up to you."

I don't push. I don't try to convince her what's best. I simply sit next to her, holding her hand in the in-between.

She closes her eyes. When they reopen, their contentment catches the morning light. She smiles, squeezes my hand. I know what she's saying without saying it. We won't be visiting with palliative care today.

If we're lucky, aging happens quietly. Years slip into decades. Bodies change and gratitude grows. So, too, does helplessness—and our innately human struggle to reconcile the two.

I'd watched Grandma Bea lose my Grandpa Harold, then her firstborn daughter, Cheryl. Then she parted with her breasts, her home on East 35th, her autonomy.

And yet she did everything with strength and grace. She didn't hide the heartache, but she didn't deny God's mercies either.

They say everything you need to know you learn in kindergarten—but I learned it from my grandma. She taught me life is wonderful and rich and full, even when it's hard and sorrowful and long.

Some years after that morning in the hospital room, we sat together in a memory care unit. She was in her final days, peaceful and content. We didn't talk much—we didn't have to. But I'll never forget her words to me as we sat in the comfortable silence. "You're a good friend, kiddo. It's nice to have a good friend." She smiled without opening her eyes in the golden afternoon sunlight filling the room. "You're marvelous . . . you've been marvelous."

Yes, Grandma, you sure were.

Carolyn Moore serves as editor in chief of *Her View From Home* **and is a married mom of five in the Midwest.**

A Grandma's Hands Write a Story of Love

AMY JUETT

"Mom hated her hands, and now mine look just like hers did. Just look at these spots and cracks." Grandma's declaration drew my attention to her hands folded on the lace tablecloth in her assisted-living apartment.

"Oh, Grandma, at least they aren't man hands like mine," I quipped, holding up my large hand for her examination and receiving a chuckle in return.

I've thought about that conversation many times, and how I'd have so much more than that quip to offer Grandma today in response to her disdain for her hands. If I could go back, I would tell her how a grandma's hands write a story of love in the hearts of her grandchildren.

Grandma's hands wrote love in the batches of chocolate chip cookies we made together in her kitchen, her hand above mine on a wooden spoon, teaching me how to fold in the ingredients. Her hands spoke of patient love as she quietly folded them over her flour-covered apron, waiting for me to attempt to roll the pie crust, yet again.

On cattle sale day, Grandma's hands showed love as she packed ham, butter, and cheese sandwiches, cans of pop, and a bag of licorice for our lunch when we went in the truck with Grandpa. And then there were those cold winter days when Dad and I would stop at her house and Grandma would busy herself making me some of her special hot cocoa, her hands writing love as she dropped two giant marshmallows on top.

Her hands shared love as I grew from a little girl to a woman in every hug hello or goodbye when life took me far away. Then there was the happy day I watched her hand scrawl love as she signed the papers selling her house to my husband and me so we could raise our children in her home. What a delight it was to watch her hands dole out love to my own children—edging baby blankets for them, rocking them, and patting their tummies as they cooed up at her.

But not all the times her hands loved were times of delight. There were heart-wrenching moments when her hands blew love with kiss after kiss to us through the window when the pandemic prevented us from spending our usual Sunday and Wednesday afternoons with her. And when I held her hands in mine during her last days this side of eternity, I could feel the love seeping from them straight into my heart.

From my birth to her death, Grandma's hands were always there to tell the story of her love for me, beautiful hands writing a beautiful story. And now, my mom's hands—small like Grandma's—overflow with the same love as she writes her own story of love in her grandchildren's lives.

My mom's hands write a story of love each time she presses the shutter on her camera to make sure special moments of our lives are captured and preserved.

The love flows out of her hands as she searches with my daughter for the best bargain at the rummage sale and as she moves the pieces of a favorite board game with my boys. Her hands write a story of steadfast love as she holds my toddler daughter's hand while they walk across the uneven ground.

My mom's hands dole out love in the pancakes and syrup she serves when her grandchildren come to visit. Her hands teach lessons in love as she helps them take care of the baby calves, points out the different birds and native grasses, and patiently allows my children to help her do something she could do by herself in half the time.

And always, her hands tell the story of love as she welcomes her grandchildren for hugs and snuggles as only a grandma can do. My mom's beautiful hands are writing a story of love for her grandchildren to read.

Then there are my hands, so different in size from my grandma's and my mom's, yet capable of writing the same sort of story theirs have. I'm learning these giant hands are perfect for writing love as I make the extra-large batches of food and carry all the things for my family of eight. Love spills out on the pages of our lives as I fold laundry, comb hair, and rub little backs.

My hands pour love when I make a cup of hot cocoa with two extra-large marshmallows for the child who is having a hard day. Each day is an opportunity to write love with my hands for my children so that one day, God willing, I will have the privilege of using my hands to write a story of love for their children.

You see, I'm hoping that someday my children will give me a whole passel of grandchildren to love. From what others tell me, grandchildren are even more fun than children, and I can't wait to love my own. When that day comes, I'll use my hands in much the same way as my mom and grandma before me. I'll teach, comfort, welcome, bring joy—each action a part of our story of love.

No matter the size of a grandma's hands or how many wrinkles and sunspots they may have, they will forever be beautiful because they transcribe love from the heart of a grandma to the heart of her grandchild.

Amy Juett, a wife and mother of six, makes her home in the Nebraska Sandhills. She writes about faith, family, and homeschooling at *Calamus Mom*.

My Lighthouse

CELESTE YVONNE

There are kids running around now who call me "Mom," and they seem to think I have all the answers. I am lucky enough to be the first person they look for when they're excited, scared, or sad. When their tiny feet scamper straight to me, they think I'll know exactly what to do and say to make it all better. But I am simply following your lead, Mom.

I imagine you may have felt unsure or scared raising me sometimes, but I never would have known. Because as far as I could tell, you were unbreakable, all-knowing, and harbored a special kind of love fused with magic. Magic that meant kissed boo-boos healed faster, a warm hug helped slow down tears, and light drove out monsters hiding in dark corners.

Now, my kids think I'm the wise protector of their hearts; little do they know I still give that designation to you, Mom. And now, Grandma.

You're the grandma to my kids, and boy, are those kids lucky. The truth is, I couldn't imagine a more perfect mama and grandma than you.

As a child, I remember hearing your footsteps coming home from work and feeling my belly soften. *Mom's home.* I could set my fears and worries aside. I knew with you near, everything would be okay. I remember your words of strength and grace after lost sports matches, rained-out birthday parties, and hurt feelings.

It was never smooth sailing; sometimes, the darkness crept in through the cracks. As a family, we wrestled with addiction, suffering, and tremendous loss. I don't know how you persevered on some of our worst days, but you always got up and did the hard things.

I saw you blaze trails professionally, too, defying the odds and expectations of what a woman's role "should" be. I imagine you faced choices and challenges my generation and generations to come may never have to face again. You did it so we wouldn't have to.

You were the constant in a home of occasional chaos. You were my lighthouse in my stage of despair, anger, and confusion. You were everything to me growing up, and you still are.

You are still the first person I call for all of it. Happy news. Heartbreak. Gossip. Book reviews. Sometimes just the weather. Our relationship has expanded beyond mother-daughter to a friendship rooted in unconditional love and support.

You have shown me what it means to be a good mom. I think of you in what it means to be resilient, empowered, and kind. I look to you for ways to be a good parent. Everything I do now for my kids follows your example, and I hope when my kids hear me open the front door, they feel their bellies soften in the magical exhale of knowing Mom's home.

Some days, my breath catches when I think about navigating this world without you. The idea feels foreign and daunting. Today I can still hear your footsteps when you come to my door—just a little softer and more cautious. I know it's a privilege to hear those steps at all. The idea of silence in their place haunts me.

When future generations ask me about you, I won't just tell them about you—I will describe how you make people feel. *Grandma* is so much more than a noun; it's a verb, and an active one.

Your insight and perseverance inspire me to keep the cycle of powerful women going. Perhaps I can serve as a lighthouse for future generations. Maybe someday I will be blessed to carry the name *Grandma*, and I can pass on everything I've learned from you.

There are kids running around now who think I have all the answers, but I am simply following the lead of the powerful, trailblazing women before me. So when they hear my footsteps at the front door, their bodies can relax as they, too, know this great constant: *Mom's home.*

Celeste Yvonne is the author of *It's Not about the Wine: The Loaded Truth behind Mommy Wine Culture.* **She advocates for mothers in recovery.**

Her Guidance Remains

SYDNEI KAPLAN

I find myself staring at the simple white dish towel hanging on the bar of our lower oven. It's covered in beautiful familiar cursive that captures part of a legacy.

It's my mom's recipe for toffee dreams, copied from her original tattered recipe card and somehow made to look flawless on this precious towel, a gift from my daughter—perhaps one of the most priceless, soul-touching gifts I've ever received.

I'm not sure when I first tasted these delicious cookies or when I first helped my mom make them and excitedly licked the yummy batter off both the spatula and the bowl. (Yes, my mom was always selfless like that.) I do know these bar cookies were part of my childhood and have remained with me all these years. I've made them countless times for my own children, sharing a treasured memory or sweet Nana anecdote with every batch.

Nana: the name she chose for herself as soon as she knew I was pregnant with my first baby. I vividly remember looking at the positive pregnancy test that confirmed what I'd known intuitively for weeks. A jumble of emotions swirled through my head, and I furiously wrote them into my journal, trying to process everything I was feeling.

Conventional wisdom said to wait until after the first trimester to let others know about the pregnancy, but my mom didn't count as "others." I turned to her for comfort as I shared the news and all my thoughts. Mom listened and offered gentle reassurance, the kind that can only come from experience and from being connected heart and soul with me.

This was the moment the Nana in her was born.

It was as if I could feel her already all-encompassing love for me grow even deeper. She loved this new life growing in me almost as much as I did, and it somehow added to her love for me. As soon as I found out we were having a girl (my husband didn't want to know), I shared this with my mom. Through tears, she told me how happy she was that now I would know the indescribable joy and love of having a daughter and best friend, just like she did. There was something so special about this secret we shared, knowing it was Mia who would be joining our family.

At the time, my husband and I lived in Atlanta and our families were in the Chicago area. Days after we brought Mia home, my parents came to meet her, help care for me, and spend time getting to know this new ray of love in our lives. Watching my mom with Mia was like getting a magical glimpse into how she'd loved and cared for me when I was a baby.

It was so hard not living near each other during this time in our lives. Even though they visited every few months, each time our families came, it took Mia time not to cry when I'd set her down or hand her to my mom or dad. My mom was patient and allowed Mia to slowly remember and reconnect. She'd feed her a bottle and talk softly to her, making eye contact and smiling with a heart full of love. They were building their own beautiful bond.

Two years later, we were visiting Chicago for a wedding, and I was seven months pregnant with my son, Ben. My mom left the wedding reception to help put two-year-old Mia to bed. I shared my worry about not loving my new baby enough because I loved Mia so much. My mom looked me in the eye with her smiling, sparkling brown ones and reassured me my heart would expand without even having to think about it. She told me I would have more than enough love for both of my children and for any other babies we might welcome.

Then I shared news I'd been waiting to tell her: we were moving our family back to the Chicago area after Ben was born, to raise our children near our families. The pull of family, love, and connection was powerful. My mom lit up, visibly radiating deep happiness and gratitude words can't properly convey. She hugged me and held me, and when we finally spoke, we validated that this was something we'd both been longing for.

We shared just two years living in the same city before my mom passed away. But in those two years, precious, unbreakable bonds of love were built and solidified. It was clear "Nana" was a natural extension of her as "Mom," both roles fueled by infinite love.

Losing my mom was something I never fathomed and was one of my biggest unspoken fears. And though it's been more than twenty years since she passed away, she is still present everywhere. She's part of who I am. She shines through in many of my mannerisms, the way I think, traditions that became mine. How highly I value family and keep us connected, the way I remember special dates for family and friends with a loving call or text—they're gifts from my mom. When I prepare her stuffing recipe on Thanksgiving morning and craft potato latkes every Hanukkah, I feel my mom in these treasured traditions. Her beautiful light glows within and radiates from me, and for that, I'm richly blessed.

I see her in how I've raised my children, and more importantly, in how I love them, in the echoes of her gentle guidance, her endless support, and the way she made me feel valued and heard, even when she didn't agree with me. I see and hear her in my daughter, in the ways her shiny brown eyes smile and in many of the loving and wise things she says. Sometimes Mia tells me how proud she is of me. Mixed with Mia's loving encouragement, I unmistakably hear and feel my mom, and for a moment I'm once again held by her.

We may have lost the physical presence of Mom and Nana, but we hold on to her everlasting love.

Author of *The Heaven Phone*, Sydnei Kaplan shares inspiration and connects with readers at *Mom in the Moment* and *The Heaven Phone* on social media.

Nobody Loves like a Grandma

CHRISTINE DERENGOWSKI

One of the first times my mom watched my son, her first grandchild, she was so excited to get her hands on that baby, she lit her coat on fire.

She whipped into our driveway on two wheels, a half hour early, and flagrantly parked with one tire on the grass. Bursting through the door like the Kool-Aid man, she stripped off her coat, set it on a lit candle, and marched straight to my sleeping newborn's crib to pick him up.

As I tried to give a few instructions over my now wide-awake baby's coos, I noticed smoke rising from the table.

She laughed it off, but I had second thoughts about leaving as I extinguished her sleeve in the sink.

If new grandmas are guilty of being overly excited, new moms are guilty of being overly worried. About sleep schedules, feeding schedules, and the competence of our caregivers.

Their excitement seems to feed our worries.

When they show up early and wake the baby, throwing off their sleep schedule.

When they stuff our kids with candy, sweets, and pop, ruining their appetite.

When they spoil our kids with toys, giving in to whatever they want.

Add a house fire to my new-mom worries, and I felt I had legitimate cause for concern.

I'd leave page-long instructions for my mom and blow out the candles before she arrived.

Around birthdays and Christmas, I'd warn, "Not too much!" but she was not too much on the listening and always went crazy with gifts.

It drove me nuts that she wouldn't follow my wishes. For years, I bristled when she'd barrel through the door with an armload of clothes, toys, and treats.

But things start to get real for parents when the second baby arrives or the title of "new mom" no longer applies.

That's when we give up on perfection and the illusion of control. And what we desperately need is a break from the chaos and our kids.

Suddenly, Grandma's excitement doesn't seem so threatening, especially when the sound of your kids squealing with delight drowns out the squeal of your mom's tires tearing up the drive.

You realize they are as wild for her as she is for them. And maybe you were a little silly to try to contain it.

I fought the good fight against my mom for years before I realized it wasn't a battle worth winning. It wasn't a battle worth fighting at all.

There were no serious boundaries being crossed. Those held firm.

I had to admit new clothes were always a help, even if there were so many I couldn't shut the kids' drawers.

And having someone I could call when I needed a break, when I wanted to go out with my husband, or when one of my kids got sick was like winning the lottery.

But a grandma isn't just "someone," and she's not meant to be a replacement for you. She brings her own brand of love to the table, and it's as much of a gift for a child as it is for a mom who needs rest or can't be in two places at once.

I remember the first time I called my mom to pick up my son, who had gotten sick at school. I'd barely hung up the phone when she pulled into the parking lot. She could sense the mom guilt twisting my heart, so she sent pictures of him throughout the afternoon convalescing in a nest of her blankets, a Happy Meal at his side and her iPad on his lap. There was a smirk on his face and a twinkle in his glassy eyes.

Kids deserve to be pampered. Kids deserve to be spoiled. Kids deserve to feel loved.

And nobody pampers, spoils, or loves like a grandma.

I want my kids to carry that love with them forever, like I carry my grandparents' love with me.

I never want to take the love they have for each other for granted. And I want to remember it's equally a gift to me.

As my kids grow up, so do I. I no longer bristle at the sight of my mom with an armload of goodies for my kids.

But for as long as she is on this earth to love them, I will prudently blow out the candles when her car zips into our drive.

Christine Derengowski is a freelance writer, wife, and mom. Find her advocating for kids on Facebook and Instagram or wandering Michigan trails with her dog.

There's Beauty in Seeing Your Mom as a Grandma

DANIELLE SHERMAN-LAZAR

My mom walked through the door as I heard the bubbling sounds from my pot of boiling water and started throwing in penne pasta.

"Mimi!" I heard loud echoes in unison.

There's beauty in seeing the girls swarm her, covering her with hugs.

My mom was holding a big shopping bag filled with clothes. She always thinks about the girls when she's out. I used to get annoyed by all the gifts. I'd give her a hard time and say, "You're going to turn them into spoiled brats who won't appreciate anything," but now I don't. I know this is special for her and them.

The girls looked at their new clothes as I finished preparing dinner. I made four separate bowls of penne pasta with tomato sauce.

Everyone was happy until I set a plate in front of Diana, my second born.

Diana looked at it, the corners of her mouth twitching as her gaze dropped to the table. She crossed her hands over her chest and shook her head.

"What's wrong?" I arched my brow.

"I don't like the sauce." Diana's eyes slid away from me, then returned to my face.

"Diana, you should try it. You can be part of the Taster's Club." When I was little, my mom always enticed me to try new foods by including me in a made-up

GRACEFUL

club in our family called the Taster's Club. It worked for me. I'd try all kinds of food and say, "I'm in the Taster's Club!" like I'd just won a gold medal.

Diana thought for a moment. "No, thank you." Clearly, Diana didn't care.

My mom took the bowl away and returned with a fresh one of penne and butter.

"I don't want it," she sulked.

"It doesn't have tomato sauce on it, and you'll really like it," my mom coaxed. Diana and the noodles continued their standoff. Then she fidgeted with her fork as if debating whether she was going to do it or not.

"But it tastes bad," Diana finally said, glancing at me.

"Diana, it does not taste bad. You didn't even try it," I argued.

She shrugged. I heard her stomach make a noise like an injured wolf.

"Fine, what else do you want?" My mom shook her head. "Do you want me to heat up a pizza slice, or can I make you a peanut butter and jelly sandwich?" She didn't even grumble. Her shoulders were relaxed. She was completely calm. Was that a smile on her face?

"Are you the same mom I grew up with?" I let out a laugh. My eyes widened at how my mom was letting her get away with this. She caved before I did, and I always give in.

There's a beauty in seeing her lighter.

My mom was strict with my sister and me when we were growing up. We only got dessert if we ate what was in front of us. My sister wasn't afraid to speak her mind and didn't care about the consequences. She'd take a bite, and if she didn't like it, she'd spit it out. "Ew, this is terrible," she'd say for dramatic effect. I always ate it.

My mom was fair but tough, but here she was, letting Diana get away with not even trying her dinner.

But my mom has transformed from mother to grandma, and it's different when you're the grandma. She's not raising them. That's my job. Now she gets to enjoy her precious girls, and her joy is as radiant as the sun when she's with them.

She puts my kids to bed during sleepovers by letting them snuggle close in her bed until they fall asleep. When I was little, I remember sneaking in on my dad's side in the middle of the night because I knew Mom would send me back to my bed if she caught me tiptoeing in.

She has time to be sillier with them, dancing with the baby in her arms instead of carrying the mental load. She can live more in the moment with them.

She answers yes to "Will you play with me?" every single time. She loves brightening their day, whether it's with a new toy, a much-needed hug, or a book she reads to them.

She lavishes them with unconditional love, because you can never spoil a child with too much of that. She makes my kids feel accepted, wanted, and loved.

As a grandma, she has more time to make endless memories and enjoy the moments together.

And as a daughter, I get to see this beautiful evolution.

Danielle Sherman-Lazar is a mental health advocate and motherhood writer. Find her work on Instagram @livingfullaftered and Facebook at *Living FULL*.

Lessons in Sipping Slowly

EMILY BRISSE

My grandmother and my mother were best friends. I'm not sure either of them would have used that term, but it seemed obvious enough. Despite the hours between their homes, they bridged this distance with regular phone calls, visits, and the kind of shoulder-to-shoulder meal-making, card-playing, gossip-laughing intimacy I knew from my relationship with my down-the-street best friend, whose likes and dislikes were as familiar as my own. I watched the two of them—my mom's dark hair long, my grandma's dark hair short and styled in a salon bouffant—in the unselfconscious way children watch adults, though I wouldn't have been able to say then what I was watching for. I just liked the way they laughed together, the way their confidence in the other's presence seemed to make even the dust motes floating in the air between them shine.

So when Grandma called me in one day from the backyard, where I likely had mud pies baking away in the sun on some stump, knees dirty, dandelion fluff in my hair, to "come join us," I felt the secretive pinpricks of invitation.

Of course, I joined them all the time: at the breakfast table over bowls of Cheerios, on the couch while viewing the televised Thanksgiving Day parade, on lawn chairs at the lake. But I registered a special kind of twinkling in my grandmother's eye, and after rounding the corner into the living room, I saw why: there on the coffee table sat a serving tray, and on the tray, a kettle pungent with sweet tea, plus an array of dainty china teacups.

There were blue cups and purple cups, green cups and yellow cups. I fell to my knees, examining them all. But my favorite one, the one I chose almost each time this tea party was repeated, as it would be time and again in the following years, was snow white with an intricate pattern of brilliant red around the rim. I called it Cherry Lace, a name that delighted both my mother and grandmother, and seemed to confirm, for my grandmother especially, some private success, which she might improve upon by next taking down her fancy hat boxes from her closet, insisting that with these, too, I have first pick. Most days, I would select the hat with the tilted red brim, something—someone?—telling me ladies should match.

We assembled ourselves atop the prim cushions of my grandmother's newly upholstered living room chairs, teacups in hand, and I listened to these two grown women speak about grown-up things. I can't remember anything they said, but I remember the light falling on their hair and the way I sipped slowly, drinking in both the tea and them.

Even as I grew older, my notions of adulthood expanding from fine food served in fancy dishes to driver's licenses and graduations and kegs of beer, I never entered my grandmother's home without peeking inside the hat boxes and handling her fragile china with utmost care. Some kind of truth had been embedded within these items; as I held them in my hands, I could hear women laughing, could believe some things would never change.

My grandmother developed dementia at eighty-five years old. By then, I was in my twenties, but still I watched my grandmother and mother move about a room, awed as my mother did everything possible to help this twenty-five-years-widowed woman maintain her independence, hold on to memory. For a while, the power of their bond stretched what seemed possible.

But even a best friend, even a daughter, cannot stop time.

Two months after my grandmother's funeral—she lived until she was ninety-three—I returned with my mother to her childhood home to begin the necessary process of cleaning, boxing, and storing away. We traveled with a degree of trepidation; it would be difficult work. But I had learned about work and the value of memories from my mother, so once we started, we progressed through the house harmoniously. We were diligent with the shelves and cupboards and closets that held sixty years of bobby pins and ragged playing cards, patient when we came to perfume bottles with their reminiscent scents and a penciled note in my grandmother's flowing hand.

It was late into the night, both of us sticky with sweat, when we arrived at the closet with the hat boxes. I knew this part would hit both of us hard. After all, I had simply been an addition to the tea parties; those afternoons were also how my mom had learned about holding delicate handles, chewing quietly, the love of her mother.

"Let's just leave these here for now," she said wearily. She fingered the worn ribbon on one box.

"No," I said, "let's see."

We stood shoulder to shoulder. She stared at me, her eyes simultaneously grateful and aged. Then we reached up together, brought down the boxes, and opened them, exclaiming at the bursts of color and feathers and lace we found.

"Oh, she wore this one when . . ."

"She'd come home from Minneapolis, so proud . . ."

" . . . walking back from church and an actual bird, a blue jay, I think."

"Do you remember how beautiful . . . ?"

We ended our evening in the living room on the faded sofa cushions, sitting side by side, with fancy hats atop our heads and chipped, delicate teacups warm in our hands. She reached over, took my hand.

"I couldn't have done this without you," she said. "Not like this."

I looked at the teacup I held. It had taken a while, but I'd found it. Cherry Lace. Before we sat down, I'd brought all the fine cups and saucers to the sink and washed them gently, my mother drying. When I was young, these roles had always been reversed.

"How do you think I learned, Mom? By watching both of you."

I was still a few years away from becoming a mother myself. What would my children learn from me? What would they learn from their grandma? I didn't own any teacups, any fancy hats. I didn't know what would become of my grandmother's fine but dated things, if my mother would bring them home or if she'd let them go. *Wasn't it impossible*, I wanted to ask her, *to lose someone so close to you?* Nothing would ever bring her best friend back, and no one would be able to replace her. How could I even begin to inhabit the space she left?

In my hands, Cherry Lace felt so small. But small did not mean insignificant. I brought the teacup to my lips.

I thought of Grandma those years ago, calling me in from the backyard, asking me to join them. The secret in her eyes. How I came in. How I didn't need to do anything else. How sipping slowly was enough.

Emily Brisse's essays have appeared in the *Washington Post*, the *New York Times*, and the *Sun*. She teaches English in Minneapolis and Instagrams @emilybrisse.

Pink Confetti

SARAH LUKE

As pink confetti fills the sky above our heads, they tell us we're having a granddaughter.

This son of ours, beginning his family with the love of his life, looks at me through the pink cloud, and I sense the shifting of our world as we know it. I'm still his mother, his younger brothers are not quite grown, yet my son is this baby's daddy . . . and I am her Nana.

Discovering what it means to be all boy, three times over, defines my motherhood. I had no idea how wild it would be at times, but I absolutely loved it. When our oldest got married, the delight of having a daughter-in-law took me to new places as a mom. He loves her with tenderness and strength, while she loves him with care and respect. Which leads me to today, and this baby girl on the way.

What kind of grandma will I be for her? Immediately I think of silly things, like I don't know how to sew or quilt or anything like that, and I have no desire to learn. I can cook and bake, but I definitely wouldn't call them my hobbies. I don't scrapbook or do crafts, and I have no artistic ability of any kind.

Then I feel a whisper in my spirit saying, *You, as her Nana, are going to love her all your life.*

I waited an entire generation for this little girl. Oh, the times we will spend together and the love we will share! Soon I will look into her newborn eyes and think of all the women who came before her in our family. Will I catch any glimpses of them in her? My grandma loved cactus plants, fishing, and baseball. Will my granddaughter love any of those things? Sometimes my mom and I think the same thing and say it at the same time. Will that happen with my granddaughter and me? I wonder if I'll hear her laugh and think of my niece.

I picture us snuggling up on the couch with books I used to read to her daddy and how the phrases will feel like old friends spending time with us there. Maybe she will like to play with my Cabbage Patch dolls (I knew I saved them for a reason!). Maybe she will want to play with cars, trucks, and LEGOs. We saved those from her daddy and uncles too. Maybe she'll want to play with all of them. I wonder what I will see in her that will remind me of my son. Will she have her mommy's smile? Her daddy's eyes and playful mischief? Getting to know her will be like watching multiple generations come to life in this new little person. She'll carry traits of people I love, but she will be unique, her very own self.

When our granddaughter is born, this Nana will be born too. I hope my love gives her a soft place to land as she grows. When she tells me her thoughts and her dreams, I will hang on every word. Her interests will become my hobbies, and I can't wait to see her grandpa love her. I have a feeling she will put a twinkle in his eye I've never seen before.

Nana's pace of life will be different than it was for her daddy's mom. I imagine there will be lots of opportunities for me to say yes to whatever she wishes for. Maybe she'll wish for ice cream, because I will always say yes to ice cream. I hear people say being a grandparent is the best thing ever. Now that I get to be a grandma to my very first little girl, I can't wait to find out for myself.

I gathered up a small pile of pink confetti from the yard. It sits on my bathroom sink as my glimmer of hope for the future. Our family is growing. Not only in number but also in the span of time. My granddaughter will live and see things beyond what my timeline will allow me to see. I hope as she moves into those unknown territories, she'll carry whispers of her Nana's love with her.

Little granddaughter, I am here, waiting for you. I am ready to be your Nana.

Sarah Luke lives in Nebraska with her husband, three amazing sons, one incredible daughter-in-law, and brand-new granddaughter. She cherishes God, family, and friends!

She Always Brings Me Flowers

LORI E. ANGIEL

"I'll bring you white roses." That's what my grandmother said to her daughters when they asked her, "How will we know you are here after you leave us?"

We weren't ready for her to leave; she was such a central part of all our lives. It was hard to imagine us without her. She lived a full life and, along with my grandfather, raised six children, had eleven grandchildren, in-laws, and all the chaos that comes with a large family.

She never wanted much for herself. She had faith I admired. She had a smile that failed to hide her mischief. She was fiery, wickedly funny, and had little patience, especially for us.

We all adored her.

As I moved from childhood into adulthood, even though I lived far away, I kept her close. I called her often, and she knew the details of my life. She would update me on hers, tell me about who she saw (and didn't see) at church, let me know what the neighbors were up to, and share family gossip. We could talk for hours.

Whenever I came to town, she was always my first visit. On the way, I'd stop at a local farm stand so I could bring her flowers. I didn't recognize it as a habit until I heard her say to my aunt with pride, "When she comes, she always brings me flowers." I knew it meant something to her, so I never came without them after that.

The first time I went back after she passed away, I stopped at the farm stand where I usually stopped. As I got out of my car, I realized definitively she was gone. Still, I bought the flowers, which I brought to my mother. Mom smiled, understanding what they were, and hugged me. This was a habit that would be painful for me to break. We both cried.

After my grandma was gone, white roses started turning up at the most unexpected times.

Once, shortly after she died, I was getting off the train in my morning rush to work, and outside was a street vendor selling flowers. He had two buckets, all of them bundled white roses. I stopped and bought them all.

It was the first time she brought me flowers.

To this day, whenever I come across a bundle of white roses, I buy them.

On my wedding day, I carried a bouquet of white roses in her honor.

The flowers have come to mean a great deal to me. A sign, a signal, a way to connect me to her and her memory.

White roses have even shown up in my dreams. When my husband and I were having a difficult time conceiving, I was discouraged and heavyhearted after a year of trying. One night, I dreamed she was sitting next to me, holding my hand—and next to her were the most beautiful white roses. She told me everything was going to be okay. I cried and told her I was ready to be a mom, that I missed her. I woke up with tears on my face, realizing it was only a dream and she was still gone. A month later, after doctors told us they'd done what they could do to help us, we found out I was pregnant. We had a healthy, beautiful baby boy. I always felt like she was the first one to tell me about him.

There has been no shortage of white roses in my life since. More than twenty years later, I still find myself looking for them, whether I'm at a farmers market or grocery store, and if I come across a bundle, I smile. She always brings me flowers.

My grandmother was my first real loss and one of the people I held closest to my heart. I have never stopped missing her . . . or looking for white roses.

Lori E. Angiel is a devoted wife, emotional mom, and proud *HVFH* **contributor. She lives in Buffalo, New York, gratefully surrounded by family and friends.**

PART 7

SO GOD MADE A GRANDMA

generous

Grandma's house was a gift, but you don't know some things while you're living them.

SHERRY WHITE

The Recipe

LESLIE MEANS

I knew his favorite dessert, but I didn't have the recipe. The Internet wasn't like today—I couldn't hop online and search for something similar.

Which meant I had to call *her*—my boyfriend's mother.

I can't remember if we had met at that point. Did she know we were dating? Did she realize just how much I absolutely adored her son?

Terrified, I dialed her number.

"Hi, Janet? This is Leslie, Kyle's girlfriend. I want to make his favorite vanilla dessert for his birthday. Can I have the recipe?"

I can't believe I did that.

What if it was a family secret? Something passed down from generation to generation—only to be shared with next of kin?

Surprised, she said, "Sure, let me get it for you."

There was no need for small talk, no discussion to fill empty air, just items on a grocery list.

One by one I wrote them down.

Eggs.

Vanilla.

Flour.

I thanked her and hung up.

A few days later, the dessert was presented.

"I called your mom for the recipe," I told him.

We were married that winter.

I don't know what I expected in a mother-in-law. I suppose movies and trends of my time tried to tell me she would be awful.

But I heard how her son talked about her—she was loving, hardworking, and devoted to her boys.

For twenty years, she's been the same to me.

I adore my husband. He's an incredible dad to our three kids and adores me right back. I know I'm blessed to call him mine, and I have his mother to thank.

She raised him to be kind, loving, and loyal. She taught him about Jesus and made sure he knew how to clean toilets and do laundry. We are equals in our marriage; he respects me, and I respect him.

I'm forever grateful for her guiding hand. And now that I'm raising my own children—Janet's grandchildren—I recognize the generosity in her heart. When kids grow up and spread out and make their own way, mothers have to let them go, learn a whole new role. Then grandkids come along, and a grandma has another new role.

And while that looks different in every family, in every relationship, she has so much to give. Maybe she sews the softest baby quilts for each newborn. Maybe she drops off a cheesy casserole on a busy Tuesday night. Maybe she offers up prayers for each person who holds a piece of her heart.

Whatever it looks like, one thing is for sure: Grandmas are givers. You'll see some of the ways they share their love in the next essays.

Stitch by Stitch

KRIS ANN VALDEZ

My foster brother, now in his late twenties, still has the quilt our mother made him when he was a boy. He kept it when he was shuffled to other homes, moved out of state to live with an aunt, and went off to college.

At seven years old, he and his two sisters came to us with nothing, not even a battered suitcase or a change of clothes. My mother immediately pulled out her Viking, a dente sewing machine with graffiti etched into the frame, a remnant from its home-economics-class days, and made three cotton patchwork quilts.

After two years, my foster brother and his sisters moved away; my family welcomed more foster children. Without fail, my mother returned to her Viking to sew a quilt for each new arrival. A cowboy pattern for Raul. Blue surfer fabrics for Juan. Vintage cars for Julian. Seafoam green and soft pinks for Estrella.

Swaddling her babies for quiet, middle-of-the-night feedings, my mother stared into their wide, trusting eyes, clutched their stubby fingers, and fell in love with each of them.

Sometimes, out of an unpredictable, solemn blue, one of her precious babes was reunited with his or her biological family. My mother always suffered heartbreak when they went, unable to eat and crying until her tear ducts dried up. Even after the physical symptoms subsided, her loss was forever pressed into memory. "I could never take in foster kids," people used to tell her. "I'd get too attached."

If I don't let my heart break for these children, she would silently rebut, *who will?*

I was fifteen, standing at the laundry room door, as she pulled all Raul's things from the dryer and packed them in a duffel bag. The brown cowboy quilt lay folded on top so it wouldn't be forgotten. The uncertainty of his future was a hundred-pound weight crushing our hearts. But it was the smallest comfort to know his quilt—which smelled of home and meant security—would go with him to his new crib.

The Viking gave Mom twenty good years, but it's gone now. She has an unreliable replacement, so sometimes she resorts to hand stitching, her readers balanced on her nose. Hours spent with a needle and thread—in and out, in and out, stitch by stitch—tedious and long-suffering work.

While her friends are off exploring the world and settling into empty nests, she still meets the endless needs of four adopted children at home, ages nine to nineteen. In her late fifties, her life continues to be given over to others.

To her eight grandchildren, she is Nana. Each of them is also the recipient of a homemade quilt. Every pregnancy, I helped select the fabrics for the mysterious human growing in my belly. An orange lion pattern for Ezra. Hot pink flowers for Vera. Tan horses and navy dogs for Mateo.

At each baby shower, I remember the *ooh*s and *aah*s as I unwrapped the quilt she'd made for her coming grandchild.

But more importantly, I remember the quiet, middle-of-the-night hours when I wrapped my new baby in it. When their wide, trusting eyes looked up and their fingers clutched mine, the fear of upcoming case hearings and visitations flooded my mind—until I remembered the comfort of a single thought: *This one's mine to keep.*

It was in those moments I better understood the significance of what my mother had done: She loved, without abandon, children who were hers only temporarily. Sewing quilts was her way of creating permanency in situations that never were. With each stitch, she bound fabric to thread, an offering and a promise: *I will wrap you in this blanket and hold you. Here, in my arms, the world is a safe place.*

Kris Ann Valdez is a proud Arizona native, wife, and mother to three spunky children. She's a freelance writer and novelist. Follow her @krisannvaldezwrites.

She Was a Mother First

EMILY SOLBERG

No one understands a mother's dreams better than a grandmother. Because before she was a grandmother, she was a mother.

She was a mother first, so she sees things now from a softer viewpoint, tempered by years and experience. She was a mother first, so she knows all too well the demands of taking care of young children. She was a mother first, so she realizes how little time is left for self-care after days that feel interminable. She was a mother first, so she appreciates how much support is needed to raise a family.

She was a mother first, so she understands the inherent sacrifice and selflessness of putting her dreams on hold. And because she was a mother first, she will do whatever she can to help her children realize their own.

My mother and I shared the same dream of military service. We were both young moms in the Army Reserve, three decades apart. Not much has changed since she was in my boots—one weekend every month, we both got up at the crack of dawn, kissed our babies goodbye, and headed to drill.

But while I stayed in after becoming a mother, pumping bottles in the bathroom, texting my husband for pictures and updates, and striving for the next promotion, my mom left the Army.

Our paths diverged with her dreams deferred, but she always supported mine. When my son was two and my daughter was nine months old, I received orders to a month-long Army leadership course required for promotion to the next rank. I desperately wanted to go, but it was too much time away. It was too much to ask of my husband, who was active duty himself. It was too disruptive for my babies. It was just too much.

But it wasn't too much for my mom. She heard both the question and the longing in my voice, and she didn't hesitate. She insisted I go and assured me she would take care of my family while I was gone. As I waved goodbye while she cuddled my daughter in her lap on the front steps and my son picked dandelions at her feet, I had a peace of mind she never did all those years ago. I knew my children were in the very best of hands, second only to mine.

I worked the hardest I ever had, and at the end of the month, I graduated at the top of my class as the Distinguished Honor Graduate and earned an Army Achievement Medal for my performance. When I got home, I swept my babies into my arms and melted into my family's embrace while my mom stood back and watched, beaming with pride. She packed her things and slipped away the next day, her heart full and content, her mission accomplished. After I watched her drive away, I found a note on a memo pad she left on the counter.

The words blurred together as I read them through tear-filled eyes. She told me how much she had loved this precious time with her grandchildren and how happy she was to have helped me accomplish my goal. She asked only one thing in return: "The most wonderful and meaningful way to repay me is to someday help your children by giving your time. There is nothing else that could replace that gesture in the future," she wrote. "In the meantime, always strive to keep the big picture in mind. Take the long view in life. Love and cherish your family deeply. Thank you for helping me to vicariously achieve my goals through you, thirty years later! Love, Mom."

Someday my daughter may choose to continue the legacy of military service her mother and grandmother began. And someday she may choose to become a mother herself. If and when that time comes, I will do everything in my power to give her the same precious gift her grandmother gave to me: time to chase her dreams.

No one understands a mother's dreams better than a grandmother. Because before she was a grandmother, she was a mother first.

Emily Solberg is a mom of two, a soldier, and a military spouse. You can find more of her writing over at *Shower Arguments*.

All My Love, Grandma

KARA LEONINO

As I step off the elevator, a mix of anticipation and anxiety battles within me. I move down the hallway with walls a neutral color meant to be soothing and comforting. To me, they feel cold and uninviting.

I search for her face in the sea of vacant expressions and muffled groans. When I see her, my breath catches. Her face is bruised and battered, a wash of purple, blue, and yellow, evidence of her recent fall. But I would know her face anywhere.

With cautious steps, I approach, not wanting to disturb her, my heart heavy with expectation. Her head is bent, gaze fixed downward, and I wonder if she is sleeping. I say her name, noting the slight tremble that has crept in. She doesn't move. I say her name again, desperate to see the spark of the woman who has loved me my whole life. On the third try, I bend down and softly touch her knee. She shifts and looks up, a flicker of recognition dancing across her features as her eyes meet mine, and the edges of her lips tilt upward. In that instant, memories flood my mind, a tapestry of moments both cherished and bittersweet, etched deep into the threads of my being.

I'm running through her house, a sanctuary of love and resilience where she raised eight children. Each room holds a piece of her, the woman who shaped my world.

I stand in her kitchen, where she whipped up home-cooked meals, washed dishes, and doled out bowls of M&Ms, each one holding the same amount lest someone argue over who got more.

In the quilting room, I feel the layers of beautiful fabrics waiting to be stitched together for graduations and marriages, the arrival of new babies, or warmth and comfort on days when both are needed. I listen as she teaches me how to sew; I want to learn, so she takes the time to teach me.

In the dining room, I get lost in photographs that have captured moments of joy and sorrow, memorialized behind silver plastic frames she bought at the dollar store, her favorite place to find treasures. Each image is a testament to a life well lived.

On the screened-in porch, I feel the warm air on my cheeks as the swing sways gently back and forth. We sit side by side, sharing secrets, laughter, and quiet moments, her soft hand in mine.

I hear her giggle as she plays Uno with my siblings and me in the living room, her sweet voice mingling with my grandfather's rough timbre as he lets loose one of his many kid-friendly curses that often flew from his lips when he wasn't playing well, which was most of the time.

I taste the butterscotch on my tongue from the many candies in jars stashed around the house, because of course my Irish grandma has butterscotch candies.

I watch as she tends to her hair in the bathroom, a daily ritual of care and exasperation. She uses the front mirror to catch wisps trying to free themselves, the one behind her to make sure the curls are tight and perfectly in place. No empty spots, no big holes.

The memories spill beyond her home.

I see her in the crowd at my graduation. I hear her cheering at one of my many softball games.

I feel her resignation and sadness upon learning she needed shoulder surgery. I help with her physical therapy exercises, knowing this is painful but the only way for her to heal. Despite her venomous words and accusations, I coax her through the discomfort, offering solace even with the tears in my eyes.

I see her pen moving swiftly across the page as she writes in her calendar, something she did for more than sixty years. I'm not surprised I have taken up this same routine, her granddaughter who loves words.

I think of the many tears she shed over the years. First when she said goodbye to my grandfather after a lifetime together, then at the loss of a grandchild, and later, her two sons. The day we said goodbye to her oldest—my dad—her face was again a watercolor painting of sorrow. Hands intertwined, we both struggled to say goodbye, neither knowing she would follow less than a year later.

Emerging from my reverie, I meet her gaze, catching the pale pink blush mark on her forehead that starts blooming, mirroring my own. Gratitude floods my heart for the moments we shared. I reach for her hand, tenderly embracing her fragile form, cherishing the warmth of her touch. I wonder how many more days I have left to hold her.

As she gently brushes my cheek, I turn toward her, longing to hear her familiar refrain shared over the years. Though whispered softly, these words resonate deeply within me, etching themselves into the fabric of my soul.

All my love, Grandma. All my love.

Kara Leonino is an editor by day and sun chaser, adventure seeker, dessert devourer, and glasses wearer the rest of the time. Find her online @karaintheworld.

The Secret Ingredient

LEAH PETERSON

There was a line worn on the floor of the kitchen linoleum where her feet went back and forth between the sunny spot in front of the west window and the farmhouse sink. The Formica countertop was almost worn away as well, right where she rolled out thousands of cinnamon rolls over the years. Flour, sugar, and cinnamon in their giant glass jars, just at the end of her reach, always on standby.

I can't begin to guess how many cinnamon rolls she's baked over the years.

As a child, I remember walking quietly behind her, clinging to my little sister as we walked to the door to leave rolls for the new family. I remember her gentle tone of enthusiastic greeting and soft whispers, always with declarations that made people feel seen and cared for.

She baked every time new people arrived in the community.

I watched her carefully as she rolled out dough in our old farmhouse kitchen, talking to herself and my siblings and me of long to-do lists for celebrations to recognize, community efforts to support, or deep grief to acknowledge.

She did it all through her hands and her heart.

She made sticky buns, some with nuts. Others were frosted with her signature glaze. At Christmas they were shaped into a wreath. We kids got to adorn them with red and green sprinkles. As adults, we still stand at the ready while she works her magic, always in wonder of her talents and full of admiration for the kindness she pours out of her kitchen.

The older I get, the more I see how my mother loves others through her acts of kindness. She was and is the grandma many children and adults never had. I watch how young and old line up for one of her homemade rolls, each recalling when they were first introduced to Shannon's rolls and how no one has made any that could compare.

Sometimes I'm filled with envy at how many people love my mother, as if I'm worried there isn't enough love to go around.

When she first became a grandmother, she baked her rolls and goodies for my sister and brother-in-law. Who knew that bread dough held such majestic power for postpartum recovery and the ability to add an extra dollop of joy to what was already so special?

Now, in my forties, I follow her cinnamon rolls recipe meticulously. I have for years. Even so, my own children say they are wonderful but not quite as good as Grandma's.

She has been baking them for fifty years, holding on to the same tried-and-true recipe gifted to her in secret in the 1960s by the "Yaya" of one of her best friends. It's a recipe so special and so secret I'm not allowed to share that exact recipe with anyone but my own girls.

They are just regular ingredients, nothing exquisitely special or magical about them—so she always says.

But I know the difference, the thing that makes them extra special to everyone who has the opportunity to taste one: It's the love, rolled up inside. The love she has rolled into them for fifty years. The gift she has baked in her own kitchen and in the kitchens of others as she traveled, visited, and cared for loved ones. It's that one thing we all remember from our own childhood and beyond. It's that special thing, known simply as the way Grandma does it.

Indeed, nothing could ever match it as sweetly.

GRANDMA'S SWEET DOUGH

Ingredients
1 ½ cup milk
½ cup sugar
1 teaspoon salt
¼ cup unsalted butter, softened
½ cup warm water
4 ½ teaspoons yeast
2 eggs, beaten
7–7 ½ cups all-purpose flour, divided
Filling, optional

Scald milk.* Add sugar, salt, and butter. Cool to room temp. Dissolve yeast in warm water. Let the mixture bubble and foam. Combine yeast and water with milk mixture. Add beaten eggs and half the flour, and stir until smooth. Add remaining flour and stir again. Knead well. Place in bowl and cover with a damp cloth. Set in a warm place. Let rise until doubled in size, approximately 1 ½ hours. Punch the dough and roll out. Customize with favorite filling. Cut rolls into desired size, and let rise for another hour. Bake at 375 degrees for approximately twenty minutes. Frost or glaze as desired.

*Take the time to scald the milk. Trust me.

Leah Peterson loves Jesus and her family, and is a fifth-generation rancher in Nebraska. She shares all about her life at *Clear Creek Ranch Mom*.

The Rooster and the Chick

MELISSA NEEB

"Rise and shine!"

Every morning when I was a kid, my mom would wake me up with those three words in a singsong voice.

She loved to sing, and she loved mornings.

I hated mornings. It aggravated me how chipper and energized she was. No one should be that happy in the morning.

She was the rooster. I was not a happy chick.

Years later, grown up but not, I sat my conservative, religious parents down to yank the Band-Aid off (more like a full-body pressure dressing) and tell them I was pregnant with their first grandchild.

This was not the Plan. Never in the Plan. I was unmarried—not even in a long-term relationship—not done with college, far from financially stable. The carefully ironed maps of my future were about to be torn into bits and tossed out the window doing eighty miles per hour.

We were young. I was twenty-two; my new boyfriend was twenty-three. We were babies ourselves.

I hated this cliché moment. My parents would be furious. God too.

I braced myself for Titanic-level impact.

The iceberg never appeared.

My mom was not surprised. "I had a dream you were pregnant," she said calmly.

My mouth fell open, dumbfounded at her low-key response.

She looked at me for seconds, or an eternity, and was quiet. Uncharacteristic for her. Once the news had settled over her like fine dust on a bookcase, a smile spread across her face, and she simply said, "We will do whatever we can to help."

I was flabbergasted. I had expected bombs to go off. I had visions of wreckage. None materialized.

Who was this woman? I didn't recognize my mom—or myself, for that matter.

There was a reason, a beautiful reason: This was the moment a grandmother was born.

Then came the tornado of preparations.

The next nine months were a blur of desperately devouring baby books and buying baby gear and floating deliriously high above this very surreal horizon—a hot-air balloon lofting in unpredictable winds. My surroundings were unfamiliar. I was a stranger in my own life.

I was handcuffed to a teeter-totter, flung wildly from pits of despair and uncertainty to dizzying heights of breathless anticipation.

My mother was in full mom mode, and what a relief it was, because I had no idea how to be one. She anchored me to earth.

She was there when my water broke in the middle of her kitchen, in the middle of eating a bologna sandwich. I collapsed on the toilet and sobbed, a tsunami of panic crashing over me.

"You are okay. It's going to be okay. You can do this," she repeated over and over.

She led, she soothed, she held fast. She took me to the hospital to meet my boyfriend. Our perfect cherub of a child was born at 5:35 a.m. after nineteen hours of backbreaking labor. I vowed through hysterics to never do it again.

My mom was one of the first people my baby met.

She held this brand-new, tightly swaddled infant in her brand-new grandma arms. She locked eyes with him, and they both smiled, their mouths wide open in exclamation.

Like old friends meeting after decades apart.

They already knew each other.

A picture frozen in time, etched by love in a deep cavern of my memory.

In those first terrifying months of motherhood, the baby and I would often stay overnight at my parents' house. I was tired of being tired. I felt permanently comatose from nursing all night, every night.

I still hated mornings. That much was the same. I was overwhelmed and exhausted and pretty certain this baby would tell on me if he knew how to talk. His mom had zero idea what she was doing.

He was always up for the day at 4:30 a.m. My singsong mom and enchanted baby would spend the first few hours of the day together. He was her happy little rooster, shrieking and cooing and toothlessly grinning while she did whatever morning people do. I had no idea. What was she even doing that early? Laundry, probably.

My mom was the pressure release valve, easing air out of me so I could breathe easier. I am so thankful for all she did then. I will never forget those early mornings of new motherhood under the safe umbrella of my parents' house. Getting some magical hours of sleep—there could be no better gift.

My sunrise baby and sunshine mom ushered in the day together.

She was always the rooster. He was her delighted chick.

As soft light poured into the room, they sang and squealed and giggled together, giddy to bask in pure love's presence, speaking a language entirely their own.

The sublime dawn became witness to this grand event: the rise and shine of a radiant new Nana and a thoroughly beloved boy.

Melissa Neeb is a wife, a mom, and an author. Find her musings about motherhood on *Never Empty Nest* **and messy faith on** *Faith in the Mess.*

She Always Knew What I Needed

JENNIFER THOMPSON

I looked at the speedometer as my foot pressed down. At some point I had to slow down. Speeding my minivan down the highway any faster was unsafe, but time was my enemy.

I had just left her bedside not twenty-four hours earlier. I knew her time left was limited, but I was needed back at home, where my nursing baby, toddler, preschooler, and husband trying to hold down the fort in my absence were waiting.

Now, as tears streamed down my cheeks and my car raced forward, I wondered why I had left her bedside to begin with. I knew this was inevitable—I just didn't want to believe it would come.

Two hours down the highway. That's all I needed.

Please, Lord, two hours.

Please, let me make it.

She's the one who took me to the ocean for the first time. Grandma, Grandpa, Mom, and I went to the beach, where my bare feet touched the sand and I ran in the ocean waves. We ate oysters on the half shell at a beachside restaurant with checkered tablecloths as people looked on in amazement. How could someone so young let oyster after oyster covered in horseradish slide down her throat? Grandma was so proud of my bravery.

She's the one who cared for me when I was sick and Mom was working. She would pick me up and take me to her house, where there was a bed made with

GENEROUS

sheets and quilts tucked tightly on the couch. She brought me tomato soup with elbow noodles and a sleeve of saltines with a small pat of butter. I never knew saltines and butter were a delicacy, but at Grandma's house, they were. We watched Bob Barker hold his skinny microphone while he talked to contestants on *The Price Is Right* as I gulped down Sprite and listened to my grandpa, wearing his usual white T-shirt and suspenders, snoring loudly on his La-Z-Boy. I loved being sick at Grandma's house.

She's the one who taught me how to be brave when her cancer came and left, then came back again—and again. First, she lost her breast; years later, it took part of her tongue. She faced it all with courage and grace and unwavering faith. She never seemed sick—she only seemed strong. When she learned to eat again and could only manage mashed foods, I started to eat like her. We would go out for breakfast at the local diner, Richards, after Sunday service. She'd order biscuits and gravy with extra gravy and two eggs, sunny-side up. "I'll take the same, please," I'd say. We would mash and mix as the yellow yoke bled over the entire meal. To anyone watching, it might have looked gross; to me it was a symbol of my grandma's resilience. She was my hero.

She always knew what I needed. After my dad moved out and we moved into Grandma and Grandpa's house while our home was being built, I was sadder than I knew a person could be. Grandma sensed it, so one day she told me I was staying home from school. I wasn't sick, but she said every once in a while it's okay to say you are, even if you feel fine. It must have been the heartsickness she was talking about. Grandma picked me up and took me to the store and told me we were going to buy stickers, my current obsession. She told me I could pick any I wanted. As I grabbed sticker pack after sticker pack and looked up at my grandma, something inside registered it was going to be okay. I will never forget that day.

Grandma made the hard parts of life not so hard. She was always there for me, for all of us.

And after the cancer returned again, it was time for us to be there for her.

My mom and I helped her to the bathroom when it was getting harder for her to walk. My sister painted Grandma's toenails while Mom and I rubbed lotion on her hands. I read her a letter about all those times she was there for me—an attempt at a thank-you for the difference she'd made. I needed her to know the impact she had on my life. How she made my world better. All the things she taught me. I read parts of the Bible and prayed with her. We watched *The Sound of Music*, one of her favorites. I brought the kids to see her, and she held their hands and laughed and smiled as she marveled at how much bigger they seemed every time she saw them, even if it had only been a couple of days.

I slept on the floor by her bedside near the end, when she was scared. I wanted to stay close.

I pulled into the driveway. Nobody had called yet. I slammed the car door and ran up the steps to my parents' house, where Grandma had lived the past many years.

Thank you, God, for answering my prayers. I made it.

In her bedroom, shallow breaths filled the air. We held her hands and whispered words of love.

Breathe in. Breathe out.

I made it.

Grandma, I'm here.

In. Out.

Grandma, I love you.

In. Out.

Grandma, thank you.

In. Out.

Grandma, your work here is done.

In. Out.

Out.

Grandma, Jesus is calling you home.

Out . . .

Grandma . . . goodbye.

Jennifer Thompson writes at *Truly Yours, Jen*. Her first book, *Return to Jesus*, was published in 2025.

Grandma Knew

VICKI BAHR

Christmas of 1956 was going just fine—until we went to my grandparents' house and opened the gifts they couldn't wait to give us.

I was six, and my little sister with the blonde curls and deceptively sweet face had turned three a few weeks before. People stopped us everywhere to comment on how beautiful little Gail was; I just wished she would behave like the angel they all said she resembled.

When Gail and I opened the big silver boxes that couldn't even fit beneath my grandparents' little Christmas tree with bubble lights, Gail insisted on dressing up in the adorable cowgirl outfit they'd given her, complete with a black vest with white fringe on it, a cute black cowgirl skirt, matching boots, and a cowgirl hat with a sparkly silver band around the brim and a little drawstring that rested under her chin.

Unfortunately, the cowgirl outfit hadn't been available in my size, so my gift was a black vest and pants, chaps, black boots, and a cowboy hat that was too big. The good news was the hat covered my short, boyish hair that was cut in a "duck's butt" style to keep my wild cowlicks that would never lie flat in line.

There were *ooh*s and *aah*s in the living room as Gail and I paraded in to show everyone how cute we looked after Mom had dressed us in our new cowgirl/cowboy attire. Flashbulbs popped, and the momentary blindness gave me a welcome chance to wipe the tears of disappointment from my eyes.

But Grandma knew.

She mumbled something about taking her grown-up granddaughter into the kitchen for a snack, as if anyone was going to notice I was gone. She poured Squirt soda into my favorite Howdy Doody jelly jar that had been repurposed as a drinking glass, added a bright red maraschino cherry, and sat me in the place of honor—her rocking chair.

I was allowed to sit in the rocking chair the rest of the afternoon while Grandma checked on the turkey baking in the oven and squirted cheese onto the celery sticks for appetizers. When it came time to put four ice cubes from the ice bucket into each fancy glass on the dining room table, she allowed me to help her because I was six and old enough to be very careful with her holiday glassware.

When dinner was over and the grown-up women gathered around the kitchen sink filled with soap suds, dish towels at the ready, there was busyness that wasn't for the children to be part of, so the little ones were all ushered into the living room to watch television with Grandpa and our dads. But I was allowed to sit in the rocking chair that had been my great-grandmother's before anyone in the room had even been born. There I sat, dozing just a little and feeling so very special.

After that, it didn't matter that I often forgot and bit my fingernails or that I didn't always remember my multiplication tables. Grandma knew how hard I was trying. I was the oldest, after all. And that made me so very special.

Grandma knew.

Now I'm the grandma, and the dinged and dented, faithfully polished, upholstered rocking chair that was in my grandmother's kitchen before any of us were born rests between my kitchen and the gathering room where we all sit when our family is together—laughing, playing card games, eating pizza, and coloring inside and outside the lines.

When feelings are hurt or noses are sniffling, or the day just isn't going well, Grandma knows.

And the wonderful chair is here, waiting.

Vicki Bahr is a wife of one, mom of four, and proud grandma of nine. She is a columnist, story imaginer, and lifelong word lover.

Bella

TIA HAWKINS

My given name is Tia, but to her I was Bella, the Italian word for "beautiful." Grandma's thick Italian accent faded as time went on, but it always showed up when she called me her Bella.

She made life look so easy and so effortless. She was always smiling, happy, and kind. She was always loving and near. She was always singing, laughing, and full of joy.

She was cozy just like a favorite blanket. She was dedicated to her church and to her family. She was my protector and my confidant, and she never paid attention to the side-eyes of condemnation or curiosity when I was with her. As a biracial child growing up in the 1980s, I was not always accepted and my family wasn't always welcomed, but somehow none of that mattered when she had my little brown hand in hers.

She was my Naunie (a shortened version of the Italian for "grandmother"), and she loved me. What made her love so special was that I always knew, without a doubt, it existed—and I felt it. Her love never wavered, and she made sure to say it and show it. She didn't just give her love to me, though; she shared it everywhere. Tossed in her perfect al dente Sunday pasta dinners. Sprinkled in her encouraging, faith-filled words. Saturated in her many, many prayers.

She was what some call "an old-school Catholic," and she prayed a lot. When I would spend the weekend with her, she would serve me Neapolitan ice cream, with all three flavors showing equally in my little special bowl, propped up beside her in bed while she pin-rolled all her hair for the next day. We would watch *Mother Angelica* and repeat the Rosary for what seemed like a million times, but I never minded because I was with her.

On Sunday mornings she'd dress me in fancy clothes and take me to the church balcony, where only she and her choir friends were allowed to sit. It made me feel so special. She would scoot me in the middle, right next to her, until her friends adjusted to my presence and doted on me just like she did. She even chanced a sin, one might say, by keeping half of her Holy Communion wafer and sharing it with me every single time once we were out of the congregation's sight.

She loved me hard through her faith, but that same love also taught me many things. How to cook the perfect pasta. How to make pistachio pudding and the best chocolate-banana cream cake. How to garden the crunchiest fresh cucumbers. How to wrap an awkwardly shaped present. How to start lifelong traditions for my own family. How to be a loyal friend. How to be a committed wife. How to give back to others. How to not give up on people. How to love with my whole heart. But by far the best thing she taught me was how to hold on to faith fiercely. She did this by letting hers constantly pour into me, even when I didn't realize it was happening.

Even though I don't follow her rigorous religious regimen, as I've gotten older, experienced life, and gained more wisdom, I understand why she did, why she had to. She had secrets, as many do, that came out in her last moments. Secrets she told us in pieces once the dementia started to kick in. Secrets she only gave to God until just before He brought her home. Secrets I wish I'd known earlier so perhaps I could have loved her here as hard as she loved me. Secrets that gave her strength nobody could understand until they were her spoken truths that explained her life choices, what many may have seen as a boring or unfulfilled life.

She worked in a factory, never drove a car, and rarely vacationed. She didn't have a degree, never owned a piece of property, and left no monetary inheritance when she passed. On her last earthly day, I was five hundred miles away in a hospital, recovering from major surgery. My mom called me so I could hear Naunie's voice. I wasn't sure if she would know who I was or recognize my voice.

"Naunie," I said, "I love you."

"Is that Tia? Where is Tia? Bella, Bella," she said for the last time with high-pitched excitement.

"Yes, Naunie, it's me, and I love you so much."

"Oh, I love you, too, Bella," she said.

In the end, that's all that mattered.

I was her Bella, and she was my Naunie. That was something she made sure was never a secret.

To me, she was and will always be the richest, wisest, and strongest human I have ever known.

What she left me, no money can buy and no human can ever take away. What she left me was all I would ever need to survive this life, because life without her requires all that faith she poured into me.

What she left me was here, her blood running deep in my veins, with the absolute best pieces of her. And that will never be a secret.

Tia Hawkins is a passionate wife, mother, and nurse sharing her voice on mental health, motherhood, and more on her *Tea Talks with Tia* platforms.

Grandma's House

SHERRY WHITE

If I could wrap up a gift to give to the whole world, it would be my grandma's house.

Well, maybe not the house exactly, but what happened in it and around it and what it did to and for us.

My dad was one of six children, and as each embarked into adulthood and parenthood, Grandma's house became the place that tied us all together. We met every weekend, Saturday and Sunday, for family dinners at 5:00 p.m. A house with a tin roof, a gravel driveway, and a large old barn used for milking cows was the backdrop.

Shortly before five, the cars and trucks started rolling in. Family gathered on the front porch and said hello while you walked through the front door, and if you were one of the children, you headed straight for the fridge. I can still see all the different sodas awaiting us—a treat because we didn't have anything but water, tea, and milk at home. But not at Grandma's house. The next stop was the counter for the jar of bubble gum, and then we were off to the rec room while the adults joked and laughed about their week. We were a loud family and a close one, all because of Grandma's house.

Those weeks turned into years, and those children turned into teens, and those young parents turned into mid-lifers, and those moments turned into the best years of our lives.

GENEROUS

All because of Grandma's house.

We all know how Jesus fed the five thousand, but what about the miracle of Grandma feeding her six children and their families every weekend for twenty years? Even as a child, I remember thinking the roast didn't look very big, but somehow it was always enough. We never took more than we needed at Grandma's house. We had to consider the next one in line, so we learned to think of one another. Because Grandma's house wasn't just for you; it was for everyone. All were important, and all were invited. And just like any great long-running series, we had guest visitors. Friends became family, and the family grew.

As children, we would make our way down to the creek on hot summer days and skip rocks. One time we found an abandoned box of cigarettes and dared each other to smoke one. Another time we sat with legs dangling over the side of the barn doors and plotted running away together. We imagined we would use Aunt Judy's pool to take baths and run into each other's homes to gather supplies when needed.

Once all the aunts and uncles came together to turn an old shed into a haunted house for our Halloween party. Then they wired electricity to the old shed so we cousins could play house. Many evenings were spent taking turns riding on the back of four-wheelers with our uncles after dinner was served. New boyfriends and girlfriends were introduced in the rec room, where cousin approval was up for grabs. The rec room was where we held dance competitions and learned to keep a fire going in the open fireplace. It's where a cousin was put into an oversize ceramic trash can that crashed to the floor as it rolled off the table and where an arm was broken from playing cannonball.

Grandma's house set the scene for the moments that got us in trouble and tied us cousins together. The place where memories that would carry us through when life got hard were made. And Grandma was like the silent movie star of the whole thing. She was the one who made it all possible by opening her home and her heart to all of us. Over and over, week after week, year after year. There were ups and downs, but we weathered it all together at Grandma's house because we all just kept showing up.

And perhaps that's the biggest lesson Grandma taught us: to keep showing up for each other the way she did, with a ready smile and a willing heart.

Grandma's house was a gift, but you don't know some things while you're living them. When the color fades to black and white, you see it for what it really was.

And Grandma's house was everything.

Sherry White is a wife, mother, and loud laugher who loves to tell stories and encourage others to fall on Jesus at *The Messy Christian*.

It's Love That Makes a Grandma

CASEY HUFF

I met my grandma when I was eight years old.

We stood in the kitchen of my dad's house, the one he had just bought with my stepmom-to-be and new brother.

"I'll call you step-grandma," I announced matter-of-factly when we were introduced.

Everyone laughed.

"You can just call me grandma—if you want," she said with a warm smile.

Grandma won me over quickly. She was funny, full of life, and always up for an adventure. Our paths into each other's lives were a bit unconventional, but we fit together just the same. From the start, she made me feel like I was her own—not a "step" anything, just a granddaughter who had always belonged.

We didn't see each other often in those early years, but I looked forward to her visits from out of state. Then, when I was in high school, she made the move to be nearer to us. We began to spend more time together around the table at family dinners and laughing over game nights.

Still, our relationship was mostly surface level. I loved her in the way that feels automatic with extended family, but I didn't really know her.

I met a boy, graduated college, and settled into my new job as a middle school teacher thirty minutes away from where my grandma lived.

Life was full, and sometimes we'd go months between visits.

"Come see us," Grandma would comment on my Facebook posts, but I rarely made the time. In hindsight, my "busy" was really just the excuse of a twentysomething who was too immersed in falling in love and exploring life to pay much mind to the grandma who lived in the next town.

Eventually, my boyfriend became my husband. "You know, I have a chest full of baby blankets that need to go to someone," Grandma would not-so-casually mention when we visited her as newlyweds. She'd wink; we'd smile. The month after our first wedding anniversary, we gave her a special someone to wrap in those blankets. Our son, her first great-grandbaby, was born.

I don't remember who approached who—if she offered out of want or if we asked out of necessity, maybe it was a little bit of both—but when I returned to work after maternity leave, we began dropping our son off at "GG's house" a couple of days a week.

I'd count down the minutes until my students went to lunch so I could check my phone for updates from Grandma. Over time, the photos she sent went from naptime snuggles and sweet potato–covered cheeks to puzzles on the living room floor, swinging on the front porch, and blowing bubbles together in the yard. I longed to be the one with my little boy instead of missing out on such precious moments, but knowing just how loved and cared for he was at GG's was the next best thing.

She patiently respected my new-mom wishes, even though she had decades of experience on me, and if my son actually took his first step or said his first word at her house while I was at work, she was wise enough to never tell me.

The two of them shared a truly special bond, and that joy only multiplied when our second son and daughter came along.

As our babies grew, the relationship between my grandma and me flourished. She went from an occasional check-in to one of the first people I called with exciting news or when I needed someone to lean on.

When I was worn down from the demands of motherhood, she came over to watch the kids and do the dishes while I napped. She never judged, only showed up in the tangible way I so desperately needed to keep me from drowning in the trenches.

When we dreamed up DIY Halloween costumes we couldn't quite pull off ourselves, we called Grandma to help us make them. She was creative in a way I wasn't, and everything she touched was laced with a little bit of extra love.

When we were evacuated from our home because of a nearby wildfire, my grandparents graciously welcomed us into their home, despite the chaos a family of five inevitably brought. I know it must have been a lot, but Grandma never treated us like a burden.

We did life together in those days—backyard barbecues, Christmas cookie decorating, and rainy afternoons playing cards and talking about life. Grandma was on the sidelines for countless milestones. She was there for birthdays, kindergarten graduations, and first T-ball games.

I came to recognize the twinkle in Grandma's eyes reserved only for her great-grandbabies and the laughter in their voices meant just for her.

She was a constant in our lives—an irreplaceable part of our village I couldn't imagine raising our kids without.

Then, a few years ago, the cough began.

It was subtle at first, but it soon became too nagging to brush off. "A paralyzed diaphragm," the doctor finally concluded—likely an aftereffect of anesthesia from the knee surgery she'd had earlier in the fall.

I watched my spunky, always-working-on-a-project grandma start to drastically decline. We worried. She was too young and healthy to be tied to an oxygen cord around the clock.

One Saturday morning, from the bleachers of our kids' basketball game, Grandma delivered the news I had known was coming but dreaded hearing. They were looking at real estate 1,600 miles away in Florida, where the lower elevation would give her a better chance at normalcy. A chance to be her again.

A gaping hole was left in our lives the day we said our last *See you later*s and my grandma made the trek across the country to her new home. Our person was gone, and things would never quite be the same.

In some ways, our story has come full circle. We're once again separated by miles and only see each other a few times a year. We can't do everyday life together anymore, but in all the ways that matter, our lives are inexplicably intertwined.

Although I'd give anything to plop down on her couch on a random Thursday afternoon, I'm grateful for FaceTime, text messages, and old-fashioned snail mail. Memories sometimes pop up on Facebook from years past when our babies spent so many days at Grandma's house, and the tug at my heart is undeniable.

I miss her so.

This woman—my grandma—has come to mean so much to me. She's my kids' beloved GG, and she's one of my favorite friends.

She hasn't known me since birth, and she never held me in her arms when I was little, but in the years since I've had babies of my own, she's held me in more ways than I can count. In more ways than she probably even realizes.

I'm forever grateful for the time we spent just down the road from one another. Our relationship has deepened so much over the past decade, and I'm hopeful it will continue to do so for the next one despite the miles now between us.

The bond we share is all the proof I'll ever need that it's not blood that makes a grandma—it's love.

Casey Huff is mom to three amazing kids and wife to a great guy. She writes to help women find community in motherhood @caseyhuffwriter.

PART 8

SO GOD MADE A GRANDMA
resilient

God hears the devoted **PRAYERS** of a grandma's **faithful** heart.

LIZ SPENNER

The Necessity

LESLIE MEANS

My grandmother never knew her father. There's a story there, one our family keeps private. I only know a few details (thanks to my sister for asking those hard questions), but most of the secrets are just that—secrets of a time long gone, never to be unearthed.

I suppose some things are too hard to discuss—especially in 1917.

When my great-grandma died, I was young. We called her Gigi. I remember very little about her, but I'm told she was a kind, hardworking woman who had no problem plucking chickens and gardening in the hot Nebraska weather.

"She did what she had to do to make it," Mom told me.

She lived with her brother, never married, and raised my grandmother not far from where I grew up.

"Gigi would put rags in the windows to keep the dirt from flying," Dad told me.

The Dust Bowl showed no mercy.

Now, as a middle-aged mother who knows just how hard it is to raise kids (even with support and a little money in the bank), I can't help but feel empathy for her. What must it have been like to bear a child in 1917 without money or support?

I can't fathom it. It makes me upset just thinking about what she endured and the secrets she had to keep.

And yet I'm inspired by her tenacity and grit, her determination and hard work.

Another one of my great-grandmas lived to be 106—most likely through sheer grit and determination. "She was most certainly a strong female in the male-dominated world of the early 1900s," Mom told me. "Perhaps she was a closet women's-lib advocate . . . She might even have burned her bra if that was a thing back then."

The women in my family tree are made of tough stuff—and learning how they overcame obstacles and loved their families fiercely inspires me to do the same.

You probably have a few of these women in your lineage too. And I like to think when we share their stories and think about how they inspire our own, a little bit of their courage and resilience rubs off on us.

It's how I felt reading the stories in this next section, and I hope you feel it as you read them too.

The Bull

VICTORIA DERKSEN

"The bull is out again."

Nana stood at the front window of her farmhouse, staring past the drive to where the large black-and-white animal was wandering across the lawn.

My seven-year-old self barely registered her words as I glanced up from the television. While summers on the farm usually meant endless adventures and exploring, that afternoon was hot, despite being overcast, and I was happy to be indoors. My two younger sisters were spellbound by the cartoons on the screen and didn't even look up.

Nana sighed as she slipped on her shoes.

"I'll be back in a few minutes."

At seventy-four years old, my grandmother was a force to be reckoned with. Born in 1919, she lived through the Great Depression, was witness to the Second World War, and saw women officially become "persons" under the law. She was resilient and stubborn in the best of ways, and though her life wasn't always easy, she always considered it blessed.

As a child, she suffered from polio, a disease that left her right leg weak and her foot malformed. The braces meant to help were insufferable, and she was embarrassed by the deformity that was painful and made walking difficult, especially in later years. The affliction didn't slow her down though. She rarely complained and never failed to conduct herself with poise and dignity. She believed in the power of prayer and consistently put her trust in God.

By the age of twelve, she had lost her older sister to rheumatic fever and her mother—on Christmas Day—to a ruptured thyroid gland. Just like that, all the women of significance in her life were gone.

Her teenage years were spent living with her father and two brothers, but through her own hard work and dedication, the early forties brought independence. Nana took a job at the Spirella Corset Factory in Niagara Falls, Canada, and as a working woman, moved into a boarding house in the city. It was there she met her husband, a handsome man ten years her senior who already had two young daughters. When she married him in 1945, she became an instant mother. Not a stepmother—she never considered herself as such, just a mother intent on learning and loving in equal measure.

Their family continued to grow, and in the 1950s, they left the city to buy a nearby dairy farm. It was a labor of love, necessitating late nights and early mornings, years of sacrifice, and more hard work. The farm evolved through financial hardship and moments of plenty. Children were born and grew up. Workers came and went. Time marched on.

Then, in October 1990, the worst happened. After years of battling cancer, her husband—my Papa—suffered a heart attack that claimed his life. Though I was four, I remember that day vividly: waiting with my mother and grandmother for help to come, though it was already too late. I remember the tears, the hurt, the confusion—raw, painful emotions that ran impossibly deep. Even still, my nana persevered. With the support of her family, she continued to live independently on the farm for years to come.

With all her experience, it should have been an easy thing, turning a cow back to its pasture. After all, escapes were not all that unusual. My mother could tell you plenty of stories about the family having to corral animals over the years. But for whatever reason, this time was different. This wasn't a cow; it was a young bull, and it had no intention of going quietly.

So engrossed were my sisters and I in our lazy afternoon, it wasn't until an ambulance came flying down the driveway in a blaze of lights and sirens that we even realized something was wrong. Nana had been gone for far too long.

Her attempt to lead the bull back to its pen had gone awry. Instead of complying, the thing had pinned her to a wooden fence pole and rammed her body relentlessly with its head. By the grace of God, a neighbor happened to be driving by and took notice of the situation. She immediately pulled in the driveway and called 9-1-1. The sound of her vehicle scared the bull off, and she was able to stay with Nana until help arrived.

My mother and uncle were hot on the heels of the ambulance, having come straight from work in a panic. My uncle was able to put the unruly animal back in its pen while my mother, still in shock, whisked us home to await the dreaded news.

For three weeks, my nana lay in a hospital bed. She had several broken ribs, a punctured lung, and too many bruises to count, but she was alive. Thank goodness, she was alive. Recovery was difficult, but as always, she was determined. As a favorite among the hospital staff, she was lovingly teased by the nurses. One even went so far as to wave a red blanket at the end of her bed, calling, "Toro! Toro!" Nana begged her to stop because laughing was still too painful. Her body may have been broken, but her spirit endured. Even having faced death, she maintained a sense of humor and grace.

When she was finally released from the hospital, Nana returned to the farm, where she remained until the ripe old age of ninety-nine. A sudden illness finally called her home to heaven, but at the end of it all, she wasn't afraid; she was full of hope.

My nana was stubborn and proud and fierce. She had no problem speaking her mind, whether for good or ill. She was also strong, patient, kind, and generous. I see her in my mother. It's what I hope for my own daughters and what I strive for in myself. When such sentiments seem trite, I remember the bull. I remember her.

Victoria Derksen, currently a stay-at-home mom to four little mischief-makers, has a love for history, writing, and a good cup of tea.

Straightening His Shirt One Last Time

BRIGITTE SHULAR

As I gently swayed my youngest baby, my grandmother leaned over the casket and sobbed.

"My baby, my baby." The cries were hushed but guttural. The pain was so tangible I was certain I could grasp it.

As I rocked my baby, she was saying goodbye to hers. The juxtaposition was cruel and stark.

I looked down at my sweet boy and imagined a younger, equally beautiful version of my grandmother rocking her youngest boy. I'm sure she sang as she swayed back and forth. I imagined her tending to every cry and praying big prayers over him. And of all the dreams she dreamed and prayers she prayed, I am certain she never imagined laying him to rest.

For just a second, I looked at my baby and allowed myself to envision what that pain must feel like.

I watched her straighten his shirt one last time and wondered how many times she'd done a similar motion. Straightening his shirt before church. Straightening his shirt before graduation. Straightening his shirt before his wedding. It was tender and intuitive. Suddenly, the generational gap closed as my grandmother was stripped down to a mama who just wanted her baby. I let myself see her just as a mother—a mother like me. A mother whose body stretched with new life. A mother who kissed boo-boos and prayed nighttime prayers. A mother wrecked with worry over teenage impulsivity. A mother whose pride swelled with each accomplishment. A mother whose love had been intensified by decades of memories.

Now she sneaks to the front porch and rocks in silence, an unfamiliar pain etched on her face. She seems to be calculating what days without him will look like. She appears to be lost replaying a reel of days long gone. Her jaw is clenched to hold back tears.

In the quiet moments, she weeps. She rocks back and forth in the recliner, the familiar rhythm soothing to her shaky soul. I wonder if she feels connected to him as she rocks. I wonder if the gentle sways transport her back to a time when he was here and he was hers, when her days were dictated by beckoning little boys. I wonder how many moments she spends reminding herself that he's gone, or if it's a constant ache that never seems to fade. I wonder if anything can truly soothe a mother's broken heart.

I think of her often when I rock my youngest son. As his little eyes stare at me, I sing about Jesus. If I've ever wondered if it amounts to much, I think of my grandmother bent over that casket. When they lowered her son's body in the ground, I was certain a part of her would be buried too. It's easy to assume the hardest steps she ever took were the ones away from the cemetery.

But my grandmother loves Jesus more than life itself. She didn't just walk away from the cemetery—she walked toward heaven. With a broken heart but a renewed purpose, she continues to pursue the heart of Jesus. She knows the grave is temporary because death has been defeated. Her eyes are fixed on heaven, where her son waits. She fills her time showing others the love of Jesus. She tends to widows and visits her sisters. She attends prayer meetings and loves her family fiercely. She never misses a church service or an opportunity to serve. She video-calls her great-grandbabies and gives virtual kisses. She ends every phone call with "I love you."

And she prays. She prays with passion and fervor. She prays for the people she loves. She brings heaven to earth on behalf of her family. She tells about Jesus, who rocks her in the night.

Perhaps more than anyone, my grandmother understands 1 Corinthians 15:55: "O death, where is your victory? O death, where is your sting?" (NLT). The passage continues: "But thank God! He gives us victory over sin and death through our Lord Jesus Christ" (verse 57, NLT).

My grandmother has endured the greatest heartache, but she displays the greatest hope. She's walking toward heaven because she knows death is simply temporary.

Brigitte Shular is a wife and mama to three kiddos. She writes what she's learning about motherhood at *Mama Unscathed*.

Strong like Me

ALIETTE SILVA

My grandmother, Hortensia De Castroverde, put her only child—my mother—on a plane to the United States, unsure if she would ever see her again. My mom was seventeen, and my grandmother knew it was the only way to give her daughter a chance at a better life.

It was 1961, and the drums of revolution were forever changing my grandmother's beloved Havana. She worked hard to make it in the music business, known as "La Alondra Tropical" and had achieved success as a Cuban singer that most could only dream of.

But all she had achieved was in jeopardy. Cuba was under the rule of Fidel Castro, a dictator with little regard for human life. My grandparents were members of Cuba's high society, and my grandmother was one of the famous people the regime hoped would give a face of support to the revolution. She refused. Their assets were seized, and everything they owned became the property of the Cuban government. All my grandmother had worked for was stripped away, and she was left a prisoner in her own home.

Soldiers ran inventory checks inside her home. Every fork, painting, and dress had to be accounted for. If anything was found to be missing, my grandparents would go to jail. It was a tumultuous and frightening time, and my grandmother knew she had to get her daughter out of the country.

Many children in Cuba were sent to "reeducation" camps. Castro believed he would gain loyal subjects for his revolution if he could indoctrinate children from an early age. It was their parents who were the problem. This is why many mothers, including my grandmother, sent their children away.

Operation Pedro Pan was a collaborative program between the US State Department and Catholic charities to help Cuban children escape the country. From December 1960 through the end of 1962, more than 14,000 unaccompanied Cuban children were sent by their parents from Cuba to the United States.

My mother was one of these children.

All my grandmother knew was my mom was going to New York to be with a host family who would, hopefully, help her. She did not know this family or their history, or if they were even real. She had no idea if they would be kind or cruel to my mother. As my grandmother told me, "There are no guarantees in life, and this was the best choice we had to get your mother out. But I had no idea if I would ever see her again."

I try to imagine myself in her position, but it is unfathomable. Deciding between my child going to a "reeducation camp" under a brutal regime or sending my child to a foreign country with no way of knowing if my child would be okay or if I would ever see them again—my heart shudders at the thought.

"*Tienes que ser una muchacha hecha y derecha!* You have to be a grown-up girl!" She would say this to me often. You must be a woman who has her life together, because you never know what life will throw at you. Life had taught her this lesson painfully, and she wanted me to be prepared for anything.

When my abuela finally arrived in the United States years later, my mother was already in her mid-twenties. Having lost everything, she came to the United States with nothing. Before Castro, my grandmother had a personal chef and lived inside a penthouse in Havana. Now she lived in a tiny apartment with mice in New York. It was a far cry from the life she once had.

She found work at the Bergdorf Goodman luxury department store, wrapping presents for the high-society clientele she used to belong to. She went from being La Alondra Tropical to having no one know her name, much less her beautiful singing voice.

But she never stopped singing. My grandmother held her head high and pushed forward. She knew who she was and never allowed circumstances to dictate her story or her future.

Eventually, she made a life for herself in the United States. It was a completely different life from what she'd pictured, but she was grateful. "I got out, and many did not," she would say when thinking of her beloved Cuba.

My grandmother told us people can take everything from you, but they can never take your spirit. "Castro took my world, so I left and made a new one," she said. Until her last breath, she had the soul of an artist, and she stayed true to who she was.

A diva in every sense of the word, she wore high heels well into her eighties, and even if her clothes no longer carried a designer label, she dressed to impress. "It's all in how you carry yourself," she would say, and, "You need to carry yourself with purpose, because if you don't value yourself, who will?"

They tried to silence her, but they failed. Her voice echoes in my mind when I'm faced with my most difficult moments. The "Ave Maria" she sang brings me to tears when I hear it. She taught me resiliency like no one else could.

At her lowest moment, the world told her, "You've got nothing now. No singing career, no beautiful penthouse, no famous friends—you don't even have your daughter! What do you have left?" But they didn't know my abuela. No one could take the song out of her heart. And with resounding strength, she replied, "I've got me."

Aliette Silva is a bilingual freelance writer. When she's not writing, you can find her chasing sleep, her children, or a good Cuban sandwich.

The Messy Makings of a Matriarch

KAITLIN CHAPPELL ROGERS

The hand she was dealt isn't one most would choose.

Poverty, abuse, teen pregnancy, her mother's drug addiction, abandonment, ridicule, and loss. Those are a few of the struggles my mother endured from a young age and continues to battle today.

It wasn't until I had kids of my own that I understood the pain my mom felt and the tenacity she has because of it.

When she found out she was pregnant with me at seventeen, one of her school administrators sat her down to tell her what a disgrace and disappointment she was, that she'd never amount to anything. Only God could rewrite that narrative and have her working as a secretary at the same school, serving more as a counselor to the underprivileged kids struggling to show up each day because of battles at home.

She was on track to cheer in college, but those dreams disappeared as quickly as the two pink lines appeared. Her dreams shifted, and motherhood became her priority. She and my dad, who was only twenty at the time, were married in February 1992, and I made them parents that August. She never considered any path other than growing up with me.

She and my dad found a trailer they could afford, and we lived in north Alabama for several years until we moved to a "nicer" trailer when my first brother

RESILIENT

came along. I was so oblivious to our lack of money as a child that I thought we lived in a large "wooden cabin" instead of the old wood-paneled trailer. From birthday parties to magical Christmas mornings, my parents somehow made our dreams come true by sacrificing theirs.

My mom's mother, "Maw Maw," struggled with prescription drug abuse most of her life, and the addiction was amplified after she suffered a debilitating stroke. My mom begged Maw Maw to quit, voicing her fear of being the one to find her dead. Unfortunately, that fear became a reality one cold December morning when we were supposed to bake Christmas cookies.

I watched my mom bury her mom on Christmas Eve that year, and we woke up to another magical Christmas morning the very next day. I'll never forget peeking through her bedroom door to see her raw eyes closed as tears streamed, her head resting on her best friend's shoulder. She never knew I saw her. I wish she would have known I could handle holding her grief, but her next greatest fear was ruining the holidays for her family—and that's the one thing she could control in a moment when life felt out of control.

In her forties, she connected with a brother she'd never met. They instantly clicked and became best friends. We had six years with my uncle before COVID-19 took him from us. I was devastated to lose him, but I was more devastated to watch my mom suffer yet another blow. I was angry at how unfair it all was, even as I was encouraged by the way she kept going and leaned into the gratitude of getting to know him at all.

The resilience and tenacity forged in the fires of her life are what have made her such a strong matriarch for our family. Married for thirty-two years to my father after everyone said they wouldn't make it, giving back to students after an educator tore her down, raising three children who love God and people, showing up for her three grandchildren in the most beautiful ways.

So much of the way I mother my boys is because of how she mothered me and my brothers. So much of the way she celebrated the big things and small things even when we had no money is what keeps my drawers stocked full of balloons and confetti for the days my boys bring home artwork they're proud of or help a friend at school.

Seeing my mom interact with my children shows me how being a mom was her redemption story, but being a grandma is her resurrection story. What was dead in her came back to life the second she started seeing the world through their little eyes.

This grandma, our CiCi, shows us what it means for God to be strong when we are weak and reminds us to keep going when the days are dark—because joy will always come in the morning.

Kaitlin Chappell Rogers is a writer, speaker, and host of *The Comeback Couch* **podcast. She lives in Huntsville, Alabama, with her husband and two boys.**

A Faithful Heart

LIZ SPENNER

She always passed on holding the babies.

Younger me understood why in part, but never fully, until I became a mother myself.

At thirty-eight years old, my mom gave birth to her fourth baby and first son. He was born with a genetic condition and birth defects undetected before his delivery that contributed to him making his way to heaven just before turning one.

My parents were completely heartbroken, especially my mom, who had spent all day, every day caring for him, leaving her job as a cardiovascular nurse to be a stay-at-home mom and caregiver. They would have loved to have more children, but the risk of experiencing another complicated pregnancy with a similar outcome was high. So, with shattered hearts, my parents decided after my brother's diagnosis and subsequent passing that their family was complete. Three daughters and a son in heaven.

Just four years later, at age forty-two, my mom spent over a year battling three different types of breast cancer—undergoing a double mastectomy and further treatment. She lost weight, she lost confidence, and she lost all her hair, but she never lost her faith. Her trust in God became stronger than ever. As she fell to her knees in prayer, her greatest wish was to simply live long enough to see my two sisters and me graduate from high school.

But our heavenly Father had other plans in mind.

Over the years of growing up and visiting with extended family and friends, my beautiful, kindhearted mom always remained quietly on the sidelines when babies were being passed around. I remember watching her gently interact with—but never actually hold—babies. She had a void in her heart that only grew larger at the thought of missing her son and holding another new life in his place.

My sisters and I each met loving husbands, and shortly after getting married, the question came: "When are you going to start a family of your own?" While my husband and I wanted to wait a few years to grow our relationship, we couldn't have prepared for the lengthy wait God had in store for us. He had big plans to mend a mourning mother's broken heart and empty arms. He just needed us to be patient. And we never would have understood until His love came full circle.

On Christmas Eve, fourteen months after wishing and hoping to begin a family of our own, God finally blessed us with a positive pregnancy test, along with a huge flood of emotions. But our favorite part? Telling our parents they were going to become grandparents.

Only God can stitch together a story of a mother's heartbreak into one of a brand-new grandma's heart bursting.

Only God can take a mother's faithful heart and fill her once-empty arms with fresh, newfound love as a grandma.

And only God can orchestrate it all in such a way that my mother's first grandchild—a new life abundantly hoped and prayed for, the first baby she'd held in twenty-five years—would be placed into her arms the very day before her son's birthday.

Our oldest daughter was born on August 15, 2009.

My brother's birthday? August 16, 1984.

Twenty-five years of sorrow, emptiness, and prayers for healing.

One of my last memories of my little brother was going with my mom to our local children's hospital on my fourth birthday, just three weeks before he passed away, so we could visit him and give him a bath together. I felt so unbelievably special to have that day with her and my little brother.

Nothing ever quite compared to that memory until my mom, a new grandma, showed up at our home to give her first grandchild her very first bath in our kitchen sink.

The way she looked at her granddaughter. The gentle way she sang to her and cleaned her up so delicately. The way she so carefully wrapped her in a warm towel and carried her to the couch, with arms overflowing. Only God can orchestrate such a full-circle moment of love.

As my mother, faithful in prayer and filled with fear, hit her knees to beg God simply to allow her to see her own daughters graduate high school, never would she have imagined thirty-five years later she would be flooded with the overwhelming joy of holding eleven of her own grandbabies.

When God heard the devoted prayers of my mom's faithful heart, He wasn't finished with her story—He was simply preparing to unfold even greater plans for her as a grandma with full arms, a mended heart, and a sacred kind of love.

Liz Spenner is a Christian motherhood writer and blogger who lives in the Midwest with her wonderful husband, seven beautiful children, and energetic boxer dog.

Theresa's Teacup

MANDE SAITTA

I don't dust my home as often as I should. I suffer from dust blindness, perpetually unable to see the particles scattered on surfaces until they're suddenly all I can see. Then frantic dusting ensues. I make my way from top to bottom, room to room, item to item, sweeping the gray fallout away to reveal the shiny veneers beneath. The result is a peaceful satisfaction.

I am extra careful with some of the objects perched on shelves and ledges. Knickknacks that guard memories of times and places I hold dear.

One of them is a singular teacup. Delicate and vintage, the white background is adorned with royal blue toile scenes. It boasts a country portrait with willowy trees, picket fences, and rolling hillsides. Fluffy clouds are scattered near the cup's rim, lazily looking down on cozy homes with thatched roofs. From afar, a church with a towering steeple looks broadly over the idyllic little town.

The teacup is pristine; I've coddled it for years, using only the gentlest of touches to handle it. It calls a dining room bookcase home and sits near a wide window, enjoying ample sunlight throughout the day. Sometimes when I pass by, the pretty china basking in the golden beams catches my eye, invoking a soft smile.

The teacup belonged to Theresa, my paternal grandmother. It was gifted to me upon her death, about twenty years ago. It was given to her by my father when he was twelve years old. He picked it out from Baum's 5 & 10 department store, a treasure to present to her when money was scarce and times were tough. My father is a thoughtful gift giver, and my mind's eye can picture him making the purchase, propelled by kindness and pride.

Grandma Theresa was born in 1914, a year marked by world war. Tell City, Indiana, was a small and simple town, churning out few notable figures—and not much has changed. She called it home for nearly half of her years, meeting her husband there and welcoming several sons before heading west to Evansville.

A striking beauty with silken hair and fair skin, Theresa reminds me of Snow White in her wedding photo. She was blessed with the same facial structure the sirens of the silver screen possessed, her cheekbones oozing a chic elegance. Her eyes were rich and gleaming, but they also seemed sad, awash in a shadow of melancholy. My father sports the same eyes, and so do I. Those eyes have traveled downstream through the generations, evidence of brawling with the blows of everyday living.

By the time I came on the scene, adversity and age had set in, etching lines through her skin and graying her hair. Things didn't get easier for her either. Her nine decades were congested with struggle, rolling through one world war, then the Great Depression, then another world war, all while navigating the heavy burden of a spouse bound by alcoholism. She never escaped poverty or found herself in a position of ease.

And she waded in the dark waters of grief many times, burying a husband, a grown son, and two little daughters before passing away in 2005. An existence of living hand to mouth, soaked in devastation, until relief came by way of heaven.

I had limited visits with her, but my memories of my grandmother are situated high and bright in my memory bank. Playtime together was imaginative and carefree. I dust off the album of moments and see us lining up kitchen chairs to mimic a train, pulling board games out of her bedroom closet, standing next to her on a stepladder to help wash dishes, or brushing my hair at her vanity mirror, a little girl pretending to be grown. Theresa's garden grew the sweetest of tomatoes, a tasty treat that relieved her strained grocery budget. Her home was sparse and rundown, but I always felt drawn in and safe in her company. Her gentle tending to me belied the currents of suffering just below the layers of her skin.

She floats into my mind from time to time, when my back is against a wall and I am dog-paddling through my days. I think of her tenacity and her drive to simply survive. Theresa put one foot in front of the other for all the hours of her lifetime, even when the hours felt arduous.

The teacup bears none of the marks of her hard-knock life. The pretty vessel paints pictures of a life she never experienced. It sits spotless and whole in my home, reminding me of the unexpected gifts birthed from the hardest of labors. A standard-bearer to grit and resilience, her steely spirit is present in my bones, and I can sense her tearstained sparkle in my eyes.

She is gone. But not far.

I am Theresa's granddaughter, and I am the keeper of her hope-holding, legacy-fashioning teacup.

Mande Saitta works in vocational ministry in Nebraska. Married to a good man and mother to two beautiful daughters, she blogs at *Handiwork of Grace.*

I'll Remember for Her

KELSEY SCISM

I stood in my kitchen rolling the soft, sticky dough in my hands. Reaching for more flour, I pulled a piece of dough to the center, pinched it with my thumb, rotated, and pulled another piece. Satisfied, I set the round ball onto the cookie sheet and tugged at the next clump of dough.

With the hamburger buns baking and the timer set, I picked up my phone and dialed the number from memory—the same number I'd called countless times throughout my childhood to let Grandma know we were on our way, to ask for a ride, to see if I could stop by after school to change before work, or to ask how much of this or that I needed for a recipe.

"Yello," Grandma answered.

"Hey, Grandma, it's Kelsey," I said, remembering to identify myself in case she didn't recognize my voice. "I was just making some homemade hamburger buns for supper tonight, and it made me think of you. Thanks for teaching me how to make them."

"Oh, you don't have to thank me," she replied. How many times had I heard her say that? Some grandmas nag about manners or get offended when a thank-you is forgotten. Not Grandma Ileta. She never needed a thanks.

Our conversation continued but didn't last long. Grandma repeated many of the same phrases she'd become known for. She told a story (or two) I had already heard (probably at least twice). Love and sorrow danced a strange, complicated waltz in my heart as I hung up the phone and pulled the golden buns from the oven.

I remember the first time Grandma called me for a recipe for "my" cheese dip. I told her how to cube the Velveeta, pour in the diced tomatoes and chiles, add in some browned sausage or hamburger, then heat it in a microwave-safe bowl.

She was likely sitting at her brown oval kitchen table with flour in the cracks, pen in hand, maybe writing on a green ticket pad, the one she kept in the pocket of her black apron she wore as a waitress. She wrote down each step in her distinct but sometimes hard to read cursive, the long cord of her rotary phone trailing from the wall to the phone wedged between her ear and shoulder.

My grandma taught me to bake—kolaches, cinnamon rolls, kiffles, hamburger buns. Yet when I was a young wife and mom, she called me for a recipe.

Dementia is a thief. It slowly stole my grandma's memory. And if I allow it to, it reshapes the woman I remember into someone almost unrecognizable. But I refuse to let it. Dementia will not take my grandma's legacy.

Her legacy is in the memories I have working beside her as a waitress at our small-town café, sitting across from her at the end of our shift tasting the newest dessert she tried out, a recipe torn from a magazine. She left a legacy of warmth, comfort, and kindness that often began in her kitchen.

It's in my memories of walking through the woods with her, decked out in orange vests. It's in the way she didn't hesitate, not even a little, to help field dress the deer. It's in the memories of her teaching us how to pull back the skin of a chicken gizzard to clean out the grainy insides. My grandma left a legacy of independence, tenacity, and a can-do attitude.

I remember sitting at the card table in her living room, waiting my turn in a game of Kings in the Corner. Grandma always made time to play cards with her grandkids. Being allowed to join the Pinochle game with the adults was almost a rite of passage in our family. Today, when we gather and deal the cards, someone is inevitably referred to as "ol' aces Ileta." I'm not sure Grandpa ever did figure out the reason the women always won was because his woman had a way of knowing where those aces would land. Grandma's legacy is found in a deck of cards, her fun-loving yet competitive nature as real as the slick cards in our hands.

It's true dementia forced her out of her waitressing job before she thought she was ready. She continued to tear out recipes but struggled to follow them. She tried to jump in and help with all the things she'd done her whole life, and when we had to explain how to do them, she'd respond with an "Oh, I knew that" as if it were a temporary lapse, not a permanent deterioration of her mind.

Dementia stole my grandma's memory, but my memories? They're still crystal clear. And I remember a strong, independent woman who loved with all her heart, who gave with everything she had, and who worked hard without ever complaining. Those are the memories that shape my grandma's legacy . . . and the woman I've become.

Kelsey Scism, author of *One Year with Jesus: A Weekly Devotional Journal for Middle School Girls*, **prays her life and legacy point to the Lord.**

Riding Out the Storm

MICHELLE KOCH

One, one thousand.

Two, one thousand.

Three—*BOOM*.

It was one of those thunderstorms that kept getting louder and louder, and the air felt electric. It wasn't forecasted to be severe, so we didn't go to the basement. Instead, my grandma and I huddled at the table in her cramped kitchen counting between lightning bolts and rumbles of thunder.

The room gradually grew darker, and at each flash of lightning, we'd jump and start the count again. Each time, our count grew shorter. Full of nervous energy, we'd giggle at our startled reactions and say over and over, "That was close."

Then a bright flash lit up the house. There was no time to utter a syllable before thunder rattled the dishes.

We laughed as we squealed, "That one was *really* close!"

We cautiously got up to investigate. We walked to the window above the sink to look out, and sure enough, the maple tree just outside was smoldering.

The rain put the fire out, and the tree continued to shade the backyard for many years to come. And I think that day made me love thunderstorms.

Before her stint as grandma, she was a homemaker who raised five children. I wasn't her first grandchild, but I was the one blessed to have the most time with her. She taught me many things, like how to make homemade fried chicken, and that a cake from a box doesn't mean you're any less loved. She taught me to read books as an escape and to go for walks in the rain.

She led a modest life and found joy in simple things, like fresh tomato sandwiches on a hot summer day and wildflowers picked from a ditch. The pace of her life allowed her to notice and appreciate simple pleasures.

She also taught me to weather the storms.

When I was little, it didn't always seem my grandpa was as kind as he should have been. Grandma tried to keep the house up, the grass mowed, dinner on the table, and his preferred brand of beer in the fridge. She put on lipstick minutes before his arrival home. But sometimes, too many times, it wasn't good enough. He was tired from physical work and a long commute, and a few beers in, he'd lose his filter. I often wondered why she stayed, but that's what women of that generation did.

Years later, he quit drinking and spent most of his retirement doting on her. It seemed he was making up for lost time, making amends. Relationships—especially those that last decades—don't come without storms. They rode theirs out together, and I'm grateful I got to see the rainbow.

Grandma's life, by today's standards, was old-fashioned in many ways. While women today may have more options, I sometimes envy the slower pace of her life. Her main job was to care for her people. Sometimes, I wish I had more time to focus on just that.

Today, when I hustle to make ends meet and do all the things, I have to force myself to slow down and be present. I want to be a mom who loves like my grandma loved me. Because when I look back, there were no elaborate outings or trips—there were ordinary days that built a lifetime of memories.

In a season when the proverbial Joneses seem to have unlimited financial resources for spring breaks that require passports and teens getting nicer vehicles than I can afford for myself, it can feel like I'm failing.

Then I realize nearly all my most impactful memories were made at home. Time spent sitting in the shade, next to a fire, around a table, or on a swing—that's time well spent.

Life was simpler then; Grandma's schedule wasn't packed, and she wasn't distracted by technology. The expectations were lower. We had time to just be.

The world today feels fast, and people so often seem on edge. Her pace was slow, and her demeanor was welcoming. For me, she was a source of peace. A calm place in any storm, and I'll always be grateful for it.

A middle-aged, young-at-heart storyteller, wife, and mom, Michelle Koch is a gratitude enthusiast celebrating small things. Find her blog and socials at *One Grateful Girl*.

I'll Face the Mirror

ANGELA ANAGNOST-REPKE

The dreaded day had arrived: My mother needed to have her head shaved due to the chemotherapy for her uterine cancer. And on this day, my four-month-old daughter had a fever. I couldn't escape the guilt of leaving her, but I had no choice. I had to be with her grandmother on this momentous day.

With my daughter on my hip, we waited for her grandmother to pick me up. I stroked her black hair. She nuzzled, calm and warm, in my arms. Growing up with three brothers, I never realized I ached for a daughter until the moment her cheeks landed on my chest. I cradled her and gazed through the blinds. Outside, a few white clouds contrasted the crisp blue sky. Our maple tree was ablaze, and its stoic beauty calmed the torment inside me. Flames danced around one another before settling on the grass. Soon the fire would be extinguished, and the maple tree would prevail, naked. No one would stop to look.

My daughter's brave grandmother pulled into the driveway. I handed our baby to my husband and headed to the fancy wig salon, where my mother would have her head shaved and be given a wig. The salon was like any other hair salon, posh and modern. Only the stylists there didn't trim real hair—they sculpted wigs to perfection. They made women, mainly sick or aging women, feel comfortable with their new appearance.

Back in the confined room, I spotted the electric clippers. I didn't want the red switch turned from *off* to *on*. The buzzing would eviscerate my mother's spirit—something I'd never seen happen before. She always wore her hair long, shiny, and wavy, like she was the star of a Pantene Pro-V commercial. But without hair, I was afraid she'd look wounded.

The man who shaved my mother's head placed the black cape over her shoulders. It granted no superpowers. The valiant grandmother stared at herself in the center of the mirror. That day in the fancy wig salon, she was a woman, but cancer threatened to steal her womanhood.

The man prepped her by reciting a monologue I'm sure he'd repeated hundreds of times to other cancer-stricken women. I steadied my eyes on the black clippers. Time was almost up. My ears dreaded the buzzing from them.

"Are you ready?" he asked.

"Yep," my mom said.

He responded, "Some women choose to have their backs to the mirror, and some—"

"I'll face the mirror," my mom interrupted.

He turned on the clippers, and buzzing filled the room. She stared. The man separated and lifted the first chunk of my mom's hair straight into the air. He placed the clippers at the top of her forehead. The clippers stumbled backward, lifting the hair off her head. Her scalp was gray-white, with black and white sprouts shooting through.

I waited. Nothing came. No wailing. No tears. No anger.

As my mom continued to examine the mirror, she sat unwavering. Her head was first a crescent moon, next a half-moon, and finally a full moon. There she sat—bald. Winter came. But the stoic grandmother's spirit still roared.

That day, beauty had a sound: the buzzing of clippers. We were frightened of it at first but discovered strength trumps beauty. Grandmother was new. A rush surged through me as I stared at my mother. Her courage was contagious. *My mom will live*, I thought, *and long enough to enjoy being a grandmother.*

With her new faux hair resting on top of her head, my mother drove me home to be with her sick granddaughter. I crept into my daughter's room, and my husband placed her in my arms. I fed my swaddled daughter, whose fever had subsided. We rocked. Her eyes fluttered before they shut for the night. My fingers scrolled her thick mane, a gift from her grandmother, with each strand rooted.

I studied her. Her petite nose breathed in life. Her rouge lips were sealed and delicate. I never wanted to let her go. I couldn't imagine feeling more love than this. My daughter and her grandmother filled me. I brought her to my chest, patting her back. I inhaled her. A silent energy beamed out of me and filled every corner of the room. I prayed it would land inside my daughter.

Grandmother is still with us. Her resilience is spent caring for my father, who is now eighty-eight years old. She suffers ailments left over from her cancer fight, which she seldom complains about. My daughter gets to spend time with her grandmother and has absorbed her strength.

Today my daughter is ten, a blooming preteen. Her own locks are long and full, but light brown. There will be phases when she'll stand exquisite, setting her whole world on fire. And there will be phases when she'll struggle, perhaps feeling naked and raw. But because she has the strength of her grandmother, spring will always come.

Writer and educator Angela Anagnost-Repke teaches along the shores of Lake Michigan and, with her family of four, gratefully calls Northern Michigan home.

PART 9

SO GOD MADE A GRANDMA

devoted

Love is stronger than distance or Alzheimer's or broken bones. It's the STRONGEST connection in the world.

NANCY BRIER

The Locket

LESLIE MEANS

She didn't know he was coming.

It was the 1940s; advancement in technology was years away. There was no texting or phone calls to announce his arrival, and a letter would take weeks to arrive.

My granddaddy served in World War II and was home on leave from basic training. But before he returned to war, he had to make a very important stop.

He showed up in her one-room schoolhouse that day, looking handsome (as usual) in his soldier's uniform and hat. He had flowers in one hand and a gift in the other. Both were for his girlfriend—my grandmother.

"Mom talked about this moment often," my mother tells me. "She didn't talk about many things, but we all heard about this." The kids (her students in that one-room schoolhouse, grades K–8) all giggled when they saw him.

Inside that delicately wrapped gift was a silver locket in the shape of a heart. And inside that locket was a photo of my grandfather dressed in his military best.

Grandma wore that locket on her wedding day.

So did I.

Granddaddy clasped the necklace around my neck moments before I walked down the aisle. I wore it, along with her veil, in her memory.

I stopped by their home one fall day before Grandma got sick. We all sat at the kitchen table, Grandma on one end and Granddaddy snuggled up next to her.

Grandaddy told me, "Leslie, the most important thing you'll do in this life is find your one true love."

Then he looked at Grandma and she looked at him, and they both smiled.

That tender moment lives in my heart, an illustration of love that lasts throughout the years. Of course, that kind of love is a choice. It's sacrificial. It's steadfast. It's not always easy—but it's always worth it.

Offering our unconditional love to the people in our lives, no matter what, no matter when, no matter why—it's one of the things that makes this life so beautiful. In the next several stories, you'll see what devotion looks like in all sorts of ways and in all kinds of relationships. I hope you'll tuck the inspiration they offer into your own heart as you read them.

The Best Place to Vacation

CHERYL DONELY

Other kids grew up vacationing on warm beaches, splashing in the ocean, dipping beneath the waves to hunt for shells and fish. Or they drove to amusement parks with mouse ears, hands-in-the-air roller coasters, and pink cotton candy piled high on a stick. Some went cruising on large ships with limitless buffets and sparkling pools. Their best memories stem from popular family destinations.

But not me.

Yes, we packed our car too. My dad strapped the luggage tightly to the top of the station wagon while my siblings and I raced to claim the "way back." My mom tucked sandwiches into the cooler next to the sliced apples. Anticipation danced around us.

It wasn't to build sandcastles, scream down the log ride, or soak in the sun on a ship. Instead, we drove to Colorado Springs.

This spot was better than all the Disney-style vacations in the world. Better times a million, for exactly one reason: My grandma lived there.

Tucked in a tiny home with a view of Pikes Peak, my grandma lived with my grandpa until we lost him young. We'd pull into the driveway, pile out of the car, stretch our stiff bodies, and walk straight into her arms—the best destination.

Next I would explore her house to see all her trinkets. I'd admire the butterfly suncatcher on the sliding door, the brass birds on her shelf, the brightly colored goblets in her hutch, and the array of family pictures down her hallway. Then I'd go into her closet, where she kept a gumball machine and a dish of pennies to help myself to a welcome-to-Grandma's-house treat. Everything in her home felt wonderful.

In this just-arrived routine, I felt stability and peace course through my whole body.

Throughout our stay, we'd always find our way back to her table. The sweet aroma of her sticky caramel rolls would beckon us in the morning. We'd help her dump eggs, flour, and chocolate chips into a bowl to make a cookie snack. We'd connect over hearty meals of tender roast with creamy mashed potatoes and a side of broccoli, and finish with a velvety dessert we'd scoop out after cranking the old-fashioned ice cream maker.

Through all the meals, I felt love and nourishment fill me.

But most of all, we'd simply hang out. Nothing fancy. We'd meander into the living room to swap stories, flip on the television, or circle up for card games. We'd take walks around the neighborhood breathing in the crisp air, stroll through the park throwing bread at the ducks in the pond, browse shops, or visit extended family. We'd update each other on our lives, asking for details, unpacking thoughts, and laughing a lot.

Through all the togetherness and conversation, I felt known and had a strong sense of belonging.

These vacations meant everything to me.

You see, I grew up with lots of change.

My dad flew helicopters for the Air Force, and we moved constantly. New homes. New neighborhoods. New schools. New churches. New friends. New grocery stores. New everything. Over and over again.

I enjoyed being a military kid and learned to adapt quickly. I think that's because, despite my nomadic lifestyle, I felt grounded at my core. I had constants in my life, and a big one was my grandma.

No matter where we lived, my grandma was in Colorado Springs, a phone call away.

Consistent.

Sustaining.

Grounding.

Providing security throughout my childhood.

In adulthood, I maintained a close friendship with my grandma. My husband, sons, and I visited often, her nourishment overflowing onto her great-grandchildren.

When my grandma was ninety-nine years old, hospice gave her two weeks. Again, I road-tripped to see her, this time with drop-everything speed. I got to return the love she'd poured into me my whole life; I didn't leave her side for many of her last days.

Then, in the middle of the night, Jesus came into my grandma's room. He stretched out His hand and asked, "Are you ready?" I imagine my grandmother hesitated for just a minute because she knew how much she meant to all of us. But after one last look back, she took Jesus' hand and walked into eternity.

When I heard, I collapsed to the ground in grief. It turns out that almost a century on earth is still not enough time for me. But on the floor, truth stirred.

I had an entire childhood through midlife of my grandma loving me well. Lucky me to have known her and been called her granddaughter. Her voice, her face, her love, and all the memories will be with me my whole life. Her legacy lives in me.

All because my parents chose to vacation at a place that was sacred to our family—my grandma's house.

Cheryl Donely is a wife, mom, and high school teacher. She writes about parenting big kids on her website and socials, *Empowered Moms and Kids*.

Grandma Lu's Kitchen

CHRISTY WALTER

Our family is growing, and we are officially transitioning from man-to-man coverage into a zone defense. Three kids versus two parents. This means making room for baby and utilizing our current space in new ways. It also means we need a new kitchen table. More bodies require more seats.

The first words out of my mouth as we searched were "Oh! I want one with a bench!" My husband was on board, probably because of the practicality. He likely assumed I wanted it because it's a trend. But my reason went deeper—one that brought a feeling of nostalgic comfort.

When I think of a dining table with a bench, I don't think of how trendy we could be or how practical it is.

I think of my Grandma Lu's kitchen.

I think of meals shared, recipes prepared, stories told, and memories made. The bench in my grandmother's kitchen was the best seat in the house. The house she raised my dad and his five brothers and sisters in had multiple floors, including a basement, and several rooms with plenty more seating options. Our massive family had no business congregating in the smallest common area. And yet everyone flocked to the cozy kitchen and crammed on the bench and four accompanying chairs.

Perhaps we sat there because the smell of freshly baked cookies beckoned us.

Maybe it was the pot of kielbasa marinating in that tangy sauce alongside pineapple and lil' smokies that we'd taste-test a little too often. Oftentimes, around the holidays, it was because Grandma Lu needed us to help in the ham roll-up assembly line. She'd explain each of our jobs each time, though most of us could put those together in our sleep. We didn't just cook in the kitchen. We reminisced, we exchanged stories, we burst into tears from laughing so hard, we had heart-to-hearts, and so much more.

This bench sat in its place hosting countless memories for generations. I grew up on it right along with my sisters, my cousins. My dad grew up on it along with my aunts, my uncles. It was a kitchen staple—a dominant part of core memories for decades.

So when the house sold and all the possessions inside had to be moved out, it was heart-wrenching. My dad has since acquired that bench. And maybe someday I'll get to have that incredible treasure.

Grandma Lu downsized her kitchen table when she moved, but that hasn't stopped her, or us, from congregating in her kitchen. She still beckons us with the smell of chocolate chip cookies and asks for our help in the ham roll-up line. We still laugh until we cry and recall days gone by.

Because as it turns out, it was never about the bench itself. It was about the people. It was about the moments. It was about how my grandmother created a home, a space, a family that cherished each other so much they could be utterly content wherever they were together.

My husband and I did end up buying the table with the bench and the four accompanying chairs because nostalgia always wins. My hope is that our bench becomes the best seat in the house. I pray our table is filled with an immeasurable amount of family and friends and shared meals and memories for years to come. My deepest desire is that the spirit of Grandma Lu's kitchen lives on in my own.

Christy Walter is a SAHM of three. Raised in Texas and living in Kansas, she's navigating this beautiful life one chapter at a time.

Living Far Apart Doesn't Change the Love

NATALIE HAYDEN

It's 323 miles, driveway to driveway. From the moment we part until we meet again, the countdown always begins.

We may live far apart, but there's no one closer in our hearts.

They're always asking, "When do we get to see Yia Yia?"

"How many more days, Mama?"

Like an endless paper-link countdown in our heads, we anticipate those big, celebratory hugs and happy tears when we're reunited.

They climb on you like a human jungle gym, never able to get close enough.

Every accolade, athletic accomplishment, and exciting experience from school must be shared with Yia Yia right away.

What we'd give to see you on the daily. Motherhood is extra challenging when your mom is your lifeline and your idol, but she doesn't live in the same town or state.

You juggle babysitting multiple days a week for your grandbabies who live near you, and you spend the rest of the time talking or traveling to see us. Always going above and beyond to offer a helping hand.

We may live far apart, but there's no one closer in our hearts.

The pride you show, the efforts you make, the genuine interest—it's all appreciated. You are the true MVP of our family.

You make them laugh. You bring out their best selves. You have patience in the difficult moments and a sense of calm. They feel safe and happy in your arms and by your side.

Whether it's typing random words in your phone and you sounding them out in a silly voice, asking for an updated grocery list so you can have all their favorite (constantly changing) foods and snacks, or allowing them to snuggle up with you in your bed for a sleepover, you are what every grandmother should be.

You never miss a birthday party, braving blizzards and snow-covered roads to attend. You make brief trips in for dance recitals and doctor appointments, and answer calls around the clock. You're always at our beck and call.

Those sleepless nights I struggled with a newborn, you stayed for weeks, telling me at two in the morning, "Go to sleep, honey, I've got this."

You help me navigate big feelings when my babies are hurting and I don't know what to do.

You always have the right words and the best advice. You always know the right thing to do.

When my daughter has nightmares, she says she imagines you so she can soothe herself. I can see why.

When my son begs to stay at your house one hundred days instead of five, I wish it too.

When my youngest looks up from his car seat and says, "When do we go home to Yia Yia's?" I feel it. Because no matter where we live, you are our home.

And when I thank God every day for my family, I thank Him first for giving me an angel for a mom and giving my kids a grandmother like you.

I may not get to have you by my side on the playground each day. I may not get to have you over for dinner after a soccer game on a Wednesday. You may not get to attend the midweek pre-K graduation. But we get so much more.

You show up more than anyone in our lives. We get quality time, every single time. We never take the bond for granted. We savor every visit that's never long enough. And before we part, we always know when we'll be together again.

So as we gear up for goodbyes and all three of my kids hug you at the same time, holding on tightly and refusing to let go, I hope those moments show you all you're doing right. How lucky are we that God gave us such a wonderful person to miss.

We may live far apart, but there's no one closer in our hearts.

Natalie (Sparacio) Hayden is a mom of three who blogs at *Lights, Camera, Crohn's* as a woman who takes on motherhood with chronic illness.

To See My Baby Holding His Baby Is a Gift

MICHELE PETERS

"Today?" I gasped. "But it's too soon."

When I got the urgent phone call at work, my heart dropped. My grandson was still several weeks away from full term. I paused and mentally counted the days in my head.

"He's a month from his due date." I stood up from my desk and stepped into another room, needing privacy. "It's too soon, right?" I repeated in disbelief.

"She's not well, Mom." My son's voice wavered. "At her checkup today, the doctor said her blood pressure is too high. He sent us straight to the hospital." He whispered, "I'm scared, Mom."

I was scared too.

I took a deep breath and steadied my voice. "It's going to be okay, Son." Despite the turmoil in my head, I needed to be calm for his sake. "I'll be there as soon as I can, okay? I'm coming to help," I assured. "Today. I promise."

We ended our call, and I jumped into action. A conversation arranging time off with my boss, a call to my husband at work, airline ticket reservations, and a suitcase thrown together. Five hours later, I finally took a breath in my seat, forty thousand feet in the air. The three-hour flight felt like ten, leaving me time to worry.

Will I make it in time?

Will my daughter-in-law be okay?
Will my first grandchild survive?
How do you get back time you haven't yet received?

I landed at 11:30 p.m. and arrived at the hospital just after midnight. Visiting hours had long since passed, but the nursing staff granted me a waiver so I could be there. My son met me at a side entrance and held me in a long bear hug, his relief at my arrival tangible. "It's going to be okay, Son," I whispered into his shoulder. "I'm here."

The reality was, things were about to get frantic. Scary frantic.

We walked briskly up the steps to the birthing room and rushed to my daughter-in-law's side. In the dim lighting, she lay connected to a fetal monitor and an IV bag with medicine to induce labor. With a drowsy smile, she reached out her hand.

"How are you doing, honey?" I gently squeezed her fingers, hoping to quell the concern in her eyes. She started to reply, but alarms sounded, and the medical team barged into the room. I stepped out of their way.

"The baby's heart rate is dropping," the lead nurse announced. "Her blood pressure is at stroke levels. We need to get her to the OR and prep for a C-section before she has a seizure."

My son stood in place, a scared little boy with his entire world on the precipice of slipping away. He looked from me to her and back again, hoping for direction.

"Go, be with her. I'll wait here," I assured him. "It'll be okay."

They handed him scrubs to put on before heading to the OR, but he struggled, his hands shaking.

"Here, let me help," I said. I pulled the surgical scrub top over his head, tucked his pants into the bottoms, and slipped the blue paper coverings over his shoes. The clock in my mind rolled back twenty-five years. I was no longer in that hospital room helping a scared man prepare for his first child—I was a young mom helping her first child pull on his snowsuit and boots to go outside and play.

"Let's go now," a nurse directed my son, snapping me out of my flashback.

I nodded in encouragement as he left the room and sat back in the chair, finally catching my breath. I tried to rest in the dim room, but the darkness amplified the weight of my worries. The ticking of the clock provided faint background noise, but my mind was anything but quiet. Thoughts raced through my head like a whirlwind, each one more troubling than the last.

What if? What if? What if?

Forty-five minutes later, my son entered the room, snapping me awake.

"Is everyone okay?" I asked, guardedly hopeful.

He ran into my arms. "They're okay, Mom. They're okay." He let out a huge breath and stepped back to look at me. "You're a grandma."

Tears welled in my eyes, and I squeezed him harder and whispered, "Congratulations, Son. You're a dad."

Before you have a grandchild, you may wonder how you could love anyone as much as you do your own child. You discover love isn't a resource that diminishes. It transcends generations and fosters a connection to the past, present, and future.

To see my baby holding his baby was a gift. To know I helped foster and ensure the legacy of love in our family line, a blessing.

The love in my heart multiplied a thousand times that day.

Michele Peters is a survivor who writes from the heart with the intention of bringing light into dark places. She believes in love first, always.

Love and Hamburgers

AMANDA MCCOY

Valerie was one of those women you noticed when you entered the room. She was tall and regal, with strawberry blonde hair and flawless skin the color of milk. She radiated confidence and rebellion. She didn't talk much, but her eyes flashed the fire beneath. You were drawn to her mystery. She possessed an elegance that can't be taught. You wouldn't know she was a farmer's daughter who ran around barefoot, sneaking out to smoke behind the barn.

Valerie was engaged to the son of a farmer. "He was a nice man," she said. "Sweet."

One night, Valerie went out with some girlfriends. She'd been existing simply in her life, and her engagement to the farmer's son made sense. Then Tom, an outsider in her small town, walked into the room. Italian, he was the epitome of tall, dark, and handsome. He couldn't take his eyes off Valerie—he would tell everyone later she was the most beautiful woman he'd ever seen. He asked her to go out for a hamburger. She laughed and wiggled her hand at him. "I'm engaged," she said.

"I'm not asking you to marry me," he protested. "I'm just asking you to get a hamburger." He persisted; she finally relented—but insisted it not be considered a date since she was engaged.

They did, indeed, get a hamburger. And after that date, she broke off her engagement and eventually married the man who would become my grandfather.

As a child, I heard my grandfather tell this story. I'd sit with him on the porch and ash his cigar for him. I'd walk carefully to the edge of the deck and gently tap the thick cigar against it. To this day, when I smell cigar smoke, I float back to the quiet moments with him on a porch. When I'd ask him to tell me something, he'd tell *the* story, and I'd imagine the younger versions of my grandparents sitting in a diner, biting into juicy hamburgers. I remember thinking he was bold and she was brave, and this is how you live life. I wanted to be like her.

As I grew older, I wondered if my grandmother made the right choice. Did she wish she'd taken the safer route and married the farmer's son? Tom was the charming man who convinced her to get a hamburger, but he was also intense, moody, and self-centered. Valerie's life with Tom was full of sacrifice. She raised five children while he worked too much. He was tough on all of them and had high expectations. He butted heads with his children, especially his older boys. I picture Valerie as a young mother, standing over a sink of dishes, looking through the window and wondering what her life could have been. If she had married the farmer's son, she would have had a simpler life.

But her choice was the right one. She chose love, knowing it was full of challenges. She and my grandfather built a legacy of five children, fifteen grandchildren, and nine great-grandchildren (so far). I hope her fire lives in me so I can pass it to my daughters.

At the very end, my grandfather was bent over and bound to a wheelchair. He couldn't use his hands much; his arthritis was excruciating, and Parkinson's made it difficult to speak. My grandmother couldn't hear or see him well, but they talked to each other anyway. All they wanted was each other. Seven winters ago, they passed away within months of each other, as if they couldn't bear to be apart.

Love like theirs is not accidental. It happens to those who make a choice, take a risk, and plunge into the unknown. My beautiful, rebellious grandmother was determined to make her life her own, even if it meant letting go of what was comfortable. Their kind of love wasn't a fairy tale. Their love was the result of living, forgiving, and never quitting. True love happens to the bold and the brave.

The last time I saw my grandparents together, they were holding hands and repeating their love. I wanted to freeze the moment and tuck it somewhere inside. That kind of love is rare and beautiful and devastating. I'm fortunate to have seen it.

Here is the short version of the story: Many years ago, my grandma was engaged to a farmer's son. She met my grandpa and made a decision that changed all our lives. Their relationship was never perfect. So many years later, after all they'd lived and lost, they were still reaching for each other, still holding each other, still loving with all they had left in them.

And to think, it all started with a brave woman who said yes to a hamburger.

Amanda McCoy lives in Ohio with her husband, children, and dogs. Her Substack platform, *The Write McCoy*, features raw, real writing about motherhood and marriage.

One Carrying Forward the Love of Two

LISA APPELO

Never did I ever think I'd be solo grandparenting.

Like so much of life, I imagined just how my grandparenting years would look. My husband was a great dad, and he'd for sure be the fun grandpa. I could see him doing lots of hands-on projects with the kids, taking them fishing, and exploring the outdoors like he'd done with our own children.

I'd be the nurturing grandmom. I'd set up a toy room with trains and tea parties, make my famous chocolate chip cookies, and rock each baby to sleep every chance I could.

A few years ago, I got a sneak peek of what grandparenting might look like for us. I'd gone with my husband to his work conference in the Florida Keys, a rare trip together away from our seven children.

While he was in meetings that first day, I went down to the hotel beach with a book and a water bottle. I snuggled into a hammock, ready to savor the luxurious quiet in the shade of palm trees.

A few minutes later, an older man and woman with three towheaded children made their way to the beach and set up not far from me. Hearing their conversation, I peered over my book to take in the sweet scene.

I gathered this was a grandfather and grandmother taking their three young grandchildren snorkeling for the first time.

The grandfather seemed well-versed in snorkeling. He worked with one grandchild at a time, adjusting each mask until it fit just right, attaching the snorkel, guiding small feet into flippers, then walking each one into the clear, shallow water, where he showed them how to breathe through the snorkel while swimming.

The grandmother, meanwhile, was tending to their beach spot. She brushed sand from the towels, handed out snacks, and organized the buckets and bags they'd brought with them.

That will be us someday, I thought. *We'll tag-team grandparenting like we've tag-teamed parenting.*

I could just imagine it. This was how we'd grow old together, grandparenting the next generation of our family.

As I watched this older couple and their grandchildren play and swim and explore together, I tucked away my "someday" dreams.

Three days later, we were back home and those dreams shattered. In the dark hours of the early morning, I woke to my husband's last breaths on the pillow next to mine.

His death came without warning. In the deep grief that followed for my children and me, I wondered if we'd ever smile again. I worried how it would affect my kids and how they'd react to this loss.

God so faithfully walked us through that raw grief. Most of my worries for my children never materialized. The older kids graduated college, married, and started families of their own.

I'm now Nonni to thirteen and counting. It's both an incredible joy and a tender ache, because I never thought I'd be a solo grandparent.

I'm not just the grandmom who gets to set up toy trains and tea parties, bake the homemade chocolate chip cookies, and rock babies to sleep every chance I get.

I'm also the grandmom stewarding a legacy for the granddad who's in heaven.

I'm one grandparent carrying forward the love of two.

It doesn't mean I'm trying to be both grandfather and grandmother. I can't do that.

And it doesn't mean I'm trying to force-fit the grandparenting picture I'd always imagined. I can't do that either.

While I never saw this coming, being a solo grandparent in the wake of loss has given me even more purpose.

I know, more than ever, what a gift these years are. I get the privilege of loving these children, sharing family traditions, and creating new memories.

I understand how meaningful a legacy is. I realize now that a legacy isn't something handed off at the end of a life but a relationship lived out day after day.

And I'm more aware than ever of the responsibility of passing the baton of faith and the values our family holds to my children's children.

Never did I ever think I'd be solo grandparenting.

But just because my dream of grandparenting looks different from what I imagined, it doesn't mean it can't still be abundantly beautiful—because it is.

Author of *Life Can Be Good Again*, single mom to seven, and Nonni to thirteen, Lisa Appelo writes on hope in grief at Lisaappelo.com.

Forgotten Grief

STACEY SKRYSAK

The room was filled with a flurry of doctors and nurses as a chaotic scene unfolded. The air was tense, my body filled with fear. I was in labor more than seventeen weeks prematurely, delivering my triplets with almost no chance of survival. After our first baby arrived, we received news no parent ever wants to hear: Our baby girl was too weak and wouldn't survive.

I looked from my husband to my mother, the only other family member in the room. I could tell her heart was breaking into a million pieces, yet she kept her composure through tears. Her face was full of concern and sadness, but she exuded strength as my husband and I were about to lose our firstborn child.

It's a vivid memory I'll never forget. My mother held our daughter and rocked her gently during her short time on earth. She smiled at our sweet girl and, through the tears, told her what a beautiful family she had joined. My mother was the shoulder we leaned on as we faced devastation, comforting us as only a mother can.

In the days and weeks that followed, both sets of our parents flew in from across the country. They helped us plan a funeral, arranging for deli trays and flowers to be delivered as our friends and family gathered to say goodbye. They made sure we were eating and sleeping, caring for us when we felt as if our world was at a standstill. And just two months later, they arrived back in town, planning yet another funeral after our second child passed away.

In the throes of grief and in our darkest hours, an army of supporters arrived to comfort my family. Neighbors prepared meals and cleaned our house. Friends sent donations to help with medical expenses. And our parents remained pillars of strength. Yet as they offered empathy and support, their own grief took a back seat to mine.

While the pain of losing a child is unbearable, imagine watching your own child lose her baby. As a parent, you never want to see your child facing deep anguish or hurt. You would do anything to take away their pain, yet your heart hurts with grief—even guilt—as you mourn the loss of your grandchild. That's the reality for grandparents who lose a grandchild. It's a powerless feeling, one my parents know all too well.

On that day ten years ago, our lives changed. As the years go by, we find ways to live after loss, but our family never forgets. You never get over the loss of a child; instead, you learn to survive with that missing piece of your heart. And on those days when the grief creeps up, I often find myself calling my mother. She was there that fateful day when life took a turn for the worse. Over the phone, we cry together and confide in each other as we remember two precious babies in heaven. We reminisce over my triplets, her three beautiful grandchildren.

As a parent, now I understand. I want to shelter my daughter from pain. And as I think back to those early days of loss, my heart hurts, imagining what my parents went through. It takes enormous strength to survive the loss of a child, and it takes just as much love and courage to be grieving grandparents comforting their own child.

To the grandparents who have lost a grandchild, your grief doesn't go unnoticed. You may be holding your head high when the world around you is breaking, but we see you and we thank you for your strength when we needed it the most.

Stacey Skrysak is a TV journalist and writer specializing in child loss and premature birth. She's mom to a twenty-two-weeker surviving triplet and a rainbow baby.

Grandma's Masterpiece

NANCY BRIER

"Just whack a little butter in the pan," Mom said.

I'd watched her do it a hundred times. She dragged a chair over to the stove, and I climbed up. Giving Mom a glance, I dropped a pale yellow glob in the frying pan, its color soft against the black cast-iron. "Now flour," Mom said. "About the same amount." My older brothers and sisters didn't like helping in the kitchen, but for me, making dinner with Mom was the best part of the day.

I reached my hand into the green canister we kept on the countertop, just like she always did. My fingers came out white and furry, and I liked the way the flour felt on my skin, powdery and delicate. A trail of dust followed my fist as it flew from container to skillet. I sprinkled the flour on top of the melting butter and stirred it with a wooden spoon. "That's how you do it," Mom said. I watched the butter bubble up, change color, thicken. Its sweet, burnt fragrance filled the air. "Now just add stock."

I plunged the dipper into our big pot simmering on the other burner, dodged the soup bone hiding beneath the surface, and scooped out liquid glistening with fat. "Let's do this part together," Mom said. Her hand clasped over mine, and we lifted the ladle and poured it into the skillet. It sizzled when it met the heat. "A little more," Mom said, and we did it again and again until there was just the right amount. I stirred the gravy slowly so it wouldn't slosh over the edge or splash up and burn my skin. Outside in the driveway, I could hear a basketball pounding against the pavement, my brothers vying for their turn to take a shot.

"Let's taste it," Mom said, "just to be sure." I climbed down from my chair, got out two spoons, and handed them to her. A minute later, both of us positioned our spoons by our lips, the gravy steaming. We each cupped a hand to catch any drips and blew gently until it was cool enough. "Perfect, Mom," I said, sliding the clean spoon past my lips.

By the time my daughter, Lauren, was born many years later, Mom and I were living in different parts of the country, and her memory was starting to fade. Sometimes, when I made dinner for the family, I yearned for Mom's presence. I'd drag a chair to the stove, Lauren would climb onto it, and we'd temper eggs for pudding or melt chocolate for Mom's legendary sheet cake, and I felt her absence. I wished the three of us could cook together, that my child could know my mother, and that both of them could feel our connection the way I did.

Then something terrible and miraculous happened: Mom fell, shattering her hip and one of her shoulders. After a long stay in the hospital, she needed a quiet place to recover. My siblings and I discussed it, and to my delight, we decided my house was the best option.

By the time Mom arrived, we had everything ready—an easy place to shower, a quiet room to herself, all her favorite foods. She was thinner than I'd ever seen her, having recently endured the loss of my dad and the trauma of broken bones. Her memory came and went, but underneath, she was the same loving person I knew her to be. "We'll fatten her up," I told Lauren. "We'll help her feel better." Lauren was the same age I was when Mom and I started cooking together, and she loved messing up the kitchen as much as I did.

After we got Mom settled, I dragged two chairs into the kitchen, one for Lauren to stand on and one for Mom to recover in. Mom's chair was an upholstered lounger with a built-in leg rest, a tight fit for the space but exactly what we needed. While Mom's bones grew stronger, I got out the ingredients. One day, we made Mom's favorite chocolate cake.

Lauren pulled out a splattered recipe card, written in Mom's perfect penmanship, and laid it on the counter. She scooped a measuring cup into the flour, a trail of dust following her hand from container to bowl. Then she added cocoa powder, sugar, eggs, and butter, and we started to stir. "That's how you do it," Mom said from her chair. I sensed she remembered the smell of vanilla, and I hoped the flavor of this dessert she'd served so many times would wake other sleeping pockets of memory. "Let's taste it," I said, "just to be sure we got it right." Lauren pulled out three spoons, dipped them into the batter, and carried one to Mom, her little palm cupped beneath the spoon to catch any drips. In that moment, I realized my dream had come true, the way I'd visualized it.

A few weeks later, we were able to move Mom's lounger out of the kitchen, and before I knew it, she was strong enough to go home. When we said goodbye, I didn't know if she'd recognize Lauren or me the next time we saw her or if she'd stay physically strong enough to avoid another fall. But that glorious time we had together was a lasting gift, a reminder that love is stronger than distance or Alzheimer's or broken bones.

It's the strongest connection in the world.

JOAN'S ONE-BOWL CHOCOLATE CAKE MASTERPIECE

Ingredients

1 3/4 cup flour
1 3/4 cup sugar
3/4 cup unsweetened cocoa
1 1/2 teaspoons baking soda
1 1/2 teaspoons baking powder
1 teaspoon salt

2 eggs
1 cup buttermilk
1/2 cup vegetable oil
2 teaspoons vanilla
1/4 teaspoon instant coffee
1 cup boiling water

Combine dry ingredients. Then add all remaining ingredients except boiling water. Beat for two minutes, then stir in boiling water. Pour into a greased 9x13 pan and bake at 350 degrees for thirty-five minutes.

When she's not writing, Nancy Brier loves to mess up the kitchen with her husband and their daughter. For more of her work, please visit NancyBrier.com.

PART 10

SO GOD MADE A GRANDMA
to leave a
legacy

Grandma is our matriarch, and we are her LEGACY.

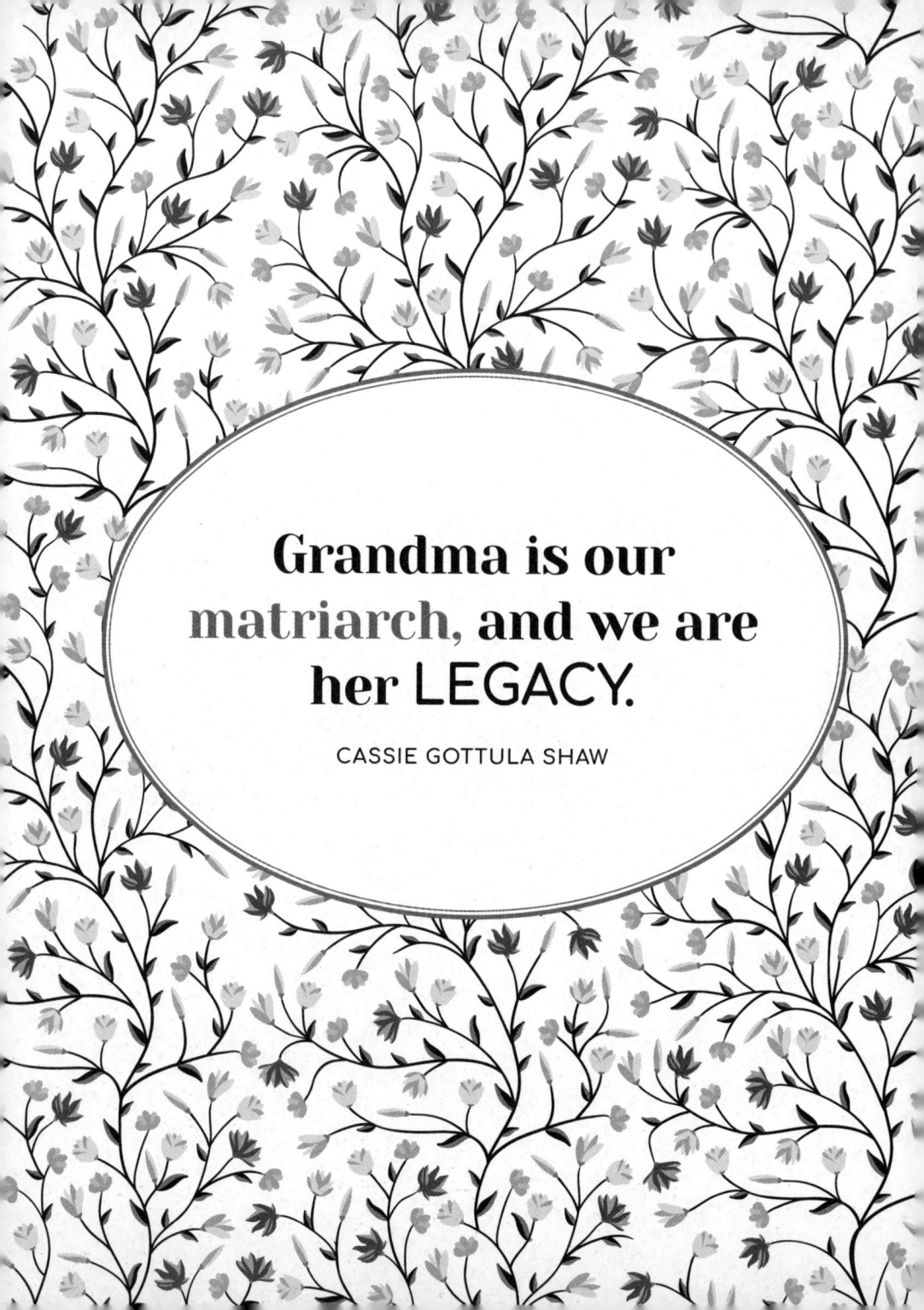

CASSIE GOTTULA SHAW

The Rosebush

LESLIE MEANS

There's a yellow rosebush on our family farm. Every spring, this plant produces beautiful, fragrant yellow roses.

"It's been there as long as the Jesus tree," Mom jokes.

We nicknamed one of our trees "the Jesus tree" because it's been there for a long, long time—at least since 1901, when my great-grandfather first owned the land.

Yes, I realize Jesus' time was more like two thousand years ago, but you get the picture.

It's been there forever.

So has the yellow rosebush.

"Things grew wild back then," Mom tells me.

This means no one planted this bush—it likely just appeared as part of the natural landscape.

This plant is hardy and has survived many storms. Webster County, Nebraska, is often dry and incredibly windy, and it sits in Tornado Alley. Have you ever seen the movie *Twister*? If so, you're likely familiar with the part of the film where a cow gets picked up in a storm and almost hits the truck.

"Cow. Another cow!" Helen Hunt says to Bill Paxton.

"Actually, I think that was the same one," he tells her.

I've never seen a cow fly (movie magic at its finest), but I have seen a tornado in all its glory.

As a kid, I watched a twister lift our stock trailer into the air and place it back down on the opposite side of the fence. Then it ripped a few doors off Dad's machine shed and started toward the yellow rosebush.

But suddenly it disappeared. Good thing, too, because next to the yellow rosebush is the house that's been in our family since the Jesus tree.

And as you now know, that's a long, long time.

Each spring, my grandpa picked a rose from that bush and placed it in the pocket of his denim overalls. Mom and Dad picked them too. I'm sure my great-grandmother and grandmother also enjoyed that plant. My sister, who lives on the farm now, picks a few roses each spring and brings them inside her home.

"The rosebush is blooming," she'll text my mom, sisters, and me—and we know warm weather season has officially arrived.

Each spring when I visit the farm, I stop and smell the roses. And when I do, I can't help but feel a bit closer to all my loved ones who once lived on that dry, windy land in Nebraska.

"What's that phrase people say?" Mom asks me. "'You don't die until the last person who remembers you dies?' Or something like that," she says with a laugh.

I told her she's in luck—since her story is now in print, people will read about her long after she's hanging out with Jesus.

I'm sure the rosebush will still be around, too, blooming each year on schedule. I hope one day my own great-grandkids can pick the same flowers I once loved. It's a reminder that even when we're gone, our legacy leaves an imprint forever.

And just like each of those roses is beautifully unique, so too are the tender moments we hold in our hearts. They create a kaleidoscope of love and loss and joy and heartache and hope—all the things that fill this life with meaning and memories.

The stories in these next few pages give us a glimpse of the strong roots a grandmother plants, the kind that bloom and grow as generations go by. And aren't we the lucky ones to breathe in their sweet legacy—one that will mingle with our own one glorious day.

Her Shoes

JENNI BRENNAN

To my eight-year-old self, there couldn't possibly have been anyone in the whole world who owned as many shoes as my grandmother.

Sorted neatly by color and heel type, the perfectly placed pairs of shoes spanned the closets of three large bedrooms. I'd spend my weekends at her house, my only safe place as a child, working my way through all those shoes. With every new pair I slipped into, I pictured a future version of myself and the magical life I would live.

Leaning over her sparkling, mirror-topped dresser, I'd pluck through her many jewelry boxes, searching for a shiny set of clip-on earrings to coordinate with whichever pair of shoes were hanging off my little-girl-sized feet. Once I was pleased with my selections, usually the most over-the-top options, I'd turn my focus to her bottomless collection of Estée Lauder lipsticks. After all, the right lipstick shade could pull the whole look together.

While I tried on life as a grown-up, she was usually in the kitchen snapping green beans for dinner, watching blue jays from her deck, or eating cookies with tea. I wonder what she used to think when she'd putter down the hallway to check on me and find me, so very different from her, trying to be just like her.

Her feet were narrow, tiny, and petite, while my feet were wide, flat, and too big for my age. Her complexion was as fair as the faded porcelain faces on the

Hummel figurines that lined her shelves, while my complexion back then was somehow always tan and dark. Her hair was short and dyed bright red, while mine was long and brown with auburn streaks when the sun hit it just right.

When I'd look in the mirror and catch her gazing back at me, as if willing me to keep dreaming, I didn't see any of the differences between us. Our age, build, complexion, hair, and style didn't matter. All I saw when I was standing in her shoes were endless glimpses of hopeful possibilities for my life.

Her shoes showed me my future.

Shoes I'd wear to my first school dance with a boy.

Shoes I'd wear to my high school graduation, because failure was not an option.

Shoes I'd wear when I became the first person in my family to go to college.

Shoes I'd wear to my first job, because I would never be dependent on a man.

Shoes I'd wear to my wedding, because I wanted someone to love me the way my grandfather loved her.

Shoes I'd wear when I became a mother, because I knew all the mistakes I wouldn't make.

Shoes I'd wear when I became a grandmother who tried her best to fill in the empty spaces with love.

But in all those countless times I stood before her mirror staring at myself in her shoes, I never once thought about the shoes I'd wear when I lost her.

The shoes I'd look down at after being ushered out of her hospital room because the morphine just wasn't helping her pain.

The shoes that held me steady when the funeral director smiled sadly at me as he closed the door to the viewing room, because surely a seventeen-year-old was too young to see the truth.

The shoes I rocked back and forth in as I stood at that pay phone and learned every last bit of her was gone. Sold. Donated. Lost.

Every last porcelain Hummel.

Every last chunky earring.

Every last tube of Estée Lauder.

Every last perfectly paired shoe.

TO LEAVE A LEGACY

Gone. Just like her.

Sometimes now, even all these years later, when I find myself searching for the right pair of sensible flats, hurriedly sorting through my own jewelry boxes, or overthinking which lipstick to wear, I am transported back in time.

There I am again, standing in her shoes.

There I am again, the little girl she let me be.

There I am again, facing my future.

There I am again, learning how to hold on to hope.

There I am again, seeing all the possibilities in front of me.

And for a few moments, there she is again, her reflection gazing back at me in the mirror, silently reminding me to keep dreaming for something better.

Jenni Brennan is a grief therapist, college professor, and podcaster. She is the founder of *Changing Perspectives Online* **and author of** *Confessions from the Couch***.**

My Heart Remembers

LAURA CHILDERS

(Written with my ninety-eight-year-old mama, who suffers from memory loss)

To my dear children and grandchildren,

I've watched you grow to be parents and grandparents. I'm so proud of you all! To know my children's children is a blessing some never get to enjoy, but I have seen many generations.

Please know when I can't recall your name when I see you after an absence (and the absence may have been short) or I can't remember recent events that are important to you—I still love you.

When you know I am confused and I am not the same as I was—I still love you.

I hope you will not let your heart be sad or fearful about this. My love for you remains strong, because it's in my heart I know you best, and it's there you will always be—and I still love you.

My heart has all the years we've shared. All of them are there. Some may have seeped out of my memory somehow, but they are in my heart. Every moment with you is there, and each moment is precious to me—and I still love you.

I know each of you, even in adulthood, still needs my love, and you may believe it's no longer there when you see me as I appear now. You may think I've forgotten you and all you mean to me because I can't say your name without being reminded—but I still love you.

TO LEAVE A LEGACY

The glory in the passage of time is a mystery. Somehow the harshness of memory may fade and richness may increase; purity is distilled that may have always been there to enjoy if only we'd grasped it the first time through. So I may remember the past as being better than what you recall. To me, those memories are accurate and fresh. In this way, you become more precious to me with each passing year. I don't know how it can be possible, but I love you more all the time.

You may even wonder if your worth—or mine—has diminished as my memory weakens.

Although it's true my brain has lost the ability to make some connections, the way from me to you is more direct than a brain pathway—and I still love you.

The connections in our hearts transcend the words I may not be able to say when I see you or when we talk on the phone—and I still love you.

Each one of you has a perfect and unique share of my love, and that love—all of it—is still here now and will always be in my heart.

And when I leave this earth, do not believe for a moment that my love for you will leave too. God has worked that out, and my heart will remember—and I will still love you.

> My goal is that they may be encouraged in heart and united in love, so that they may have the full riches of complete understanding, in order that they may know the mystery of God, namely, Christ.
> COLOSSIANS 2:2

Laura Childers and her husband live in Oregon with their soon-flying teenager and Laura's ninety-eight-year-old mother. Find her on Instagram @llsauce5.

We Are Her Legacy

CASSIE GOTTULA SHAW

The girl sat down for a picnic with her imaginary friends (Buddy, Putt-Sutts, Caucus, and Beets), her golden ringlets bouncing as she parceled out the fruit. World War II had recently ended, so she could afford to be more generous with their rations, imaginary or not. Her tiny hands moved quickly and with intention as she cared for those she loved. She was barely six years old, but she was certain of her calling.

In 1952, she met a boy and fell in love. They spent their weekday afternoons at the roller rink and their Saturday nights at the movies, and soon they knew . . . they'd each found the one. He didn't have much to offer this girl in the way of material things. But he opened his heart to her, and that was all she'd ever wanted. She was only twelve years old, but she would love him all her life.

On their wedding day, she was radiant. She wore a perfectly fitted white princess dress with a sweetheart neckline, floral lace sleeves, and a ball gown silhouette. Her curls were pulled back and draped with a veil; her signature glasses were perched on her nose. The boy she'd always loved was now a military man, and he was waiting at the end of the aisle. He slipped the diamond on her finger, studying the steadiness of her delicate hand. Yes, indeed, she was certain. But their time together was brief. Her new husband had his orders—he'd be stationed in Korea. She was just seventeen years old. They exchanged letters for more than a year.

And still, they persevered. A couple of years later, they welcomed a precious newborn son. They didn't have much money, but love accounted for everything else. They had two more children in quick succession, one of them my mom. Their fourth and final child arrived in 1969, the year of Woodstock, the Stonewall riots, and a man walking on the moon.

They bought a little white house with solid bones in the town where they'd grown up. They worked humble jobs with their heads held high, for they understood their value. They spent their days raising children, nurturing friendships, walking with Jesus, and loving each other. That little white house became a haven for many neighborhood kids. The love was so thick in that space, it practically seeped into the walls. Life was filled to the brim with beautiful things for a very long time.

Now I watch my grandmother sigh as she looks in the mirror, and I wonder what she sees. Is it a memory or merely a reflection? Is there really any difference?

"Getting old is for the birds," she jokes, but I'm in awe of how she does it. She's eighty-four.

Her achy hands might shake, but they still tend to those she loves—they move purposefully in prayer, and then they get right down to work. And wrinkles or not, she's still the girl she used to be—imaginative and determined, made of resilience, moxie, and heart.

She suffered her greatest sorrows—the loss of her husband and son, both decades ahead of their time. She's been gutted by those deaths and by voids that can't be filled. And yet her life still offers purpose. We need her, so she keeps going.

When I ask my sweet grandma if she can capture the essence of her life in just a few words, she is almost brought to tears. "So many blessings," she whispers fondly, as if only to herself. "I can't believe how I've been blessed."

This woman is so much more than the sum of her pieces. She's the amalgamation of every version of herself, every stage of her life, every choice she's made, every minute of love she's been given. She is our matriarch, and we are her legacy. And together, we've forged a foundation of love that will last for years to come.

For me, there is simply no one like her. And yet her life tells a common story among this generation of mighty women.

May we honor them. May we follow them. May we respect what they can teach us. And may our granddaughters cherish these stories . . . even as they light their own way.

Cassie Gottula Shaw writes about motherhood and mental health at *Girl, I've Got You.*

I Have a Praying Grandmother

VICTORIA RIOLLANO

I will never forget the day my grandmother met my fifth child.

As a woman in her eighties with eighteen grandchildren and more than fifty great-grandchildren, it seemed unlikely she would be able to recall each one's name. After all, keeping up with the names of my (now eight) children is a challenge for me on a good day!

But when she saw my child for the first time, she said, without pause, "Is this David Jeremiah?"

My response was "Grandma, how do you know his name?"

At this, she looked a bit shocked, as if I wasn't aware of her secret.

"I pray for all my grands and great-grands by name, every day."

I couldn't believe my grandmother not only knew my children's names but had been praying for every one of them. I couldn't help but think about the most trying times in my parenting.

When my daughter started having seizures, my grandmother was praying.

When my son struggled with reading, my grandmother was praying.

When my daughter had RSV and stayed in the hospital for a week, my grandmother was praying.

Knowing someone cared about my children was reassuring and reminded me I wasn't alone in my parenting journey. And there are days I desperately need to know I'm not alone. The days sickness outweighs health, when I'm so exhausted I get lost in the middle of a task, the days I mourn the loss of my expectations about parenting—I need to know I'm not alone. The truth is, in the shuffle of it all, there are days I forget to pray for my kids. Thank God for a praying grandmother to fill in the gaps.

I have an insatiable desire to follow in my grandmother's faith. It was her faith that carried her through Jim Crow laws in the Southern United States; it was her faith that helped her face the challenges of being a pastor's wife for six decades. It was her faith that helped her when she had to bury one of her six children. I think she prays so deeply because she knows that without trusting God, she wouldn't have had the strength to carry her through. When my grandmother prays, it's not out of routine but out of necessity. I can't help but wonder how her prayers have helped shift things in my home, unbeknownst to me.

Now I challenge myself to be a praying mother. I'll be the first to admit my prayers for my children may not be daily or as extensive as my grandmother's. In fact, there are times my children have to remind me to simply pray for my food. But here's what I know: When we pray, God listens. I never want to stop talking to the God I claim to love, the God I want my children to serve. I hope I will pray for my children's safety, health, purpose, and their hearts every time they come to my mind.

My grandmother taught me what legacy really means. Her legacy may not be one of wealth, fame, or worldwide ministry. She may never become a household name. But she's the one who encouraged me silently from the sidelines. She's the one who bombarded heaven when I felt hopeless. She's the one who called my children by name when my strength was fading. My hope is to carry this same story of faith for those who come after me.

A praying grandmother is one who can never be forgotten.

Mom of eight, pastor's wife, and psychology professor Victoria Riollano desires to inspire women to walk in victory through her blog, *Victory Speaks*.

Apron Strings

MICHELE L. PETERS

With permanent wrinkles at its edges and fading with age, my great-grandmother's handsewn apron holds more value to me than diamonds or gold.

I inherited the treasure along with hundreds of her handwritten recipe cards, now aged and yellowed. Though she left this world three decades ago, her spirit lives on in these cherished items I pull from the closet for every holiday and special dinner.

If you examine the tattered apron, you'll discover more than fabric and thread; you'll find a steadfast love meticulously woven into every stitch. When I was growing up, she showed me how to sew doll clothing from scraps, how to use a pocketknife to whittle sticks when camping, and that warm tomatoes from her large garden were better than any you could buy in the grocery store—all with her delicate manner of teaching, shaped by a lifetime of experiences. We'd walk hand in hand on the river's edge, looking for colorful rocks to put in the rock tumbler on her porch.

When I tie the apron around my waist, I am wrapped in a comforting embrace of tradition and heritage. Blye Adams, a farmer's daughter and one of eight children, came of age during the Great Depression. Her example instilled in me the value of frugality and repurposing, as she saved everything from margarine containers to bread clips. On sunny spring days, I can still conjure the scent of freshly washed clothes hanging on the laundry lines she used instead of the brand-new Whirlpool my great-grandfather had bought for her at the local Sears & Roebuck.

I would leap with joy at the opportunity to select from the array of canned fruit in her storage cellar to accompany our breakfast. The memory of the fresh peaches atop homemade ice cream, prepared with her love, lingers in my mind. Her cherished recipe cards serve as a catalog of our family's culinary history, with each relative's name inscribed at the bottom to denote their contribution.

The cotton fabric of the apron, aged over time and many washings, is soft on my skin. When I hold it in my hands, I recall her gentle hands, adorned with constellations of age spots, holding mine. As a little girl, I'd trace each spot with my fingers when I sat in her lap, my head against her soft chest. She radiated peace and calm; her presence provided a soothing balm to this child from a broken home. To this day, when I hear the click of cards being shuffled, I think of her in her red vinyl chair playing Solitaire. I give thanks for the quiet strength and stability she exemplified.

The subtle hues of the apron, with their gentle greens and blues, echo her tender nature, revealing her intentions with quiet grace. Never once did I hear her raise her voice. Whenever my great-grandfather became upset over one of the children's mishaps, she would effortlessly calm him with a simple "Now, Windy" from her post at the table. That single phrase was all he needed to hear to understand he had overstepped.

When my great-grandfather was at the end of his life, she and I sat together on the side of his hospital bed in a three-way hand hold as we listened to the monitor's soft beeps marking his last moments. When the nurse announced his passing, my great-grandmother squeezed my hand. Tears silently flowed from her eyes, mirroring the sorrow in mine.

Like the threadbare edging that unravels from the apron's seams, my memories wane with each passing year, and I am left to wonder, *Did she have blue eyes, or were they green? Was she right-handed or left-handed? What was she like when she was young? Did I ever make her mad? Did she know how much I loved her? Did she ever realize the powerful influence she had over me? Will my grandchildren and great-grandchildren remember me with the same fondness?*

I have a lot to live up to.

The holidays come and go, and I return the recipe cards to the shelf. I hand-wash the apron and gently put it back in the drawer. With each tie secured and every stitch embraced, I am reminded of the tranquil grace she imparted to me—her legacy woven into the very fabric of my being.

Michele Peters is a survivor who writes from the heart with the intention of bringing light into dark places. She believes in love first, always.

How Is It Possible?

ESTHER JOY GOETZ

The soft scent of the roses surrounding the urn makes its way to me, and I audibly sigh.

We are burying you today. Saying our final goodbye.

Your husband of almost sixty-four years, your son and his daughter, your daughter and her husband, sit in front of me, the sight threatening to undo me. I feel a catch in my throat.

I glance down my row to see my four children and their people as I tightly grip the hand of my husband, your son. Each face expresses a mixture of sadness and gratitude, eyes brimming with tears, and I can't hold mine back any longer. I reach for the crisp paper towel shoved into my pocket on my trip to the bathroom only moments before, so distracted earlier in the day that I left the darkened hotel room without any tissues. I delicately wipe underneath my eyes, praying my mascara won't run.

My heart sinks once again, the way it has in all the days since we received the dreadful call that you were gone—in a flash, without warning.

How? How is it possible?

How is it possible that what feels like only moments before, you were making the six-hour trek to our home to meet your first grandbaby, the one you were dreaming about every night since she was born?

How is it possible that you, whose eyes lit up every time one of my kids walked through your door and who made them believe they were the most special and only person in the world, are gone?

How is it possible there will be no more card games, shopping trips, beach visits, laughter, or popcorn eating with you?

The surreal scene of cold, stark grave markers with fake flowers in plastic vases and wiggly six-year-olds whose parents are shushing them leaves me dazed and confused.

How is it possible this is happening?

You, who we call "Grandma," were the personification of unconditional love.

Love that looked like a sparkle in your eye and a long, gentle hug.

Love that smelled like Red Door perfume and Christmas casseroles and cookies.

Love that sounded like "passing the peace" in church and giggles and wholehearted expressions of "Love you, honey."

Love that felt safe and special and sacred, the kind that should never go away.

I feel the shuffle in my pew, remembering that my daughter, that first grandbaby of yours, now a beautiful grown woman herself, has prepared a short reflection about you. She scoots around me, our eyes locking for just a moment, and makes her way to the front of the cemetery chapel. There is a new life (a baby girl) burgeoning in her womb.

She speaks eloquently, grief sneaking through as she chokes back her own precious tears.

"I had the privilege of knowing my grandmother for the last thirty years. She never failed to tell me how beautiful she thought I was or how much she absolutely loved me. She said it with the deepest sincerity in her heart. From sliding down the little ramp at the Brandon courthouse to stuffing our faces with oversize bags of popcorn to trying to keep up with her and Aunt Karen during Black Friday shopping to countless hours of cards to finally holding her hand one last time during Mass just a few weeks ago, my grandma was the sheer embodiment of love. I can without a doubt say I have never met anyone else who loved so genuinely. My life, the lives of all her grandchildren, and the lives of anyone who knew her knew love."

As she returns to her seat, dabbing at her eyes, my earlier thoughts echo again in my heart.

How? How is it possible?

How is it possible a five-foot-four bottle-blonde simple woman from Pittsburgh, Pennsylvania, having only completed high school, would change the world for the better one heart at a time, and especially one grandchild at a time?

How is it possible one person's small, ordinary acts of love ripple out so far that hundreds of folks pack a small room on a chilly Saturday morning, each soul having experienced her gentle, honest, caring, and patient love?

How is it possible nothing kept this beautiful wife, mom, grandma, and friend from loving deep and wide, up close and far away, strong and especially tender?

Right then and there, I sigh once again, knowing the answer.

It's possible because love is the strongest force in the universe.

It doesn't stop because it's tired or afraid or frail.

It frets and falters at times but fights its way to the surface, spilling out freely on those in its path.

It's the answer to the questions, the hope in the heartache, the safe harbor in the storm.

And unconditional love, wrapped up in you who we call "Grandma," wins in the end.

Nothing, no one, and not even death, can take that away.

It's here forever. And so are you.

Esther Joy Goetz is a spiritual director, author, mom to four, and creator of *Moms of Bigs* and *Esther, the Dolly Mama*.

If Only She Could See

REBECCA COOPER

It was a humid Saturday. Her hair was graying. Her glasses, a little crooked. The wind was blowing, and it was the time of year that felt hopeful. Spring was just turning to summer.

She pushed the pedals of her bike and yelled loud enough for the entire neighborhood to hear, "YOU'RE DOING IT! KEEP GOING! COME ON!"

My son, trailing behind his Nana, was learning to ride his bike. In the middle of her quiet street, she slowly rode beside him, cheering him on with every single pedal rotation. He smiled and teetered, and she kept yelling. I ran behind him, and before too long, they were both on their own. My mom and my son—riding together.

I remember thinking right there—right on that street—that is exactly what her own mother must have been like. Unabashedly supportive. Proud. In it, right in the exact middle of it. But before I could even file away the sound of my grandma's laugh, and before I could memorize the crinkles on the backs of her hands, she was gone. I was only five, and even then, the sadness hanging from my mother was a recognizable heavy cloak over her shoulders. That Cape of Loss has never gone away, and neither has the empty feeling that takes up the most space on birthdays, holidays, or during life's storms. The grief of her passing is like an old acquaintance we've all known for decades.

I watched them ride back and forth down her street. She shouted encouragement the whole time. "Just a little farther," she yelled. "Let's turn the corner! Let's go around the block!"

Standing on the warm afternoon concrete, tears swam in my eyes, and a familiar ache crept into my chest. *If only my grandmother could see the woman she raised right now*, I thought.

My mom lifted her hands off her handlebars, and out of worry for her, my son screamed. I smiled. I could hear my mom's hearty laugh, and my son's laughter soon followed. She veered her bicycle in gentle circles, patiently waiting for him to catch up.

Watching them together, I felt questions I've asked Grief a million times catch in my throat.

Would she have ridden a bike with me?

Would she have sat with my mom at ball games and choir concerts?

Would I have heard her voice rising above the others, cheering loudest for me?

Are my eyebrows just like hers? My eyes?

Did she hold down the piano pedal too long like I do?

Did she hate shoes too?

Did she get restless in the spring?

When she prayed at night, was it an argument or a conversation? And when she sang in church, was it on key?

I crossed my arms as the two of them grew smaller and smaller down the street. My mom kicked one foot off the side of her bike, then the other. I smiled as my son tried his best to do the same. His handlebars wobbled before he remembered he was just learning.

They finally turned and slowly headed back.

"I'm doing it, I'm doing it," my son chanted.

"You're doing it," she answered. "You're really doing it!"

I helped him park his bike, and his sweaty face and wide blue eyes stared at his Nana. "Did you see that?" He pointed a finger at my mom, who was putting her kickstand down. "She is, like, literally amazing!"

I looked over and smiled. She was waving at a neighbor.

She turned back to look at us in the garage. "Like, literally, amazing," she repeated, throwing her head back laughing.

My grandmother, Lois Fisher, once introduced a speaker at a luncheon. The crowd politely clapped, and she stepped down from the podium. Her hair was curled. Her dress was pressed. The camera panned the room. Centerpieces made of fake carnations dotted tables, and above the din of the transition, she made a joke with those seated nearby. Her voice carried over the group, and her loud laughter rang out. Her shoulders hunched up, and she threw her head back.

There are only ten seconds of video of her, but there it was, and right there in the garage I saw it again that day. For maybe the millionth time, I saw sparks of her in my mom. She would have been the best grandma, and that loss is often acute.

"First one inside gets dibs on the Oreos!" my mom suddenly yelled, before breaking into a run for the house. My son dropped his helmet and sprinted after her. Slowly, I followed them. Their breathless laughter formed a familiar harmony, and I knew she would let him win.

Somewhere deep inside, I recognized this would be a day he would file away. Long after she's gone, he will pull this memory off the shelf in his mind. His questions for Grief will be fewer than mine, and his memories will be more vivid. He will be able to hear his Nana's laugh.

And he will realize it sounds just like his own.

Rebecca Cooper is a mom and a lover of nachos and Jesus, and she lives every day rooted in joy. Find her latest books on Amazon.

She Is Everywhere

JENNY VANDERBERG SHANNON

She is everywhere tonight. In my hips as I sway, stirring broth made with bones and water and scraps of leftover vegetables from the bin, crushed under the weight of newer, firmer models. Just the way she taught me, with pinches of salt and bouquets of herbs tied with baker's twine and whispered prayers of thanks and desperation and hope. Spinning stories of her father, the stoic, Scottish fire chief, and her younger sister, the beautiful blonde.

Her hair was auburn. It shone like the fire at the end of her Salem menthols, the box left on the counter in perfect alignment with her red lighter. She would tap her frosted, mauve nails on the kitchen table as she waited for the bubbles to slow to a simmer, and my sister and I would sneak Hydrox cookies in plain view from the cookie jar on the counter beneath the flickering fluorescent counter light. Her whiskey tenor laugh made us bold enough to ask for another.

Her letters to Baptist missionaries in Papua New Guinea were always lined up neatly beneath her signed photograph of President George Bush atop her leather-bound Bible—tearstained and earmarked from years of desperate searching. She always had a Rolodex of emergency numbers by the rotary phone. In the mornings, she waited for my grandfather to get home from his night shift as manager of the A&P for his bacon and eggs, two bowls of Honeycombs, and a banana before he went to bed as the sun came up.

She is everywhere tonight. In the song I breathe: "Deep River." This was the song she'd played over and over on the piano as a girl, until the pages were torn in two and she patched them together with spit and cosmetic tape. The pages are framed in my house above the same piano where she taught me my scales. I can still picture her sturdy frame standing at the kitchen sink while I sat on the bench; I can still hear her calling out for different keys and modulations.

When my faulty fingers hit a wrong note, she sang out, "Again!" I knew that meant from the very beginning, in order, from the C-scale and working all the way back up. I hated her for it then. Now I sit at the piano and finger the grooves where her hands covered mine as I play the songs she taught me from her books. Thirty years later, they're the only ones I still have locked in my memory.

"I will play; you sing," she'd instruct.

She never asked me to do anything—she always commanded.

"Go outside and play."

"Drink your milk, or you'll end up like me," popping her dentures out like a jack-in-the-box as an object lesson.

"Finish your plate."

"Sing. Always sing."

"When there is nothing left, there will always be God and music."

She was right. Sometimes I'm glad she didn't live to see me struggle and rebuild. Sometimes I'm resentful I wasn't able to prove to her I was stronger—so much stronger—than I knew.

She is everywhere tonight. Lingering over my garden, deadheading my roses, clicking her teeth at the way I've poorly cared for my hydrangeas, and squishing my face against her sagging breasts as though to pass love through two bodies, fierce and determined.

I went to visit her for the last time years ago, in the nursing home. She used to stand tall. Stout. She was a rock in purple polyester and black slacks, always smelling of sweat and cooking onions and cheap perfume. But then she was stooped and bound to a chair that did all her walking for her. It had been two months since I'd seen her. It had been too long, but life got busy with a new little baby, so I brought hydrangeas to cheer her and my daughter to bring her joy. Her eyes held a glimmer of recognition before it was gone.

And then she was gone.

Now she is everywhere. In my second daughter, the one she never had the chance to meet. I see her in my daughter's fits of rage, her defiance, her courage, her fierceness, her brutal love. When she sits on the piano bench, her little blonde curls bobbing in time, legs dangling a foot above the pedals to plunk out "Hot Cross Buns," she waits a moment before calling to me, as I stand at the kitchen sink. "Again, Mama?"

"Again, love. Again," my voice answers, husky with emotion, sounding an awful lot like hers.

Jenny Vanderberg Shannon is a writer with a penchant for good coffee and fantasy novels. She lives in New Jersey with her husband and daughters.

If I Had Known the Day

SUSAN LAMBERT

The day Grandma left us unexpectedly was a warm, sunny morning in October.

The sun was shining brightly, and the sky was so blue it seemed far too stark a contrast to the sad reality of our loss.

I walked back into her home late that afternoon, and it seemed surreal, almost like I was walking in a dream.

Everything was just as she'd left it.

A room full of things stared back at me.

A cup of tea, half full. Utensils scattered on the kitchen bench.

I touched the teakettle, and it was still lukewarm from the morning.

Her wedding rings sat loosely on the bedside table, where she'd placed them the night before, and her reading glasses were nearby, ready to be worn.

Her Bible lay open on the kitchen table.

All these things, waiting for her return.

Including me.

How can we not know the day? It seems so unfair.

If I had known the day, I reasoned with God, *I could have prepared a whole lot better.*

I could have held her with a long, slow, deliberate hug rather than the rushed one I gave her before driving off to collect my children from school.

I could have thanked her more fully for the sacrificial life she lived.

I could have told her how brave she was.

I could have prepared myself and her grandchildren for the inevitable sadness that would arrive with the loss of their precious grandma.

I could have asked her all the questions I suddenly realized I didn't know the answers to about her life.

I could have cried with her, rather than sitting here crying by myself, on the edge of her unmade, empty bed.

As I allowed the tears to flow, I remembered a life that had so significantly touched the lives of so many.

And in the stillness of my sadness, I felt a comforting sense that God was with me in my pain. That God understood all my questions and regrets and deep sorrow.

And in that moment, a rush of thoughts interrupted my grieving heart. I would like to think those thoughts were from God.

I realized there is a freedom in not knowing the day. There is mercy in not knowing the day. There is a greater level of trust in not knowing the day.

I picked up her silver watch from the dresser and held it gently in my hand.

How strange it seemed that time had not stopped, despite our pain.

And yet while our time on earth is finite, God has graciously set eternity in the human heart. An eternity that gives us hope. An eternity so beautifully captured by the words of my six-year-old son, her grandson, who wrote his grandma a goodbye letter. A grandson who found courage and hope in eternity.

May this faithful child's words also bring courage and hope to you:

Grandma,
    You have finished your race.
    I will miss you so much.
    But I know I must stay here and keep running.
    I will keep running my race until I can see you again.
    Love you, Grandma.

Empty-nest mama, wife, and grandma Susan Lambert believes the power of faith and sharing stories changes lives. Find her on Instagram @mamastories_.

Conclusion

LESLIE MEANS

The world needs your story. This is the mantra we've written in our hearts and shared with our community at *Her View From Home* for years.

It's that simple. *The world needs your story.* Yes, your story.

And part of that story comes from the lives that came before yours, the heritage pulsing through your veins and in your heart.

It's why we know the world needs this book too. When we tell the stories of the gentle, wise, redeemed, creative, faithful, graceful, generous, resilient, devoted, legacy-leaving women who shape us, it connects us to more than just our history. It connects us to each other. And friends, that's what makes life beautiful.

The world needs your story . . . and the stories that came before.

Even if you think it's small.

Even if you think no one cares.

People care. More importantly, God cares.

Your story has value, no matter who you are or where you come from.

I fought against this notion for so long.

"Can it really be that simple? *The world needs your story?* Doesn't it need to be more exciting than that? Doesn't there need to be a takeaway, a lesson—a teaching moment?"

Time (as time does) has softened my heart, though. After more than a decade of running *Her View From Home* and publishing our second book, I understand why God's whispers continue to nudge me toward this work.

"Mom, tell me about the time when Grandpa came back from war and surprised Grandma while she was teaching," I asked as we finalized the book.

As I listened to my mother talk about her mother (one of my favorite parts of compiling the words you're now reading), it hit me: Stories connect us in a way nothing else can because they help us feel something. They make us seen, known, and understood. They heal broken hearts and teach us mercy, tenderness, and so much grace.

Stories are powerful.

Yes, it's really that simple.

God has authored your beautiful story, friends—a story unique to your family, your history, your hopes and dreams.

We're honored to help you share it.

Acknowledgments

You can't write a book without a team of people supporting you. It's beautiful, wonderful, and somewhat wild to have my name on the cover because it was created by so many. I don't know why God chose me to lead this book, but I'm grateful. Always.

To Carolyn: I know you could be with any major publication out there—but somehow, you stick with me. It's bigger than us, friend. It's bigger than us. Thank you for everything.

To Casey: You are a wizard with words, and you make it all look gorgeous. I'm so grateful for you.

To Claudia and Katherine, the best agents ever: Thank you for always believing in us.

To our incredible Tyndale team—Sarah, Kara, Stephanie, Andrea, Dean, Cassidy, Claire, and everyone behind the scenes who helped us create this gorgeous book: Thank you for your careful guidance and wisdom and for lovingly creating space for our dreams. Thank you for praying for us throughout this journey—we are blessed to partner with you.

To Emily, Jenny, and Kelsey: I love our random chats about the internet and all its interesting quirks. Thank you for so beautifully caring for our *Her View From Home* community and for cheering us on as we finished the book. You're appreciated beyond words.

To the *So God Made Grandma* contributors: It's an honor to include your words in this book. The world is a better place because you share your stories.

To the *Her View From Home* writing community: You make our group one of the best on the internet. Thank you for celebrating the contributors in this book.

To the *Her View From Home* readers: We couldn't create these books without your support. Thank you for loving us for over thirteen years.

To Carli Nelson, owner of our local Christian bookstore, The Solid Rock, and independent bookstores across the country: Thank you for including our books on your store shelves—we couldn't do this without you.

Central Nebraska friends, you've done it again. You show up to signings, share our books with friends, and always support me. It means more than you'll ever know. I'm so proud to live here.

To my neighbors who have become dear friends: You always make me feel awesome, even when I'm not. Thanks for cheering me on as we finished this book. I appreciate you so much!

To my sisters and your families: I love you. Thanks for always having my back.

To my mother-in-law: Thank you for your endless love for me and my babies. We adore you.

To Mom and Dad, because you two are a pair: Thank you for always loving me and my family. Thank you for loving each other for over fifty-seven years. My kids are blessed to have you, and I am blessed to have you. The older I get, the more it all makes sense. Thank you for everything.

To Ella, Grace, and Keithan: It's such an honor to be your mom. I love you. You're awesome.

To my husband, Kyle, as always. *I couldn't do this without you.* I love you so much. Forever and ever.

To Grandma W. and Grandma C.: I can't wait to hug you again in heaven.

To you, the reader, holding this book: We are so grateful you chose it. May you always remember the world needs your story.

About the Author

Leslie Means is founder and owner of the popular website *Her View From Home*, which features heartfelt contributor stories on motherhood, marriage, faith, and grief. She is a former news anchor, a weekly columnist, and an author of the national bestseller *So God Made a Mother*, and has published several short stories. She is married to a very patient man named Kyle, and together they have three fantastic kids: Ella, Grace, and Keithan. When she's not sharing too much personal information online or in the newspaper, you'll find her in Nebraska spending time with family and friends.

✢ NATIONAL BESTSELLER! ✢

Join Leslie Means, founder of the popular website *Her View From Home*, as she weaves together a powerful, emotional collection of essays from women of all ages and stages. These real-life, straight-to-the-heart stories will make you laugh, cry, and nod along.

So God Made a Mother is available everywhere books are sold.

CP1962

✣ **WRITE YOUR EVERLASTING** ✣
"I LOVE YOU."

SO GOD MADE A
mother's story
a keepsake journal

CREATED BY
LESLIE MEANS
FOUNDER OF
HER VIEW FROM HOME

So God Made a Mother's Story is a guided journal filled with thoughtful questions and inspiration to help you write about your life before and beyond motherhood. It's an open invitation to share your heart—in your own words and in your own handwriting.

Learn more at HerViewFromHome.com.

STORIES FROM THE HEART OF EVERY HOME

Her View From Home®

Connect with more stories of motherhood, marriage, relationships, faith, and grief at

HERVIEWFROMHOME.COM

Follow along
@HerViewFromHome